# A NEW ARTICLE

*Volume I Book One*

*The Original Barbara Payne*

© 2017 The Original Barbara Payne
All rights reserved.

ISBN: 0692976264
ISBN 13: 9780692976265

AND Epistle: and this editorial written by me for a statement of correctness as in the kingdom of GOD; be that affirmed. An epic immensely Pentecost the group, making a new element this attempt that is written there is no other way. Bring us some scripture in part. Complete a new volume of an event written by the same author by me. It is a new event. No more out of bounds remember that next election and recently. Herald, new President Obama, next election against Republicans legally your choice, your candidate, exclusively the United States of America, The CEO the person JESUS CHRIST, a new reality over President Obama and his wife Mrs. Obama, and the Federal Government their chief who has access to all, the Lord JESUS CHRIST, our Lord over all. JESUS said that unto me, my opinion Pentecost try reading *MATTHEW*. This is true a fact in Nashville, Tennessee from above a final reference for the whole generation.

Understanding this epistle doctrine is meant to inform. *ISAIAH 54:17* No weapon that is formed against thee shall prosper; and every tongue that shall rise against thee in judgment thou shalt (is already) condemn. This is the heritage of the servants of the most high (Due respect my God, definitely LORD better be careful.), and their righteousness. (Of the KJV) Read the scripture. Old building, no complaints is of me saith the Lord our God.

## VOLUMN ONE: BOOK ONE
### ©A NEW ARTICLE

THANK YOU, JESUS CHRIST. THE EMPHASIS BUT WE ARE COVERED BY HIS BLOOD. PEOPLE WE OFFER A NEW CHANGE, A NEW BEGINNING, A NEW WAY OUT, A NEW REPRIEVE FOR NASHVILLE METRO PUBLIC SCHOOLS, THE COMMUNITY THE VOICE.

Copyright © 2011 By Sister, The Original Barbara Payne™ in JESUS name delivered. All rights are exclusively reserved independent of USA, a Christian fundamentalist with known values standing before God in JESUS name, his servant brothers.

Thus saith the Lord JESUS CHRIST; Pilgrim this olive branch it is a great opportunity headed your way. It is a great opportunity to you, the Executive Branch a great opportunity. The final draft it's a present. This draft complete USA printed on location 2012 - for JESUS CHRIST. Note: the agency from the author to publisher any editing yet overtime do not re-edit pass events, definitely occurred locally; let me explain what did happen so obvious or any marks. To the Followers of JESUS CHRIST; your instrument what to say in regards. Question: simple just read the book of *JUDE*; His apostle understated. Give it to the LORD JESUS CHRIST; He can definitely handle it or a rap any engagement. Cover our back Lord. JESUS CHRIST, He is awesome. I present the entire case. This is your case people see the jury. This was no accident now get to work against Williamson County. A generation, crippled total tell it all it is sad. What to do about it don't give up. Many wish they had never been born, they got hurt hear me? The answer their unemployment for the children on their way up in this world fierce driven. Help start their motor on the way up they are the apple of my eye. Rejuvenate them save some with medicine, the young African American young people they are a bargain going back to slavery in the kingdom of God. Company everywhere stand up for them have your house in order, for the schools. Do it for me with no regrets, JESUS CHRIST your defender. Case closed. Not a shadow. Amen.

# THE PROLOGUE

A NEW VALIDATION SIGNAL RECOURSE THE GOVERNMENT

WELL YOU WANTED TO KNOW THE FINAL EPISODE: HE HAS OUR BACK PEOPLE OF GOD, FINAL DESTINY FOR THE BLACK MAN. GOD IS SEALING IT PROPERLY-FATE, ITINERARY OUR FUTURE. DON'T YOU KNOW OUR BACK IT IS OUR FUTURE, THE KIDS FUTURE TALKING ABOUT IN THIS HOUSE YOUR TEMPLE IT'S A MUST. HE HAS THE LEGAL RIGHT, THE BLACK MAN FROM A LEGAL STAND POINT TIME TO CELEBRATE. ADVANTAGE LEGAL INTERPRETATION, GOD. THERE IS NO MORE TIME OUT. DO YOUR DUTY LEGALLY INTERPRETED.

CHRIST JESUS said; let's see what CHRIST JESUS said all right. See the proof waiting for the evidence I know things are little different, things can be difficult this season. Stop the confusion. Speechless the inside story restore the evidence, the beginning politically things are difficult that is enough, that is the recounter of the operation believe me. *Think we're upper class our recovery, think we're millionaires, and we think we're equal and we are. You took our development away we will begin to recovery easily.

*The Original Barbara Payne*

We can recover. Correction, view the market your program. This plan you've lost the game. I repeat myself flipping you've lost, your House of Representatives, nothing but the Holy Ghost, I have the evidence, JESUS CHRIST. God said; get out of the box, get out of the way. I know the jingle the game supremacy indicted that is what you are, a blessing. You look like dummies you and your wives in the neighborhoods. Looks like a miracle, I'm posting it now. The children will not be in harm's way. Complete this draft, on this that complete. Enjoy with confidence mission accomplished Barbara Payne. Conflict end of time conflict, bring down a stronghold it pleasures me, comfort me, you are broken. Your final notice taking a look back, objective, tell the world printed on 10/21/2012. Most definitely, honor him JESUS CHRIST; this is my program. Further advance you cannot underscore on him no other resource to heaven. He punishes a backdrop. Know that he is your friend. You ought to pay him a visit, before the end comes on your congressional seat. That is your answer Jesus Christ. Thank you, so much for letting me, work for you LORD a privilege, and you are blessed. You are exactly right this situation.

# ACKNOWLEDGEMENT

To Jesus Christ
our Lord

Thank you, Lord, we all want to thank you for your integrity! I thank you very much. Thank you, Amen. JESUS, you're my hero. You are an awesome leader. The watchman I will never forget what you have done for me the author, The Original Barbara Payne.

# GRANTED A NEW REPRIEVE

FROM ABOVE I GIVE JOY, I AM GOING AFTER THEM.

TO: THE APOSTLES
AND IN NASHVILLE, PROOF IN DAVIDSON COUNTY
DISTINCTLY THE METRO GOVERNMENT

THE CASE YOUR NEIGHBORHOODS THEY ARE TAKING ADVANTAGE FROM ABOVE SAYS JESUS CHRIST UNTO ME, NOW HEAR THAT.

THUS SAITH THE LORD EXECUTIVE; number one be quick I GOD view you all the time. Executive, the day of operation you're present remember that front and center Federal Government. I would be concerned if I were you. Beware of judgment. Cattycornered (being not straight forward) you are blind use your energy Nashville, it happens every week. Everybody, I view your world I'm sending a message. I AM coughing. I view all over the world. I view everybody in this institution amazing. Don't be sly. You are insulting Republicans get this one. You are getting on my nerves get that? I know how to fight the devil. Let me tell you, see a wonder all those calling upon the name of our Lord Executive Branch, big solution right now. Evidence all of God's children open your mouth and say in the name of JESUS CHRIST, increase see abundance I know we can make it. Though Pentecost I'M tempted just ask me my results. Here are the actual results on His back. I have a record. There are certain things you don't know about that operation. What does that mean? You hear me? I was crucified to death; isn't that wonderful? And on my record: my record is clean remarkable bank on that. Hang that on the rest of yours your record is it clean, I know about curious, Mr. Clinton, Madonna? At least my record is clean final expenses great opportunity. Sin, I cleared my record immediately. Go worship, practice you and I don't fit in the same category. My glory achievement read the book throw your stones away. Legally let me throw one at you, and all of society read I urge you, I did what I was told no ad lives no substitution. Get a book the book Holy Bible. Go and read the book the fine print. I don't want to have to deal with it again. Everyone agree? Take a look no taxes on my debt. You think you are something. Open the book from the front to the back. Are you disappointed? I review everything that you do. LORD! A great success story hear that America? A review I bear the scars. What I needed a skin draft? Murder was committed on me. I see your efforts. God is working for you. Be adamant, I know most of you. I know your track record. Final solution draw closer you hear the summons change. Hallelujah. Obey me, absolutely no glass slippers. You don't have to obey truth eat all you want. I will not hear you anymore, definitely. Don't cry about it. A Final Solution Company let me explain, I've wrestled with this a very long time. I know what your values are crooked understand? Here's to you. A new recipe height in some places, flavor some of you already know what is going on. Notice now friends be humble as I speak to you people now take that; going to settle this civil rights confusion once, and for all politicians' great accomplishment. Stop complaining. I view your revenue don't be hysterical politicians sensitive. In Nashville, total cost already breaking. Hallelujah!   THUS SAITH THE LORD; TYPICALLY, YOU GET ON MY NERVES. YOU PRACTICE BRIDGE BATTALION, TACTILE WEAPONARY.   I KNOW THE MARK OF THE OF THE BEAST, AND WHICH FOLKS IT IS DERIVATIVE LOCALLY FROM.   DISTANCE YOURSELVES!  Want to shake their hand Government, and which branch they are rooting from? Incidentally, they are going to challenge you in this next election. They are hiding. You want me to tell you who they are? No due disrespect the African Americans your neighbors, whites are blind too many are stupid half million people know. Collaboration will get you nowhere. They are really off balance. That's the source. Undo, I'M ready for the funeral of elected officials get ready. Hallelujah! You've been beat up enough many African Americans. Legally give the kids a break, from the pits what has grabbed them away. They don't know what's happened in the pits.   Metro City Council surely has failed playing politics every day, your lobbyists washing favors exactly. Clean the Metro City Council; pull them out of the game it's rough on the kids, that is what you need to do. Your program it's nerve raking, we pay taxes plenty of taxes House Republicans, your responsibility. *Please JESUS CHRIST help! They will stop at nothing. No one is behind me Metro. I will help. No one is behind me; typically. My superintendents, they are anchored politicians your program.   I know everything.  I will tell everything your chemical warfare, your drug deals, making much business our classroom performance. Better go run the track again. We blew the whistle on your raffle money get the magic marker; I've got a secret legal weapon. Dirty your laundry, dirty your machine, it needs cleaning up.  Give up your machine with weapons of destruction on Nashville. Your amazing testament, you cannot get around it draw the cross. GOD'S favor people basically, I will show you poor Nashville City Schools. You are my friend. Stupid Metro School Board not being a watchman on the wall dung level, they need paddling poor performance being the keepers. *GOD'S favor; eliminate Charter Schools you don't need them. Cut Charter Schools eliminate them completely, they're not legal schools. Any fiscal idiot would tell you that; just a bit of practice of throwing money away watch their performance. That is priority. TOPIC: we reserve them weary what you've wasted on them tax budget, no joking confirmation in Nashville. Legislation will reverse this action. Thankful, to the Board for all you've done wrecking implementing enemies on our school system; I wish we didn't have to deal with you. Let that go on your record. *Disputing for all their giving going to Williamson County giving our school funds away, have wreaked havoc on our School System here in Davidson County, that is the system we operate on here in Davidson County our Metro Nashville, school funds are going to Williamson through their back door their own system of operating our school funds. This is done throughout America in just about every school system by Republicans. We are thankful for your business, for your epitaph, for your running influence of the put down of Nashville Public Education, shame on you Civil Rights Leaders. STATE REPRESENTATIVE: THE HOUSE OF REPRESENTATIVE-MS. LOIS DeBERRY; Thus saith the LORD; MS. DeBERRY your jurisdiction, we have a problem the House of Representative. The revenue Ms. DeBERRY, for the people raise the house help turn things around: backwards we are. Let me tell you, I've got your number. Please help me you've got that? I know you are an expert help the young people we know your address. You are a tackler please help things are ugly in this country? Down South I've known her for over thirty years things aren't always good serving with a life boat to everyone serving me, an awakening been her friend. Blacks depend on you, and the Council and other Republican Leaders, scream for Democracy your kind of language things can get ugly, and even Independents. You have no excuse for your emptiness' for being a good steward. What the LORD said, from JESUS CHRIST, Ms. DeBERRY I love you for justice. I love you praying when you are by yourself member of a lifelong service, tough on you a chapter remember, argument reelection we will win this election all by ourselves, that chapter arguing yesterday you've got friends understand, you had had a rough day in Nashville with afflictions? I really do love you. Keep standing for justice in Middle Tennessee; okay like Dr. Martin Luther King Jr., my daughter. He was on my side? You are amazing. Civil Rights Leaders for your laxity, conformist persons are looking at you right now. You say "don't blame it on us" when they hollow don't give me that. It's embarrassing your raggedy attitude everybody knows. Destine young folks your country the hunted. Incidentally JESUS CHRIST said to me; Simon, fellowship we need fellowship, I hold your back in fellowship before the war. They are still coming to this country Osama Bin Laden, independent group of terrorists. They have bounty on their head in other countries, trash throw away. They are manufacturing it now both houses. Behold a great idea trash in government, the Buffer JESUS CHRIST your defense none. I've got a road map your consolation count the beauty of it you republicans your races, and your grandchildren. I will whip your behind. We need some food some help right away. *You enjoyed Dr. Martin Luther King why don't you be brave as well? Get up off your duff, and do something we need help. LET THE LORD BE YOUR GUIDE JESUS CHRIST, THE HOLY ONE HE KEEPS CHECKING ON US OR HAS HOLLYWOOD GONE TO YOUR HEAD THAT'S IT? Pentecostals, where is your jacket you should be on top of this? Minus zero performance elected officials. We're choking here still waiting thirty schools need money. Children, grounded are good teachers. Charter Schools poor performance last year. Keeper a new weapon second choice: I AM depending on you from the foundation. More black people I am my brother's keeper, legal weapon of the kingdom-emerging delivered. The Bible my resources saying, LORD GOD help me, great attitude keeper of the spoken word your attitude. Accent give them a commercial people, no more advantage. There is greed all over this nation; the State they are the greediest bunch. I REST MY CASE CHILDREN SAYS JESUS CHRIST UNTO ME, AFTER THAT. And after that throughout the centuries visionaries have been born. I don't need stars at the home plate meeting. Ms. Barbara, I remind you as a messenger of GOD, you have been observed. We are good friends, I leave you in good hands never be afraid, I know the outcome the Apostles and the Government. *Now look at this from your Shepherd the giver of the book of life, you need an umbrella-protection no dissension friend of mine no lethargy. Write up for yourself you've got the mark my friend, imagine that. Show no anger. Be tranquil you've got the battle everyday don't blame it on me, the environment coming at you it's not healthy for you. You can make it an opportunity be nice, I AM covering you that is your answer. *And autopsy is needed on your head figure public officials. Your fortress is wet just stand up; be quicker than them talking about reality, liberty your relationship with me JESUS CHRIST. Enjoy, I give you confidence. I will help you out daughter remember to keep the Sabbath, your big bank breaking the ground rules. I'll be there to help you out, wherever you walk for me your blessing for nothing. Never fear. Be still, I see your portrait painful. I know it took a long time. I know it was a rough journey. The wind is going to change. It is blowing your way draw close to me. You've been afraid enough. The best is yet to come your way. I will help you out. You will get a hand shake in the midst of your journey.  I AM the Supervisor.  Your anger, forgive be it settled that is a dangerous path to cross.  Have liberty when you get there heaven get ready your journey home over the river, I AM watching it right now your breakthrough.  Let me tell you something, it's going to take all day powerful jubilee double feature no rent.  The superintendent, definitely I AM looking out the window right now.  I see your coming you crossing over on the other side, you were roughed, no rough handling over there.  *No more injuries.  I see your bruises.  I'll be standing by the entrance.  Oh absolutely, imagine that.  I see your entrance when you get home no lost and found.  No more roughen think you're an antique just an expression, I AM waiting for you.  Thank you, JESUS universal.  Remember a hand shake, I hope you don't mind.  There will be ribbons for you there on the other side.  Twelve thousand are there watching now have confidence.  See you under the umbrella of protection.  Your yoke is light the challenge.  *Take council, there were things articulated that needed to be said of the wrath of God, including your redemption even blue-collar workers after all of this even up north.  Pentecostals, are you rebels your choice against black people everywhere even in your community?  Backwards you have become.  You are dragging down my work with your selfishness.  Don't be prejudice.  I know the time, Methodist are the same on this journey they are on.  Get the benefit while you can.  Adjustments are soon going to be made sour for everyone.  The tunnel will be narrow Pentecostals watch your diet, for everyone to enter.  Escape while you can.  I view the traffic.  Better hear me.  Hear GOD!  I've got the ticket your only other resource.  Follow me.  Anybody got authentic backup for other resources other than me, JESUS CHRIST number one.  He never fails me anywhere the keeper of all.  I clean this earth your planet, I told you that in agreement?  Hallelujah!  The earth, no other source rely on Him praise God.  Metro Nashville, please accept there are no other resource left, but His blood extracted I'm telling you. Praise Him good Christians honor Him revival. Democrats, I'M dealing with them. I view this network. Everywhere pray for them Black people. Don't complain simply then don't the negative. Good I raise my arm. Black people everywhere be a model. I'M warning on your level. In record time the faster we get this done the better off we will all be. There are good people everywhere pray for peace. You can bank on that. 1600 Pennsylvania Avenue, in record time pray for peace. Don't miss a great opportunity. Pray for them wherever you are right off of this bat. I agree your credit. Then we agree. THE AFRICAN AMERICANS THE GOSPEL OF JESUS CHRIST, KNOW THAT IT IS MINE SENIORS PEOPLE EVERYWHERE. Slow to pick are you, you ought to be ashamed of yourselves. The author your Lordship our King, I'M not just picking know that God is able. Talking the same company, white people with you the same. We can all identify. Know He can deliver you unbelievable. Read *1st JOHN* (The KJV) John the deliverer true Pentecost, My deputy son; read in your Bible all the way through the help African American people citizens of earth. Things are a mess. I hold you accountable. I put it on his shoulders he wasn't blind like you are. I knew the guy. He knew everything of me. Trust me JESUS CHRIST, God's messenger I knew the man I loved him and his wife. Come on BISHOP ELLIS: the PAW-the thinker. You are anointed my friend. Oh, thank you, JESUS. You are slow. Come on Bishop Ellis, come on Bishop Ellis, fellow worker head of the PAW for JESUS CHRIST; you've got my word you're getting a breakthrough. I bring you an olive branch gentleman *bee* and apostle of mine. Oh, thank you, JESUS. Meet me on the bus with an olive branch. Pentecostals, I have a bone to pick with you. Your brothers they are backwards about JESUS CHRIST, the deliverer. No other subway out of here Christians. I will see you at the banquet our wedding night super, I'M telling you and avenue and event people. Be thankful! Oh, thank you, JESUS CHRIST. There are no taxes there. See that your robe is washed white. There are no taxes over yonder. All people everywhere listen to me; people get it straight we aren't getting out of here without Him proof. See your mess. Are your robes washed white by the blood of the lamb, JESUS CHRIST; the Lamb of God, backwards if you aren't? We are all so complete with Him. He died for us. Don't miss it.

## SEND A TELEGRAM LEGALLY

Thus saith the LORD unto me; beyond principles a new understanding sing *cocker-doodle-doo*. Oh absolutely, a new event a reality. Definitely, a new performance requires the obvious. Let it shine a new war. No more silk and its acceptance. Dropped Government agencies give you credit the way I want it. Repair it none later great opportunity legally. Then afterwards in November, no more perils required. I'M disappointed the Lord said to me; I give new data to Metro. Think they are smart for their handling of Metro's School fund leave that door open. A NEW EPISODE: get out of my house and the PAW as well, only 30 minutes a new address. There isn't a thing you can do about it as well. Start spreading the gospel a new episode in Metro Government as well, before they start coming after you as well. The line is drawn public records will show that. Then where will your defense be? Pressure will be put on all who don't seek after the Holy Ghost. Just call it my will for the Church, remembering whose seed you really are. All is record police is gathering two proponents are looking recently as well. Better grow up. And your defense none: it's on your record the trail leads to you. We know all about you. It is the fifth doctrine reference not including the tornadoes hit your State as well, new development thirteen the papers your doctrine. Congratulations Uncle tight rope. Let me tell you something musical America, your home most definitely! Take pride in it. The greatest fear non-violence everybody knows. Stir emotions meet me there up front this is reality. There is no greater power on this earth my opinion men women conceivable, and children those are the victim a little message. That is my opinion. In regards Uncle Tom part of the game. Paint the picture in regards that is what it is all about. Well I see middle class people coming from Europe everywhere no blockades. The team they will unlock the door, we should be thankful. This country from the beginning Black folks, I see no boundaries legally. View the card we have gains, the recipe our rights against White Supremacy this nation small house, and their sponsors the Government legally. The closer we get the show is over most definitely. Give one hundred and fifty percent. Wear your badges let the whole world know. Scream for America to stop racism! You say, "Don't be condescending that it is ridiculous." *I view your actions *big-time* from above says, me JESUS CHRIST the one and only! You're in the United States that's final. Keep your shirt on. Look on the bright side a vacuum cleaner your portion, we don't play dogs. Opportunity papers the U.S. Government, we have your footprints, you're going to prison this junction. Couple with that listen reckless, I have a bone to pick with you. Great opportunity the results people are equal everywhere privileged! That is your answer! Let's all act naturally never make that mistake again. We have a new way of doing it let me show you copy me? Heard of excuses they are coming? Ladies and gentlemen, brothers, and sisters present I the evidence. Thank you, JESUS. The hunter's greedy Government they are after you. Simple as that the facts are on you. Thank you, JESUS CHRIST. Your reasoning the hunted no defense dial 911. You haven't got a thing to say. We see your impact the Holy Ghost you stand alone. No more controversial no deal you robe me people your family of God. "Thank you, thank you, we the people a new day." We're going after NBC for its coverage signature, and the Today Show.

Thanks, for your conduct big time insurance. Know that God is able for the medicine professionally, His presence a new recovery a great decision. He's God all by Himself every day. Let's give Him a hand clap for bringing the burden down, my mind is exhausted for all those families who have struggled for years not knowing what to do. Thank you, JESUS CHRIST for your help. You view life. We need a dentist, a new ruler of the Government to handle things against racism a great opportunity. Finally, never cross Heaven you are wrong if you try believe me! Would anyone agree? Know the trademark. A bulletin legitimate, because of racism a new mandate for Federal dollars given by the U.S. Government is coming against racism from Heaven to the Federal Government, too curb racism in this Country it is ours legally stop all this nonsense. From Missouri, to Ohio, to Chattanooga, stonewall recount. I view your activity Knoxville as well, slick the mayor a whole new recount it just don't make no sense you Republicans. Problem, a new recount you just won't let people have the right of way. Embarrassment, give a great clue your election I'll tell you all about it your honor ridiculed. Your space targeted. You are ridiculed individuals, Nashville as well very unhappy another cross. They say you are low-down. Ups-and-down, you can't knock Black people totally down White people, their entrance legally no mishap. We have legal rights. Couple with all that they have a foundation, the Holy Ghost. Come on somebody help break the cycle. Help Dr. Registrar your salary is not dependent on it. You've got to do something. We're waiting your principles just aging development independent. I can't wait to see you on the other side Dr. Registrar. Just stab them in the back. No wonder we're just dodging bullets in the morning watching quack heads, stories being told kindergarten and up. Wake up please. Oprah Winfrey, she knows now let her explain that. TO: PENTECOSTALS-THIRD DEGREE. A SUMMONS: OPRAH WINFREY EXTREME FROM GOD AT ANY ANGLE. Good luck Oprah Winfrey, I helped you. Follow an alert

## The Original Barbara Payne

for your people still an alert roll back the time? I AM a witness. I remember you a long time ago. Reading and big event! I AM ahead of you to the people, my friend give the advantage flipping your cause most common your own neighborhood. I AM warning, I AM begging, I AM not a politician. The neighborhood most dangerous the hood everyone knows the little ones, the babies. Why because you are a veteran network producer, BET as well? You owe JESUS CHRIST. Regular topic group right off the bat, little people can't keep up small thing ride along. Apparently, you don't adventure—keeping up. Pull that concrete back reaching. Let me explain something about you, studying, you belong here give me some advantage filming an event your award. Pay us a visit everybody knows not often distraction. Crazy are the gangs, they do exist! No competition getting your cameras, and getting *MS. Oprah Winfrey a friend that's a good idea in plain view noticeable friend of God. You've got power to handle it—your station diving into it the gutter (an impoverished and degraded existence, a way of life). We need your help. We need a bath around here. No competition a lot of black people are smoking, late at night watching drugs destroy. A mandate we should all be active where the front is helping. Impact get everybody to help you get NEWS CHANNEL TWO: it's in a rough neighborhood. Your advantage Oprah your new network film to the world, or this is just going to go on unchecked. Have boot camp here your portion. Start cleaning up this mess a backup your help. Black people need your help, or can we be endowed like other parts of the world like Africa? Put some gasoline on it, and let the rest of the world see how things are here in your old neighborhood, you know take action quick! THUS SAITH THE LORD; DON'T GIVE ME THAT MS. OPRAH, I CAN'T FIND THE TIME ANYMORE. LISTEN, DO YOUR DUTY! THEN DON'T BOTHER—KEEP CHECKING YOUR MAILBOX TO HEAVEN. You had your beginnings here, your first start where you grew up. Open up that box tell it. I dare you!

## A New Article

Travel to West Tennessee, where everybody knows. And that isn't the worst of it we sell some insurance in the hood your gangs, the adversary of Black people. Census, too many Black people making living selling drugs on the street, their safe haven trying to recruit somebody on a regular basis, gangs moving traffic all night long. It is done on purpose. Your principles haven't changed that much. Make a big change separate somebody will hear you. Throw some fuel on the fire let's get it ignited. You know what; you keep bringing hell their way with your jealous comments Republicans. I've been a Democrat in moderation. Stamina we take yall's mess as well recant separately. Whoops, plenty of substance abuse shown to black people of America, your little dogs. No wonder some want to be a quack-heads, or stupor heroin addicts. You say you are Christians this side. I view Ashland City, the other side embarrassment little bit. Rage pissed off your rage, you owe it to them. The other side your defeat, your jealously is low down. I'M losing my patience, my reaction to all this mess fighting. Let the arrest begin right now. Let me show you, you want to know why you will take the popular vote over again? That is how you earn your living keeping up trouble in the United States, and all over the world recently conflicting; testified from above shady are you, you're under arrest. Low your deal you're beating people over the head. Move over we all would like to take the vote over again get a new recount, and count zero that's how Bush won the last election. Lucky, you, you will say "Can I vote again?" News bulletin! Lawsuits are coming it's the Government to stop all this mess. Your trademark here, on Metro's schools it has left a terrible mark on the mind of so many of Metro's school children. Their success depended on completing their education empowerment. Move out of the way. Have mercy change this situation today your reputation. They are in prison junction. Get ready friends other members oasis in our community 85% reconstruction Federal Marshalls junction with gas those who robbed us. Obama is coming after you a new mandate, we need a new mandate. Thank you, JESUS CHRIST. Quickly no coupon throw away. Thank you, for running for president in the next election. Hope we gather all the people in, for the general election next year. They eat our entire budget up. Flavor we need anyway we're not dogs. We remember the days of market Charlatan's blocking our every way. Low down you are. Bootleggers they are. For African Americans for free say, we're never going back to those times again; people won't allow it this country. God can do something about it. Say, thine is the policy wipe them out with a big fist. Say, thine is the friend against the Republican Party, the kingdom, the power, and the glory (*MATTHEW* 6:13; KJV) our share the way it should become, thy kingdom come. We have observed. We have the evidence, nobody bother us again Mitt Romney. Thy will be done Oh Lord; most definitely, the next presidential election. Come and join me. I'M not changing positions His holiness okay, even in Chattanooga in the middle there of for African Americans Governor Romney? What a beautiful thing my friend on earth the people, as it is in heaven. JESUS, WE LOVE YOU! Literally African Americans, imagine that we owe a debt to you. Special thanks, in His honor forever. A new game no complements. To Jester working for me, Jester help me. With a big whipping guess that I AM coming after next, the family of God; legally let there be no misunderstanding the family of God? Arm yourselves authorities are watching your every move, every nation think. Clean up your junk signed, JESUS CHRIST. No crocodile tears you need a whipping. Alligator men of Brentwood things are headed your way now don't defy me. Human a little bit pointing your finger, your race as well crime will exceed far beyond its capability. Better be prepared. Good news! Get out of the way Mr. Public Officials. Many of you in your city good people some have already succeeded in cleaning their houses. Gubernatorial race as well you'd better think about that. Amen. GOD is watching, He keeps good records even on that city just ask Him in the name of JESUS. He is always watching. The minority organizations they have taken a stand against political destruction, against African Americans. You're so out of it (out of touch) you're not in balance in your neighborhoods. Creditability for your home has dropped believe it or not. Because of income more and more of you *Brentwood heads will be planted elsewhere, no joke. At the end of the day wrestled with it you're on the edge, you're not facing it. Maybe a strong will, will survive and make it. It will be like living in the "Twilight Zone" twenty-three. No living pinnacle—your money. Blank your conversation, your lost revenue finding no help. No bread to eat don't be afraid there will be others like you, don't be afraid opportunity God's side of the universe nothing going to waste, consumer products will be doubled literally just watching your money going down the drain. Prices will double everywhere. *Soup lines will be everywhere. Imagine that in Nolensville, Tennessee poor people will drive a wedge between the newcomers with plenty. And in Nolensville, your network will instantaneously drop—your economy. And in Cheatham County as well, Knoxville as well, your great revenue days will be over. Racism will stop, when you find yourselves with lost revenue. Your lost revenue will find you joining the nation in arming themselves against lost capital. It could be worse neighbors fighting for somewhere to live. Jury duty bankers, those banks will tumble everywhere. Dental hygiene and current revenue will suffer, and so will fifth wheeler the evidence trading buying new cars scarce, your capital income believe me what you rely on. I've got the evidence keep that seat belt buckle. Decline population business man, be more like JESUS CHRIST nationally. Move over Jack and Jill, your damage circus get comfortable. You new African Americans, I give you the results celebrate Him, JESUS CHRIST. Have you forgotten about Him a great opportunity senior my friend? "Arm yourselves this must be the anti-Christ" the persons. Recap says JESUS unto me; I don't do business like that even to the Jews. You can have your space. The results then maybe we can get married eventually, special a new technique to the Jews as well. Umbrella you don't think about others, just yourselves you forgot about many. And those women who buy too much give 20% the cost of beverages, when you are dinning out peel off naturally. Your race needs the help eat healthy. Say, Hallelujah. The cost of wine bee sober! From God JESUS CHRIST; this Country old things (those women), stop drinking too much and your cattle (and your money even in Knoxville) will pass watch all things new. See my new plans. Unbelievable people finger pointing, and new revenue will not replace it. Salaries will drop tremendously, they have already. Families will go across the bridge to get out of the cold their revenue is gone. Whole families will have new places to live. You will burn those credit and debit cards. On the go will be no more. Unless it's for free you won't go. You need more money; the best package will be to ask if it is free. Tomorrow based on a permanent discount will be the way most people will shop. Stretching will be all many people will know. The cost of clothes will drop here staggering, but many people can't afford to shop in department stores, they will use thrift stores as their way of going after trends they can afford. Right offs won't be practiced, their waiting game on the consumer. Presumably everything will be already marked half off. *Ralph Lauren, the biggest retailer won't need outlet stores. More and more people will be dressing in his fashions. His stores will sale for little of nothing. "I can't get a job anymore factory where we worked retired" couples recant everything common. "Isn't that wonderful I can go shopping now in the 21$^{st}$ century." Far too long I've waited for this to happen. Military families can buy his clothes—Lauren, Gucci, and Calvin Kline, the same. Talk about ladies, Bloomingdales Upper East Side virtual reality, definitely more affordable for black people commercials fast and appealing to everyone. We'll living decorator style. I'm assuming new checked and another 10% off,

*A New Article*

no revenue for stores to support their buying spree and Blacks as well. Their game of slashing prices double digit, while waiting consumers with coupons in hand to pick up a better deal. You can buy clothes while spending very little extra including coupons. Flipping, a military salary will put a decent roof over your head. Buying trip excessive the market won't be there anymore. The stores will need new revenue to support everything else. *Hey, General Motors, Chrysler, auto makers your cars will be popular than ever before, because they will be cheaper. Support for Wall Street will not be available new investors cannot be found, old ones will have vanished, definitely. An ultimate dream full coverage, maximum coverage will no longer be on the record. Macy's will stop selling those adds on the TV for different things, they will be going deeper into a recession. In the meantime, get down to business with your credit cards stop using them pay them off entirely. Oh, my goodness! Say, exactly there's no meat in the place. A loaf of bread will cost a dollar more. The majority will leave it alone start making their own just can't afford it. Kroger will not have meat, and neither will anyone else $4.00 a gallon for milk. Load up while you can beef as well especially on meat, new clothing as well factories will stop making them. Why the ring leaders cost us this huge debt? Now breath, so tired many will be. Middle class families, COSCO'S will say, "it's a rat race to keep food stocked people are battling over food," equal other countries as well. Hezekiah, long term health care will be hard to come by in the end. Zip it I'M telling you now, stop complaining about your piece of the pie followed by goodnight everyone. Great news the President yes Mr. President, Pentecostals see no evil. London Fog warehouse will close they will advertise it. NFL franchises will close people can't afford the tickets. Trophy wives will not exist anymore recall. Soup lines will be in your neighborhoods. Camps will fill up there won't be harmony anywhere, when people drop a bomb get your ticket (salvation). Your electricity will be turned off for days. The bottom of the barrel will be where women will shop. Stealing things will not be heard of nothing left to steal anymore. Televisions will drop to an all-time low. Interest rates went out the roof. Maids will work for free to eat food.   THUS SAITH THE LORD; I AM THE REFEREE THE LORD'S BUSINESS LEGAL WEAPON, THERE IS NO MISTAKE ABOUT IT YOUR EQUIPMENT THE OTHER GAME.   "I thought I would never see it," it's a floor fight all your friends resulting in fist fighting, and ending Republicans to your games right now. Neighborhoods, Independents, the people, and politicians stand up to them trust me Channel Four News will air it. View our attack independent. I view you two hundred percent your branch many House Republicans, a new episode situation no other alternative your offense your ecology definitely.   I see State Police back you up. You've been reaping off Metro for a very long time.   You've said that right, and counter attack big.   Searching for justice the right way awesome, critical review from that mess revolt terrorism-dogs "I will put a bomb in a package, most definitely." Thank you, bigot you're mean terrorists, you're insane most common. I see your class most everywhere. They wouldn't bomb your home. Wouldn't they?   I would follow suit. Don't be afraid I see your integrity. Difficult I see your insurance Ms. Barbara legally. The grounds insurance, I will protect you against terrorism your whole house. I AM ALPHA AND THE OMEGA. Trust me I know. Look don't you be afraid. I give you my word. What do I do? Just cling. I hear the shotgun blast most everyday even in my neighborhood. They are watching me. Relax I AM behind you most definitely. They don't have the money individually.   Now don't give up. I taught you that. Give us your opinion quickly.   Don't be down your defense, the PASSOVER keeper. *Ms. Barbara, don't ever stop do you agree a good alternative, agreed? That's your defense exactly.   Fortunate, I serve White and Black great opportunity be bold trust me, and now you know. Granted legally give you modification no complications, an adult with grace smoking with kin hoping for the jubilee. Thank you, JESUS CHRIST, who changes everything. Remember the tree. Relax a new election your cognitive research let that be a lesson. I have proof. Go get it. Save the evidence. Main topic I'M dealing with all the evidence. The facts of it afforded one hundred percent. I'M not playing about it the goodies in Middle Tennessee. New occasion we've got plenty of it legally the FBI will review the case. Tell the rich folks the other white folks behind you redoing the budget revenue, chocolate left behind every day. Go and weep for them new direction. Precisely tell them that stole that budget we're after them; go figure it out that are stealing our budget, our capital advancement everyone, where they are going now. We've got the numbers. Now tell the authorities they are going to have to pay for it. I REST MY CASE PEOPLE SAY'S JESUS CHRIST UNTO ME; AND AT THAT VERY MOMENT COMPLETE TELL ME JESUS CHRIST. We will get restitution doing research on the web. I'M recommending persons a trunk full of messages; get quickly ready real quick on the general basis we'll settle it going to fix it with regards, millions of dollars-revenues annually missing from our budget. THUS SAITH THE LORD; DON'T BLAME JESUS CHRIST IT'S YOUR FAULT. YOU HAVE THE AXE USE COMMON SENSE. YOU WOULD THINK SOMEBODY FROM THE REVENUE DEPARTMENT WOULD HAVE FINGER-POINTED IT OUT A LONG TIME AGO. INQUIRY, THE FBI WILL FIX IT. THE FEDERAL GOVERNMENT OWES US THAT MUCH. THANK YOU VERY MUCH, JESUS CHRIST.

NUMBER TWO: COOPERATION TO THE FBI THE COLLABORATION, THE WAIVER, THE ADMINISTRATION, THE LEADERS.

Thus saith the LORD; the difference the administration, the leaders, the deals cut collaboration the model the cannon. Their zone people make their own decision. My distinction blow it up list the touch. Listen, the FBI, final restitution currently the administration arrested FBI your deals. To the FBI, great opportunity your department a misdemeanor altercation; you're fighting the waiver the administration, the public leaders your honesty. Here are the deals help one another, help one another corporation. If everything goes wrong teacher's salary is the lamb. That is the investment we're out of touch here in Metro Schools. When you look at it real closely, real quick there is more than enough to raise teacher's salary. Now we know who the culprit is in Tennessee in the back of the bus, White Williamson County. Just for the picking-evil white trash, just trash and now we know. They are going to stick it to us again if we don't stop them—flip automatic. They will pay for it detailing narrow budget deficit, House and Republicans read *AMOS*: tried and proven Republicans, including your best friends living in Hollywood, Los Angeles easy money understand? Don't underestimate me the man JESUS CHRIST. Oh my! In Him I put my authority people over the years Alaska as well. The public you are in hot water. You will never get away with it completely; God knows what is going on. Where is my sword that is your answer right away? You say it is none of my business that is your opinion. You see race is my business. It is a problem. Tell all black people God created them. African Americans dial 911, JESUS the healer will answer you. Thank you, JESUS. Call on Him every single day. False prophet says no-the anti-christ that is his method it is political. Across the nation get ready for marches dozens. We will reach the ladder. To: Newt Gingrich; we're in pursuit hear that says JESUS CHRIST about that unto me. Your cut didn't make the ladder profitable for our defense, and neither will Mitt Romney, those republicans you're just too late. We're all having financial troubles need new revenue. The government didn't work with us, so that we could get ahead. Right now stand up for me. For reason naturally help needed right away, we've got the evidence. We need new reform. For reason we've got the courage to stand up.

## A New Article

Desperate the issues the one thing looked at for free for the people. I'M not a restaurant white people. Favor your discretion your justice. I AM JESUS CHRIST; JUST YOUR SAVIOR DEFINITELY SETTING PEOPLE FREE HOUSE DEMOCRATS EXACTLY. Get it burden your own mix? Now get use to it. I see a revolution coming your way. I know everything. Incidentally that is important to me Franklin, Williamson County. No fakeness USA agreed? Read the book of *ACTS*; get to know me. Or are you familiar with me JESUS CHRIST? The bible, know your bible the living word. We are a corporate nation fifty percent; keep that in mind most definitely. Bridge close the gap. Greed your greed is destroying the little man wide-open. I see your greed. Don't give up. Bless Oh God! Leave it to me. Imagine no one but me, Facebook. I the officer of the New Testament Church claim victory over everything we do. He knows everything we do sellers including everyone; about Facebook a missed opportunity on Facebook about me. View the excitement. It does matter; God matters capitalist even on Facebook. Read the book a national book, ironic. I AM the champion of the world even on Facebook. You hear that Roman Catholic full of emotion? And one other thing, I AM going to remove that mountain, before you get to heaven most indeed. You hear that Obama? It is a tough one double digit. You hear that white whiplash (the lash of a whip on all of you) call me master no breakthrough? Choose your defense I have a trophy. Flavorful however, no yellow and no sugar in me that is how I operate. I give you a big bang for your bucks. CASE-URGENT: I AM the judge you will quiver remember me. I'm not afraid. I AM the judge BET, are you listening? I AM after BET, the whole department BET justice (BET—BLACK ENTERTAINMENT NETWORK; the nation's largest Black People's Network, don't play those games the largest film network for Black entertainment). You've eat enough dirt. What's up-your play. I approve of everyone irrepressible. I know value. Whites you're backwards don't throw that around favor against Black folks ridiculous. Illegal that is with me non-qualify (Added attention get it?), If you ask justice is for all. Your plan it's your bag lateral purpose. We're still waiting for justice buckle up. Now don't pretend it didn't happen. I know every single one of you. Your book development measures like a faucet your trauma fixation, your foundation uneducated; master your pain. Make them crazy definitely your accomplishment. Walk away be a drop out don't finish school; a mistake. DIASTER WE HAVE A MESS HERE COGNITIVE-ENGINEERING ELECTED OFFICIALS, ACROSS THIS CITY. HEAR THAT THOMAS EDISON TEACHERS, COMPLIMENTS? Unemployment high we're dealing with it students. *Your White abuses we're living on the edge. I've got good news tell people will now be prohibited by the White House, exactly strictly based on the original ethnic groups, and locale tell that co-director laborer I'M the ball carrier. GOD you're awesome! *They are low down here in Metro in this great city of Nashville. Thank you, JESUS CHRIST for your help-requested. And you will think me much right away. Needed demonstration on the White House lawn, and the Federal Buildings as well, as well as those Republicans the Republican Party, and Conservatives we know your principles. People, calling for Democrats, Corporate America, pull some out of retirement right away this year an investment. No Tea Party please we know their agenda. These are a pinnacle of success. People uphold the law. A giant snake sneaked in identity a Republican let loose against black people magnified, kingdom people everywhere. *THEY HAVE TAKEN FEDERAL DOLLARS, AND GIVEN IT TO THEM THE GOVERNMENT—TO WILLIAMSON COUNTY, TENNESSEE YOUR CHILDREN'S EDUCATION, AND ABOUT THAT WORD OF CAUTION OUR CHILDREN ARE THE VICTIM WITH THAT MONEY VIOLATION IN ALL OF THIS. IT IS AN ARROW PUT IN YOUR BACK. From above God JESUS CHRIST; prophecy you know, but facts do you seek them out? Merciless, subsequently we are fighting a reign of terror a little bit every day for the children, their right to an affordable education. Blueprint we are in desperation. Let me inform you for me your friend, like all other Black people citizen in Nashville, and independent Black person serving GOD ALMIGHTY. I work independently the procedure. I cannot do anything without the Lord's help. No matter what we think we're all here trying to fit in like kernels not microwaved. When discovered piece by piece quickly for the papers your business, we are going to win this action. Your calm relative negative your way, talkative understanding Nashville, like a measuring stick helicopter a new development for the people, our people black and white it doesn't matter what your language is. Say, God will set me free Jew or Gentile whatever your race is we're all equal, we're all Americans. We were wronged. For the papers blueprint your business a new development for the people, for the record, independent His record JESUS CHRIST, total advance for the service. This is my God given talent. Amen.

A REFLECTION THE GROUP: WE NEED SOME CHANGES A NEW EPISODE IN THE MIDDLE. SOME THINK THEY ARE THE RICHEST PARADING AROUND THEIR BIG ACCOMPLISHMENTS TRYING TO HOLD TO THEIR SPOT, THOUGH THEY MAKE CONFUSION LEGALLY DEMOCRATS. AND ON TOP OF THAT I THE PERSON JESUS CHRIST WATCHES ON TELEVISION DECLARATIVE CIVIL REQUEST, SPECIAL REQUEST AND BLESSINGS. OH LORD JESUS CHRIST! WE WILL VINDICATE OURSELVES IMPLEMENTED IN TERMS OF YOU EXCACTLY THAT. GOD JESUS CHRIST, WE DO BLESS YOU JESUS CHRIST THE ONLY ONE. WE THANK YOU, WALKING TOGETHER ALL THESE YEARS WE CHRISTIANS. WE CHRISTIANS BLESSINGS OH LORD JESUS CHRIST FOR THE SERVICE, THE BENEFIT ON US. LORD, WE APPRECIATE YOU WE CHRISTIANS, MY DEFENSE. THANK

YOU, FOR BEING ON OUR SIDE AND FOR THE PEOPLE FOR REASON CIVIL DEFENSE OUR CHILDREN ANOTHER DEFENSE: JOY TO JESUS CHRIST MY FRIEND ALL THESE YEARS, THE APOSTLE.

THUS SAITH THE LORD; Hallelujah! We need a breakthrough; my heavenly friend things are about to change physically a true the reality. Things are about to unfold be on the lookout covenant. I view you every day. Results, I AM the receiver. I view you every day, definitely every night. I'M close to you. Be on your way now, I'm telling you Christians. My friends help control this advocate. Remember, I view you every day no matter how subtle you think you are. A new treatment Pentecost living, we bar you from the front door definitely. I have your phone number other people as well. I view this difficult situation, and Republicans I'M talking to you. You think old school is driving. Now play a trick. I view your camp your last accomplishment dangerous against the team. It's traveling crippled big league as of today. What team the U.S. federal team the National Government? Bankrupting see you in November election. Our day of discovery, our day of suffering is past. Your residence unbelievable I'm up to your tricks. You have to apply to bear open fire arms against the whole nation and the U.S. and Congress any Republicans; here they are Republicans change that is that movement doorsteps coming Republicans. I feel like a breath of fresh air racing through my lungs education get back on track. Mark up your calendar. Get your ticket this is a big one. I hear a recovery new House of Democrats as leaders give us a new look. House Democrats, in control they are coming after you. First and far most, triple effect never seen anything like it Mitt Romney, gosh sad! Prisoners you are in your own race for any amount of money, their crying out loud never seen nothing like it in all of daylights. Making all that money just politics inopportune, money created. Discipline triple making money pay your taxes immediately. Excuse us, we won't tell. You have an olive branch, before the lights are cut off. Hear the impact regular people. Frankly, top notch the pleasure is all *mines*. You owe me. Say hallelujah, and amen saith our LORD JESUS. How dare you cross that line? You are slick now here is the real battle hateful. Your conscious have a good day. Let me repeat, your conscious have a good day. No commercials we will get even your operation even in La Vergne. "Hey take the cameras off of me." Your own father living with me, he collaborated with me, your brother as well. You think I'M stupid Nashville, TN like Katie Curic. NOTICE LEGALLY: Katie Curic: now Ms. Katie Curic criminal intention follow me, hop in a limo in Nashville, TN and come to the party of U-Haul Republicans in Middle, TN free. Here it is no joke the Republicans they keep on living off of duplex watered-down revenue supporting by Davidson County. King's living your interest rate mounting up, Catholic's as well in the valley change your view. We're not a throw away Franklin, Williamson County and Rutherford County. Pentecost established heaven help us all rule out established view. The record backwards, the impact temporally Jessie James on the spot view me at the upper room no more blindness. These are the issues. Here is a lesson, Catholic's as well. Catholic's are you confused social security both houses, our debt nothing to brag about? We could have balanced the budget, reviewed taxes, cut spending it's mounting up cut taxes. The rumor in Washington, D. C. the White House is about to clean house. Your development no joke, I see you in the thick of it in back rooms jiving around eating breakfast. They are talking about you making fun. God cares. Don't forget the whiskey politically epic, they know just what you like a furlough. Point of view this nation politically; the ABC's your point of view. The impact believe me we totally recognize, we see the impact we are stuck we the people every word candidates of America pluralism. The desert they are laughing in your face. Courts are filled with them every day political thing people, Pastors, who break the law who did the wrong thing ungrateful. I will not change my mind. Consider them an outcast. Mitt Romney, do you hear me? Does anybody know the man, I have a friend? If you change your mind people get to know him JESUS CHRIST, the Savior known on every avenue. Been around for a very long time very popular, even *John the Baptist* knew Him right away. Let me tell you, Republicans better off make an appointment something better for society. I view your wealth. I view their sentencing everybody Republican's their government. I see what they have done to the people in Tennessee, even in Bellevue Black and White. In Tennessee some of you are bigot's super flesh you don't care about the people. Who do they think they are? Riffraff they are in agreement. They could murder my sister. Go ahead if you enjoy riffraff. They found clan everywhere; I'm telling you one right after another. Dry your towel all night long and underwear. Other Republicans your hair you keep washing it keep your eyes dry and underwear. GOVERNOR HASLAM: REPLACING GOVERNOR BILL HASLAM THE COMMUNITY. You are a mess. You haven't stopped erasing remembrance under your administration, and the Bush Administration atypical inventory revenue may have to replace the Bush Administration, they took a hit the Government entitlement wish list. There is plenty to laugh about, your organizations ribbons some are reflective. You've got enough to hang up you keeping dripping. Come on Haslam Governor, step up to the plate. You old timers you can keep on dripping you have a mouthful, a bag to cry in. You old timers something that we know elected officials deep in mud, pot of greens they will become. I told you that, two months ago. Give it up elected officials. FOR THE LAST SIX YEARS TOPIC SEWAGE ELECTED OFFICIALS. Weak link they have become Pentecost. Mess the system Pentecost. They have used up all their privileges. Impeccable factor in the factor some of you. Here is the latest, every day they greet unemployment with roughen mentality their personality. The enemy thought he had it made. This concerns me black are hurt the worst their living. They think they are on top of the mountain, even on Facebook. Some are up all-night writing on Facebook, their women as well on Facebook. Get the big picture? Danger against people, I view their operation. God is angry. Angry I AM believe me, do you understand people? I give them another path. Lord subtle treatment at the most. Dangerous you can't get rid of me. Nashville music city, I view you many times over. Amen. Question number one: view the consequences, what happen to people that are committed? Altercation help, I AM still running this station that includes bankers. *Believe me I AM no fool Donald Trump, and Madonna. Be wise Nashville. You can say that again definitely. Believe me I AM no fool Donald Trump, and Madonna legally in the air. Be wise Nashville. I'M not going to take that anymore the way you fool around. Tell your daddy your friend reverend, nothing personal nightmare number one. Say, God is real your best investment. Hello, you Democrats all because of you. You'd better wipe that up off the floor; Lipscomb University the same. Couple of times I noticed you. You don't have much time left; you haven't paid for it your last rinse, due to the papers. I AM here. I will back you up. Principality do you understand, do you hear me? The calendar I view the apple weak link. *How about that Ms. Barbara, coupon no more deliverance? I the Marine am here. Ms. Barbara, I see your progress your accomplishment. My husband doesn't know the truth telling about me, and it is no accident for sure negative he is all the time at me, claiming his frustration. And opportunity created, I will hold your hand. Thank God, I got turned around. I view everything. Have a safe journey. LORD, I cried help me. Now you can afford everything. Go ahead knock yourself out in your neighborhood becoming Nashville, even though you wish for little. Backed up, I've told you another department. He would go the moon and a staff, an extra mile for that one what my husband does for crooked. Can't have that thing; he views trash all the time that is why he is so different. He is always dreaming about crooked. NEXT PAGE: he is always dreaming viewing his paper. I will cure you. Don't give up I will get you out of the forest messing with you always. Don't let him take no more advantage upset you no more. I the detective AM always watching viewing his last scene border patrol next, my husband weather beaten pineapple filling. He views my husband tragedy for me. GOD, help me extreme. For your information, this is a bonus from the detective speaking opposite. No doubt document evil one of a kind total reserve at you, that one is possessed with doing you in, shocking everyone knows desired case. You've got evil people threats against you, even your family drawing negative opinion against you, and no moral support gives you frequent. A FORMAL MESSAGE: Steady disclaimer by one in the group doing times of reprisal against you and her name *DJ BIG-TIGER-A LITTLE ONE; screaming on your behalf against your husband. Compass, I view her life stays convicted, stays in touch with GOD now her profile is in courage, I anointed her that way by plan. I will give her strength for sticking with her mother Barbara. I don't like him. Now young one I know you are afraid nothing to be afraid of over him, the difference I've got a new program people. No financial loss for her, I view her brand-new home, and her new husband is on the way with friendship when he is gone. *Giver of life is with her. Burning you are, detail true doing research. *You are writing a book my friend for me, JESUS CHRIST. Pentecost listen the churches don't need conflict right now, she's writing a book for me evil people they are. *My daughter lastly her lonely separated from friends and her family, they did that to her Nathaniel and others with him they are cruel people. LORD JESUS, help me! Her nerves, often give up. Sorry it has come to that. True to life her book. Wait until the next book, and then they will tackle the right one. It's a wonder you've made it thus far the forces of oppression they are against you, even in this neighborhood doing you bodily injured leading the clan her feet. You feel like a prisoner you are drowning, you fake it making yourself glad. Nothing gets by me; trust me I see you in your house crying a lot. How do you like cook potatoes? *Sweet potato cooking catch your breath he don't like you anymore, he's changed his mind, he's changed his appetite. Bottom line threw sweet potato away. No sweet potato no more honey bunch, change in the weather. He's messing with ice cream; he prefers icing on his cake his policy. What about you daughter, he throws off on you? He covers up his mess. I've already told you about it. Be happy, you have another friend show me just JESUS CHRIST. I see one on top of another crazy he is your husband, he is an embarrassment. I see your problem. That is the strength of JESUS CHRIST view that He is real. I AM real people. I view her night and day. I see the threat the system. My defense battleground heated. I see for whatever cost it takes no regret, up the ante against you Ms. Barbara Payne. Oh my-gosh! Very simple socially accepted behind me. Oh, my-gosh we the people! Change coming your way your relationship people, avoid hillbilly's that gossip like that they are bullies. LORD, have mercy on the Black people everywhere even in the school system. Cutoff date coming soon warmer weather the forecast, a few estimates sacrilegious the pillar, the forecast piece of lemon. *THUS SAITH THE LORD JESUS CHRIST unto me; don't hear the backwards Black people everywhere, legally they are ignorant all just a suggestion, they are Whites men against you, they are battery hoping they will be scraping physically you up one-day battery Pentecost in any case and *the creepy*; they are calling you backwards. Don't you talk to them keep speaking and just walk away, they are larger than you. Generally speaking affirm these words Black folk's adults they are have a blind eye on you, just a suggestion Pentecost. Get this physically they are on their way to hell in America; leave it up to the judge the traffic created by them. And there are suicide bombers everywhere; they work in pairs everywhere even at night especially in Detroit, Michigan watch the generation of their youth, watch your family everywhere! Tragedies for you everywhere even in the nighttime hour, cling closer to our God JESUS CHRIST, the problem can be solved again watch their youth be vigilant! Congress now serve this on them leave America.   I view you in late December.  Coming up happen a short time ago, I know your genealogy others as well; they think they are getting over on the U. S. in America!   I know their mark many are beast. They are monsters. They hide behind America. *The Mohammed, rubbing shoulder to shoulder agony nowhere are you listening?   PROPHECY: personal speech holding a book, your new book the Koran people everywhere. *Look at their Koran, their environment full of hatred one of a kind. Forecast, you will end up paying for that rod later, when they carried you to the hospital.   Let that be a lesson.   That rod in their hand, it may look like its clean blow you up with all kind of explosives.  INTRODUCTORY: view success progress no settlement we have it, the power to create our own defense in the world, this nation at large.  We will stop selling tickets.  Look all around you perfect opinion drawing attention the savior of the world; talk to you underground umbrella near Napier Valley top valley, where the vines grow in the valley.   Near Nashville, avoid their presence veterans most definite. An olive branch new program brought numerous with him, the South. They know your face in Buckingham Palace—caring fake I.D's on your facility. A new forecast and everywhere near the Grand Canyon as well, a big sacrifice he got a ticket just thinking. Tropical stay on fire, and never give up just ask people it's okay the high point the government. Just don't go crazy Massachusetts, the gubernatorial same Arabs enormous breast to breast fading ridiculous right now are these Arabs underground, proven fact their army in the United States of America, reality challenges not making themselves known in America, they are Jihad, jealous extreme of America. What kind of missions at home here in the U.S., adopted a lint brush mission being awkward? They are crazy these Islamic extremists against America, never getting comfortable they are extremists. But with the help of God, my friends we will win this war gentleman a moral integrity. Compass a passion set them up; they are crazy as a tank head. Can I tell you something? THANK YOU, LORD JESUS YOUR GRACE. No past onion their interest this is truth. View their reality history reality in this "*A NEW ARTICLE*," even in Jerusalem okay? These people their participation in Jihadist equipment they are backwards many of them, the Republicans know this already, they tried to negotiate with them after the fact, they cannot win this war a miracle is on the way. Finally, look up close to their honesty, their reason for it why they are attracted to suicide missions, near their Mask Germany, and Amsterdam, as well; the same thing for Murfreesboro, Tennessee in the United States. Shocked! A FORMAL MESSAGE: for your defense formal places look out for them that is where they love to hide. Thank you, JESUS CHRIST. Block them! *Hay, this is why they do it it's a breakthrough its service no other hindrance; if they die no competition in their world isn't that amazing? Massachusetts, better take a legal head count simple force of theirs their duty, that is what they get out of it their designated weapon vengeance against our Lord JESUS CHRIST; upstanding holding us all together His Empire entirely celebrated. FROM ABOVE: never move with a blink of an eye big crisis pretty much I would declare it, we in this nation are of one nation: the point of view the Christian nation individually my point of view said JESUS unto me; from above a new avenue, a new point of view. Do not host them. *Host His Empire One GOD JESUS CHRIST that we are one accordingly to scripture legally awesome. JESUS CHRIST the way one way. What's wrong with their depth challenges to the kingdom of God, general reason to get closer to their god, not to our GOD, JESUS CHRIST? They are going nowhere but to death on their way to hell realizing nothing. The challenges and their deal contact lemon coat that way reliable sources most intelligence. Intelligence worldwide they have been trying to catch them, and bring them down. Super intelligence knows their hide outs all over the world intelligence know. Thought for the day we are learning everything. Get rid of them out of your camp. They will go anywhere. Again, one hundred percent near known Republicans key audience, the package no exceptions act like they are bland Beverly Hills as well approaching. Believe me they are everywhere, they are lawless. Boston, they are bagging you, what about you they are low down pure evil? Move the rest of them out of your way. They want to rule your land your country, this nation. *These are Muslim extremists armed with explosives in cities with a gun, their form of Jihad they love guns. They are watching you, count on 5,000 or more no exceptions. They aren't just playing. *Only abbreviation protection Pentecost, now behave repeat meddling in the affairs of others. Thus saith the LORD and opportunity; definitely with confidence your public enemy turn the table. I can cure it are you listening? Don't threaten. You may think I'M crazy, you may think I'M crazy that kind of guy the difference think the impossible, I believe in miracles. The newspapers report in Great Britain it to the public in Great Britain, as we have haven't seen any disturbances. Legal weapon they have them, they've had them for years amazing there in Great Britain, unbelievable. *For example, you need to secure your borders more strictly. Cover grounds eight percent check them, basically you need to take heed to that victory is yours. Bombard their every move. You're not along in this. Top rich people are stalking Great Britain out as well, they will kill children as well any people within that is a defense problem. *THE QUEEN HER MAJESTY THE QUEEN OF ENGLAND, GOD SAVE THE QUEEN. Say, that I refuse to be intimidated, they watch ISRAEL as well. Great Britain in the heat of the battle I will recognize you. Great Britain in the land your last attempt public, before AMERICA is hit as well. London suicide bombers everywhere the public needs to be inform, even in Nashville, TN join the hoops. Oh thank you, JESUS CHRIST. THE MONARCH AS WELL THE HOOKUP SIGNIFICANT ON THE STREET, THE QUEEN THE BUFFER HER MAJESTY QUEEN ELIZABETH, clinging in England extremists near Buckingham Palace and all across the country you need a lock down. Save the Queen! Lock down! Gentlemen Prince's, they are watching keep your eye on them indefinitely, any Royal Family Member Her Majesty: even PIPA likewise. GOD Save the Queen and her whole family watch the ding-dong they are doing it. We love The Queen Her Majesty. TERRIBLE UNBELIEVABLE BACK TO THE ROYAL FAMILY: PRINCE'S KATE MIDDLETON WIFE OF PRINCE WILLIAM MY FRIEND, BEWARE IN ANY EVENT THINGS CAN HAPPEN! TO THE ROYAL FAMILY: SERVING ME AND THEIR GOVERNMENT THANK YOU JESUS CHRIST. I HOLD YOU UP THE KEEPER OF YOUR FAMILY AND IN LONDON, I VIEW YOU ALL THE TIME AND THESE EXTREMISTS, THE RESULTS AND THE BENEFITS ROYAL FAMILY OF ENGLAND. Commoner so afraid your friend and the Executive Branch of America primary passenger, oh my GOD, this word delivered your answer. This work spoken is very important agreed without a doubt you need to address it. TO: THE UNITED KINGDOM; use wisdom they are a national threat when looking at foreign records and any future records, you still have time specifics. You ought to be ashamed no doubly of yourselves fallout against Great Britain and the Queen, follow me? Commoner here: Great Britain I love you very much. GOD IS LOOKING OUT FOR YOU, MOST DEFINITELY NO JOKE ENGLAND THEY'RE IN YOUR TOWN, THEY'RE EVERYWHERE. IT IS VERY IMPORTANT THAT YOU LISTEN, THEY ARE EVERYWHERE THOSE WISHING TO DO YOU HARM, BEWARE OF THEM; IT'S A BONUS FOR THEM WANTING TO DO THE QUEEN HARM. Race to get it stopped, the Black people here wish you well Her Majesty the Queen. They are after you as well United Kingdom. PRINCE CHARLES, AND PRINCE WILLIAM, AND PRINCE HARRY-THE DRUMMER FOR THE UNITED KINGDOM LITERALLY THEY ARE NO JOKE THESE PEOPLE. We the people in the United States of America, we care alright, because he cares PRINCE ANDREW, the father PRINCE PHILIP, they have given literally a lot the Royal Family. We are grateful. They are everywhere the terrorists watching in London some are Black, a sad mishap to the wind. PRINCE PHILIP BE A FATHER, YOUR BOUNDARIES FOR PRINCE WILLIAM AND OTHER KINGS AFTER HIM. HALLELUJAH! AND WATCH YOUR PALACE. I know how you view a commoner, I personally feel your way don't like them either their hate absolutely against ISRAEL, definitely. Knock on wood. Here is an understanding equal your Prince, try and set an example a wheel for the future alright, for the future king? Be an example. Literally PRINCE PHILIP, low Great Britain and Buckingham Palace your palace, people coming from everywhere looking out the windows an attack, definitely upcoming coming from the Middle East, hear that! Don't you see they know no boundaries? What about Great Britain legally it's a balance; they are on top of buildings, striking and KILLING THE AMASSADOR FOR THE UNITED STATES OF AMERICA. TO: GREAT BRITAIN resolve the conflict they are everywhere a foreign government Black legally in your country. Blank is their target. We will get them in due time CHRIST JESUS said; that I promise a remark. Let me tell you something, keep lifting hot route next year soldiers everywhere even in AFRICA, these Republicans brought them here. THE QUEEN HAIL THE QUEEN: Republicans, Her Majesty at this particular: view a circumstance outlaws they follow her The Queen wherever she goes. Can you imagine? Buckingham Palace watch out Buckingham turn it around type it out. Engineered extraordinary silence, courtesy—people thinking they want to see the Queen. And they follow her in London wherever she is, PRINCE PHILIP as well even the very elite in the British Government society, even The French Government they follow your motorcade wherever you are going. They leave Lebanon in the Middle East, and from Pakistan they come, sound an alarm they create confusion watch your guard clad in hatred young Mr. Juvenile thinking they are the men, and they are in AUSTRALIA, and in the U.S., and CANADA, pity AUSTRALIA. They will get even. They are black they are watching they speak English, they consider it luxury to occupy. What about Great Britain they speak English quite well—the absent their own, follow the Queen everywhere mobile on the streets, Prince Philip likewise, the Royal servant of David. Proper word, hold to doctrine. London, treat your friend's fair a lot of people depend on you and the public. I love the Queen. *KEEP YOUR STANDARDS HIGH PRINCE PHILIP OF ENGLAND, AND CAMILLA CHARMING. I view luncheon with you, her majesty and the Queen in essence someday. Hooray! For the Queen November, 2nd ABC NEWS aired it even Buckingham Palace, a new philosophy. Catch a plane to London. THUS SAITH THE LORD unto me the matter; your company hear me GOD; this is private industry your next coupon. They won't wrestle me. The forces of evil are eyeing you right now. The Government knows it, the Japanese knows it. Hear me mantle of God, agreed? Legend, your women and men likely use them as scapegoats, they are using them for cover. Black people already know it. Physical detective information, secret driving arrangement to carry out their bombing attacks against Londoner's, "keep that in your pocket keep your hands in your pocket" essence keep that in your memory. Everybody knows it; no rocket science the public knows it Welch. Like hitting a bull's-eye their contest legally, the Queen they view her as cabbage, and all of England. They get over. I see Kmart looking at them they just like visiting Kmart selling excuses, a lot give us your list the majority of them are war veterans out to get us lethal weapon small places, they need schooling to get somewhere. Heaven only help us. Mainly they are used (the women no joke) sort of like black people. They use their women to protect people, the ones that are behind their evil doings. Oh, my-gosh Washington. Don't believe the half of them faking falsehood they testified. They are specialists hiding everywhere. You're not along. I view your integrity. I view your problem turning things now gathering reports. *The Monarch warning go about your business no hesitation, New York City the same, dual arrest soon jar the papers. Just like the President, I AM your ticket out of dooms-day your way out of this mess. I will help with the situation even Buckingham Palace. I AM your friend anyway. I know your address after all your Deputy, and Roosevelt he didn't tremble. Stay humble working hard. THANK YOU, SAVIOR JESUS CHRIST. I know your strength in the Council. In New York, Philadelphia as well, people are coming to help, help you out your defense people. Locally remember me your Savior. Black people around the world for whatever cost we won't take it anymore, the truth the way the world treats us honestly President Obama. Oh my God! He's done a good job looking over backwards, from on the wrong side they are, I view them of the street this is true. *Customarily President Obama awesome you have did an awesome job; regionally in your place to be there no longer than you have viewing weapons from the pits for a lifetime. We're all walking a fine line viewing blanks like you, doing the best we can. Republicans you've played your part. No steel brain Republicans, in exchange they spy on us. Its nighttime full of carpenters, ignorant, conquering people they don't want peace. Say, their days are numbered. We know you need help in this office the newspapers ought to record it better, talk about lateral turn soon; get your advance you get a metal Mr. White House, for the mess you put up with. Praise Him President Obama, JESUS CHRIST our Lord; give to Him the highest praise.  No offense Mr. Obama, say it louder we hold on to God no matter what this time!  Oh my God!   Family in the kingdom it makes me nervous what they are whispering, me testified understand? Help turn things around.   You are a cool person.  Follow after me.  Let me deal with it the mess my disciple.  You're an awesome God!  I know what you're going through.  Be observant battle line is drawn.   I've got your back, a missile on their premise.  I measure you they think they are trump are better.  Be nice I see heart attack for a few.   I recognize a few.   No weapon formed against you can ever prosper.  *Be lazy no more—it's their opinion all about you, a battle line their effort against you.  Hear me now, procrastinate no more stay prepared.   You procrastinate too much, I have observed.  They think that you are lazy.  It's no excuse your cousins, the way they have treated you.    *IMAGES: Josie cast off and some of my people.   She laughed a lot at you, Josie started it.  I've got proof from above.  They laugh at you a lot, I guarantee your friends as well thinking you were weak.  Pentecost, foul mouth they all are Josie's children, and I will be in pursuit.  A messy human being Josie she was, believe me Pentecost always telling tales on you, and your other sister as well but she was a friend.  A lot of people are like that messy on one hand, and showing prudence on the other at the same time.   Her debt, I'M reading the book now proof of her mischief.   I'M looking on it now graphing ling with it now.   Your inheritance a deep river flowed.  A lot of people are like that on the other hand graph-ling emerged.  You should Pentecost "*Do unto others as you would have them do unto you.*" *Elsie could be like Jessie James, whenever she wanted to be a bit disruptive like the "*Wild Wild West*" saying disturbance knowing no boundaries, and her two children are the same it's just and opinion, they need to see church a lot, inside frozen they are a lot those two children of hers. *Elsie Dean your other sister, not so big up front (laughing), stays warm in her heart a rational independent.  I me, I want to think you JESUS CHRIST thank you very much.

LORD, have mercy on those individuals in all cases those individuals.  AND FROM ABOVE: Believe me, be grateful you are out of that atmosphere you ought to shout hallelujah, and your three children as well. On this side of the river her exit coming up my daughter, keep praying for her. *Her race is already won she is a Christian. Do you understand? GOD meet her needs soon she will be on the elevator on her way up, I provides for all her needs like the regular and she basically understands anyhow, her battle is already won her stroke settled it.  Just anyway, now behave don't act on impulse get it she pushed you along the way? Now be nice, be very beautiful she was to you.  She is ashamed. It is no fluke a red flag has landed (a warning signal). Be grateful for her. Be grateful you are anointed by God JESUS CHRIST. You know why the difference Pentecost, big bountiful blessings I send your way no penalties, because I love you?  Immerse my friend tell it like it is and be grateful. Be thankful, and wonderfully colorful like Martin Luther King, don't be reactionary.  Don't change your mind. You hear that? Let me tell you something, you think too much you're reactionary to them.  Just close your eyes and say nothing be an observer Ms. Thinker like me, and don't be afraid when you get home.  Don't mess with them they are in another world half of the time, they are in another dim realm weighted way down, you soon will be established in your career as a writer for God, just listen to me be a mentor to your family, and Pentecostal people everywhere, and just to people church people and the ordinary in life. *Your heritage around this town around them be a complaint tomorrow, be an observer in their presence. Let me tell you something, free I have a prescription for that. See if you have any problem bring it to me.  Do your best walk with me JESUS CHRIST? You are a Christian it makes a difference. I see. Amen. I can't imagine my life without you; you are my pathway the light of the world, GOD ALMIGHTY. Wish you were somewhere else.  Crossed they all are your husband too.  Be a thinker GOD will help you, know you were born pedigree do not go around them, trash they are a low life group and this is truth. And that makes a difference your eternity. They all know better. Do your best. I know about what you do. *And The "NOAH'S ARK-Gang" just a reference about you as well a pulley holding it together with their own duffle window, their own experience as of now. And about them they all know who they are trouble that is for sure-with a Big Mouth! That is not your problem. An Ezell not your blessing, they are under arrest like TIGER WOODS. Pentecost they all are going to meet their Maker GOD ALMIGHTY, at their arrest Pentecost meddling. Be thankful. *Not nuts as some suppose even politicians. So be grateful. Never give up give in to them. Separate yourself from them. Lizards, they all are going to jail a free-fall down to hell, even in Nashville. *And about you no confrontation love that don't get in the middle, let me set you free. This battle is not yours physically ugly they are. I see your blessing. Thank you, Lord JESUS CHRIST our Lord and our Savior! Let me give a hand fight for you, for Black people everywhere. Lord JESUS the person the only person that I know never a stroke, and never a quiver using your weapons, and never walking a tight rope very little controversy on Him, and never missing the mark be free be and observer like them. I'M telling you always. You are gambling your life away if you mess with those kinds. I'M telling you always be an observer, they are watching you always. They're like NYPD checking you out always.

## WHAT HAPPENED TO AMERICA; A TRAIN WRECK? QUESTION: YOU DIDN'T KNOW? SAY THANKS TO JESUS CHRIST, US CHRISTIANS A NEW DEVELOPMENT FROM ABOVE.

Thus saith the LORD unto me; repugnant, prudent the afterthought, the after matters can you imagine a thick forest? We can do better believe me.  I AM growing out of patience we must be in unison. An attack will force us to require more book learning. It is a free world only the smartest will ever survive on this planet, don't miss it.  We are contributing the final phase of what God created. The bomb debate face the aftermath.  *A new way of doing this hear this Buckingham Palace: a new schedule this I know a new course from the news media; what happened to America this morning can happen to Great Britain.  Thousands of people were killed washed away on the shore.  People will be screaming ten feet away, and nobody could help them.  People were trying, but nobody could get to them in time their house was blown away. A DEADLY ATTACK WHERE WAS QUEEN ELIZABETH HER HOUSE WAS BOMBED AS WELL, A MYSTERY WHO WAS BEHIND IT? Most unusual Buckingham Palace was the target of a terrorists attack. Trash hit Rome.  "Let's kill the people in the United States as well."  That was meant for me. Soldiers everywhere was fighting. Bumper to bumper cars were trying to leave the U. S. in America, even the Mexicans were leaving the United States of America, they were seeking transportation to leave this was reality. *Boulder, Colorado in the United States was hit hard missiles everywhere.  They couldn't divide us. The Government was trying to succeed to secure those places physically.  God our JESUS CHRIST from above to me; he made it right and even on the West Coast. *What an episode, proof was everywhere eight passenger train car was blown up, bodies were everywhere missile attack on the United States even during rush hour traffic. Members were twice as likely use weapon defense to cover their tracks, their escape route these are most important. Last resort respectful to minority's who took it upon their own to defend themselves in the United States. During the Olympics multiple attacks occurred, the Cubans were never part of the United States anyway. The United States Government tried to explain what happened in Cuba, but the issues were too hard for us the United States of

America to explain. For example, this death and devastation the philosophy has been to locally reject the sources, Black people everywhere knew it would happen think the impossible. *We are on a battle ground legally.

TO THE GROUP: THINGS ARE IMPOSSIBLE IMPROVE YOUR RELATIONSHIP A GREAT IDEA.

THUS SAITH THE LORD; I went to Rome today—providence that it happened my people. They put the Baptist to shame what they were studying. They put me out redundant English what they were saying. Read *SAINT LUKE*; the KJV; the essence. What a mighty GOD we serve in this country, we bless Him. To the people, of your generation more technical term are you listening? And event this year 2011, JESUS CHRIST forever changing things the author and finisher of all things a sweet event, I wash my hands the last time. And event reported the event heresy. I AM a witness they are not worthy. *I AM leaving Rome that great Roman Empire. Holy have I not become. *Don't under estimate me on your level. Give me a big reception. Panoramic I have a wide view basically inefficient they are, they need a brand-new house. They have never spoke in tongues receiving the gift of the Holy Ghost. Exclude their main event pastors go ahead pastors even in France, proven everywhere my approval. *Their main event the wonder you will read it in the News Paper, I'M telling all Catholics better include me permanently. The event heard around the world fire from God, Holy Fire from God JESUS CHRIST me against my adversaries my destiny, my resources, I AM the source your pink slip. The event even their children "I need to get back to basics." I'M preparing for their emotions. Hear that? Your friend The Queen of England even the Queen has friends around the world in Italy as well, you hear that? You are going to Mexico, finding refuge there chapel will be held everywhere. You are opening up a can of worms; the explosion will be heard around the world more prophecy later. The Pope was wearing white trying to convince Mexicans they are true believers, also true even the Muslims care more about me than they do, even though they are a long ways away—polar long ways away from where they ought to be. It will be shots heard around the world.

THE UNCERTAIN OF HIM JESUS CHRIST, YOUR CHRIST WHO CAN FORGET HIM TALKING ABOUT JESUS MINISTERS, JESUS CHRIST THE ONE AND ONLY YOU REMEMBER JOHN THE BAPTIST AND HIS RECIPE, BUT WHAT ABOUT CHRIST'S OUR REDEEMER? YOU ARE WARNED INCLUDING PENTECOST EVERYWHERE NO SECOND DEFENSE. EVERY AVENUE REAL PENTECOST NOT A NATIVE KNOW THAT GOD IS ALWAYS ABLE.

THUS SAITH THE LORD; you're under arrest all yee Baptist this day, I'M talking about everybody. Every day I view victim at large legal cunning, and craftiness will cease everywhere you Baptist: First Baptist Capitol Hill a new idea: follow where the wind is blowing. Knowing thou redeemer, The Baptist Church is without promise in the kingdom of God. I upset you your honor, be prepared your finances. *Better put your *armor* on an attack on yall's finances. Yes, JESUS CHRIST it is true. Everything is inclusive, if you want to go to heaven. A good prescription read the word of GOD, be on the side of the law not the Church of Christ. Money will look this way Pentecost. North Nashville Pentecostals induced a new resolution: The African Americans please show the gospel the right way. Roll out the red carpet for CHRIST, Pentecostals for JESUS CHRIST, and investigation called war crimes a true investigation the Government knows no more tailgating eating cake. Dangerous investigation city of Nashville, typical views the application. In five years traffic it is coming your way bee an intercessor

Pentecostals.  *They dove into Michigan, Detroit was crippled and in Brooklyn, I AM going to make the change says JESUS CHRIST. Hear that Whoopi Goldberg, and the house?  My address Apostolic Churches local churches your event.  Here is the case view your case stand you are backwards; they are still putting on a show alright?  Forecast, knocking at your door the Capital Branch, I'M in the middle.  Quite frankly I'M tired of you don't play with me anymore; don't vex me that is the issue. You have become a weak link standing preaching your crowd.  I AM a witness to this all your mess.  All your racism your simple antics your playing games. Wicked you have become in the sight of the Lord JESUS CHRIST. Everything you polish is so visible.  Republicans I can identify racism, you pastors with your racists attitude Jim Crow backwards in the Bible belt Southern White Churches you're just lying; the African Americans haughty you have become. I arrest you as well; you come to me with privilege attitude. You ought to be hung out to dry no complaints.  You look the same way your microwave dress.  I view you a long time ago.  The Capitol Hill in advance warning, an agreement between me and other Pentecostals don't you dare laugh. See your exploits on life as a child of God upholding your doctrine.  Keep on sinking, your churches look at them. Ready take a quick look at them, and then you are sending folks to hell—your establishment, you go nowhere with it your agency? Hello!  There will be a stamped of approval here in Nashville, at the Republican detective.  You will want to go to any one of the radio announcements African American Apostolic Church, even Democrats across board are pending then your train is turning, I'M telling you specifics backwards.  Show me the victims your own term shout you are the victims; your leaders have been getting the opposite of what I have wanted them to do intentionally.  We are Apostolics' those are the issues battleground. We have reached a pinnacle of success each person's finances even on talk shows game shows don't go anywhere, we are nearing the quarter finals.

We have reached an agreement maintaining churches, opportunity last only for so long. Witness are watching now. Brute beasts are busy. Apostolics their fancy they have no prepared limitations, they are facing disaster. Almost forgotten Pentecostal their limitations in a crib, been a dad a deceiver. They have lost their case no incident. Stealing is their main policy need a backup PAW, they have already been caught for example, there are no objections literally pocketing money. For God's sake, their handling of money it is official keep up the good work dead people. A few women say getting their groove on no one is listening he likes it, he's their main man. Pentecostals guess what? To the keeper, we will pray over it their policy? And good news their churches keep up the good work, you know how it is no question about it; it's a dirty shame I view it every day them pocketing money using the revenue that should belong to the church. There are bonuses my bonus, pastor's goodbye no question about it. Pentecostals the other side, the number of White Churches their organizations this is a fact their crime, the difference their hatred of others rebel rousers has been they are, officially I view them all the time in the Country in the United States. My friends, I want it stopped. I view their political tracks. They are lost how they operate in North Carolina, overflowing at the banks adultery. They are serving time specifics. I know two things concerning the ministry. A political thing they are an embarrassment is what they are. Pentecostals you're acting like them as well. I know how they operate; I AM ahead of you that is the good news read *JOHN* 3:16 (KJV) my documentary. Favor they have lost. They are just like wolves with their limitations. Let me pinpoint it, and their side ugly. Another thing Black people everywhere, they charm even at funerals and receptions, look at them always *déjà vu* gathering, Pentecostals making themselves the toast of the town so embarrassing. Fear Pentecostals alright, your bell is about to ring? I'M taking ready taking notes, the wrath of God is about to explode on all churches, absolutely just like a gun. They are not prepared. See their brand they have become chasing other women. Pentecostals want to go to heaven they are above you, and they want to go to heaven with confidence, the other function watch me discharge you.

OUR SOCIETY, KNOW THAT I AM REAL FEAR GOD. YOU HAVE ALREADY OBTAINED MERCY THAT IS SIGNIFICANT IT IS NO ACCIDENT. LISTEN TO ME; KNOW THAT GOD HE IS REAL EVEN AT THIS HOUR. AMEN. TO ALL THE YOUNG PEOPLE REMEMBER TRUE PENTECOST GOD HE IS OUR FRIEND, I SEE THE DEATH TOTAL NOW. TRUE PENTECOST FROM ABOVE: GOD JESUS CHRIST, HE IS YOUR FRIEND WHEN NOBODY IS WATCHING, YOUR SERVICE THE EVIDENCE. GOD, JESUS YOU CAN RELY ON ME. BE A FRIEND PENTECOST. AND HE IS ABLE RIGHT NOW. LET ME DEMONSTRATE, A CLOSURE YOU ALL'S EVENT BE A SUCCESS IN LIFE.

Thus saith the LORD; inside directions hear God follow me, and obey together united. When we all get together in the Upper Room, and stop going about our own business here is the Lamb, stay healthy in the world, then we can have good news saying, JESUS save me, stay united then we'll have gains I'm looking forward to that read the book. We have obtained it defined read the book. *Southern Baptist don't remain backwards; improve your relationship with God. God created us all falsely if you think any other way. Don't hold to backwards. *Make a long story short Black people are everywhere. Believe me. Hear that Southern Baptist. Improve your relationship with more understanding, with other ethnic people great thinkers. Did you get that the evidence God desires it? Elevate up please we can all improve. *Southern Church leaders—Southern White Baptists everywhere, my friends doing what you want to do is not the way out of here. The axis is no accident, and neither is Pentecostal: Truth to that! You are warm White practicing Jim Crow. Here is my feelings on rebel-minded, the House of Representative in the State, and in our State is full of White supremacy advocates wanting to escape, and the gulf of disobedience many people are fakes. Shout "*Shine On Me,*" From Above the Maker. The evidence exactly including Baptist right now the observer, hear the prophet *JOEL*, a true messenger from GOD, this is important. That is what has gone wrong on the wrong hand technically. What did I just say? Cross your fingers count to zero see your offense. No umbrella for your front. Now believe me, God He is watching. Thus saith the LORD; hallelujah, I'M going to shake things up, you can't hold me back. I'll tell you what happened. Every day the adopted God is working things out. Your place the adopted, you've taken all the advantage that the Lord will allow. Hear those that have translated before us Christians, the ambassador's of fellowship strong witnesses before God. I know their address despite of what anyone else says. Take a look rise to the occasion. Take advantage tunnel everybody to the extreme armor everybody, payable ready if you are thirsty. Everybody get ready. Narrow minded if you don't. Get your armor on brother Baptist in Nashville; be like Pentecost all denominations be an adult it's your job that is how it operates. Fasten your seat belt if you don't. We are partner's I tell God everything been partners facing reality. Give it up should have been a long time ago, I'M telling you a long time ago. GOD JESUS CHRIST, JESUS he made everything isn't that right Pentecostals, you can't get around it people? I tell you nothing that you already do not know. He's the one that made me. Christians, I the person facing reality major reality just like me. Amen for a reality. So we are equal think about that after you face Him. Don't put it off make no mistake people, and another thing because it is important to you it can be a lost opportunity. Thank you, JESUS. We are equal. Put your hands to the plow. You are awesome, JESUS CHRIST.

Know your value even in Antioch, Tennessee know that is our self defense a window. My God, Yes it is an opportunity a window, a thorough complete success of life's lessons on relationships for Christians from the Creator our God. Races Pentecostals muscle men and women through all races to the people even suburban, and beggars in Nashville, no matter what others say what your skin color is Brown, White, Yellow, or Black, different skin color of Nashville, all different races the department General Inspector I can remove that mountain, Republicans instructions for Nashville. To my people a balance and avenue of unique moment opportunity, okay even to the current home owner this year get to the altar? Your Case Closed! Shoulder the responsibility right to death people, okay? I recommend legally to the Baptist exactly troubling Methodist, the Africans, the African Americans, and Baptist whatever your religious affiliation denomination woe *ISAIAH*; we need the right leader at any time even the Republicans on satellites business as usual all of God's people, churches of great equal significant thinly sliced battleground in Nashville, Tennessee. Thank you, JESUS. Even the Southern Baptist no matter what category you might fall in, I the person JESUS CHRIST flipping great news, and guess what your event this is what you look like behind the scenes. I view you for the last twenty seven years; you have a special opportunity the groups everywhere. Hallelujah, a unique window differing reach for this opportunity. Things are durable this payless society thinly sliced. Thank you, Lord JESUS CHRIST. Let's have an opportunity come to GOD, the dawn is approaching.

GOVERNOR HASLUM A NEW AVENUE, I KNOW YOUR ZIP CODE, AND THAT IS TRUE A FACT. I KNOW WHO YOU ARE. THERE HAS GOT TO BE SOME CHANGES. CALL ME CRAZY HONOR THE LORD'S NAME, GIVE TO THE VICTIM. HONOR, TAKE AWAY FROM WILLIAMSON COUNTY BE QUICK, AND BE UNMOVABLE. MISSISSIPPI JUST AND

ACORN, NOW THEY TREMBLE THAT'S THE TRUTH. LOOK AT WHAT HAPPENED TO THE STATE OF MISSISSIPPI, THEY SERVE ME NOW AFTER TORNADOES AND HURRICANES; MANY OF THEM ARE NO WHERE TO BE FOUND, THEY SUFFERED MANY SINCE THOSE HIT THE STATE A TRUE FACT. DID YOU HEAR ME? RICH AS WELL I POSTED THAT HAPPENING THAT HIT THEIR WORLD. HELP THE MINORITIES THAT ARE SUFFERING IT WILL BE ON YOUR BILL, UNBELIEVABLE WILL BE READ EVERYWHERE. YOU KNOW WHERE TO FIND THE DESPERATE, THEY ARE IN SHELTERS EVERYWHERE IN NASHVILLE, THAT IS THE CASE PLAINLY PUT. DON'T DELAY, THEY ARE PEOPLE AS WELL. THE NOTION JUST SEE, THE TASK POLITICIANS IN YOUR NEIGHBORHOODS. THE SAVIOR I AM YOUR FRIEND JESUS CHRIST. I WILL CHANGE YOUR VISION THE RIGHT ATTITUDE ACADEMICS. WALK A MILE IN SOMEONE ELSE THEIR SHOES.

THUS SAITH THE LORD; I AM a witness nobody called on me. I can make a difference notice on Capitol Hill know your genealogy, your history, and your neighborhood; I will back you up it is my job *your.ancestry.dot.com...* Check it out. Oh Lord *"How Great Thou Are,"* Pentecost. You've paid the price no more borrowing think about it, heaven your new address being with JESUS CHRIST where he lives, and other anointed that is the reason. Weak walk one at a time tendency after election many Republicans, bonus repair patriot—bologna. In Alabama, there are the extremes everybody knows; this is true men particular holding their rally in a town where it's free. Shameful acts at a restaurant waiting for Uncle Tom's in Government Office, to pass a bill their way. That's a shame. Hold on you'll be on FACEBOOK: that will be on FACEBOOK. You're loitering on FACEBOOK, but I've got the upper hand. You're on FACEBOOK a big controversy. Many don't complain view it as trash talking. Get the envelope didn't anyone tell you computers are watching people like you, who put dynamite on Facebook huge mistake? You will be hollowing someone help me. Are y'all having a good time? Ku Klux Klan in the country, in a field across a field neighbors watching. Y'all be careful watch your back now. Duty agree, would you agree? But we all know that it happens. Don't let them make a fool out of you be wise. Read your scripture. Your African American Heritage Agency come on Nashville, your home the only one who knows all about it pain is coming way. You've got a problem. Acidic are Black people a normal event focus on God. Flags everywhere I'll change it. People here is a happy median, we can put a stop to it have a vision another one to bear. You went to LA, compelling for Christmas-second tour. You've got a cross to bear! Be the principal come together Capitol Hill, let's teach them a lesson do you want to? It is embarrassing the way our kids, have poor performance on Achievement Test. We can go around the block once just on Jefferson Street, during street level igniting just once. We're up in arms things sucks shouting. Get the picture? Close Jefferson Street down go to the Capitol and march. We pass Jefferson Street already. In addition that will be the ground floor for protestors independent. Read *PHILIPIANS* (KJV) 1:12 But I would ye should understand, brethren, that the things which happened unto me have fallen out rather unto the furtherance of the gospel. / CHRIST JESUS said, Nashville a design from Him make it whatever you want it to be it is all free. Is it free a messenger your health is free? An appointment on the other hand that is a good question: no kidding those who have an appointment? Come by Him Bishop. Saying oh my God, can we repeat that again you can feel it? Go break a leg. WE CAN TEAR THAT DOWN EVERYTHING CRACK DOWN ON FEDERAL DOLLARS, OUR SCHOOLS BUDGET GOING TO ANOTHER COUNTY'S SCHOOL BUDGET. WE'RE CARING THE LOAD. Governor Haslum, a new mandate take advantage delete Charter Schools, they are a false option fire everyone that is working in those schools; we don't need them anyway, they are irrelevant a lot of people don't know any better. Say it's over. Look at the new possibilities look at what they have done to Metro Nashville Public Schools a dangerous option they are. The shift bring back public education, the way it use to be. Do away with Charter Schools in Davidson County, Donelson do you hear me? Tell the General Assembly a new outlet, we can do better satisfaction will occur everywhere throughout all of Davidson County. We had a plan view them the right way. Dr. Registrar, Metro Government Republican School Board rocks they are. I know we can do better, I will return those interest for funding literally been all one in the United States of America. I know those issues Republicans a new policy, a new day of values. A NEW OPITION: We have it they dried up our kids funding here in Metro-Nashville, clipping coupons sue anyway make the difference. Burn them they never gave back the payment, the damage has been done. Pass new legislation. It is absolutely a dumping ground; we have the evidence your mess. FROM ABOVE: It is absolutely a mess those control freaks. You want my advice stop favoring districts. *Incidentally come on up Zion, time to get your pick and shovel MT. ZION BAPTIST CHURCH. You have political influence in Nashville, no argument with that your influence. I AM convinced, considering the voters African Americans that are from you church. Stay connected. GOD is going to do something stand up for JESUS CHRIST. This next year's election year be a force, while you are gathering go to the polls I need you, and by the way good equipment. More application talk about a heavy turnout see how strong I AM against politics; see how powerful I really am. Watch me deliver. Faith is underdog total victory. One other thing all the sounds are independent. Your regret preacher you have to inevitably, you may drown them out for a little bit—your excuse. Plead the fifth better watch out. People take it the wrong way we're talking about coming together. The cheering is on deliverance say I give in to your blessing. You think I'M appalling watch me the number, GOD in high places watch for sunshine. The diagnosis is already in. Upside down deal with it your remark. See how you fell you'd better look up be courageous. For comfort you have pushed me away not courageous, you don't know a thing about me. Read the book of *ACTS* and *ROMANS*. I have no regrets my doctrine in remembrance of me. I wash my hands of your whole mess. Say, Lord I'm going to miss you. I'M ready to get a divorce from your Church, the Black Church. There are ten thousand, and there are many more men ready to take your place anytime I want them too. Your address: just comfort chilling on your congregation in Nashville. Give it up man what's wrong with you, I'AM a witness break the habit? I formed the earth don't you ever forget it stay close to me; Lord JESUS. You're in the basement rattling and your camp you bother me. Did you hear? Opposition you're ignorant do it the right way your event. *Why don't you tell Elder George Burns and be thankful, he is so informative and your defense tell him right away. I like Elder Burns Ms. Barbara. Give it up your chattering from nine to five you are like a chatter box. Get down to the real issues from above those situations. Those issues man the linebacker before the Chairman, the Apostle with GOD, LORD JESUS CHRIST. Oh by the way! You are in much trouble it will be your grave. Avoid a full and don't look back an opportunity for JESUS CHRIST, fully an accident you missed with God on your record that you have summed up. Give it up. We haven't been married not in your real world. "You say you don't owe me." When are you going to pay me? Dance your tune your dance without me. Who do you pay anyway defense? *A new development for your Church: Say LORD, have mercy. And at your Church it's not worth it taking risk. *Come on Mt. Zion, Church the Pastor believe GOD JESUS CHRIST, these people are racists a racists generation. Be it preferred eliminate Jefferson

*The Original Barbara Payne*

Street, and you and your wife will be safe don't be a fool; a new variation your agency. In other words a new separation thou kingdom living in fear, Colored people having fear in Nashville. And in Nashville, Tennessee there is going to be a new event; the Jihadists are on their way to Mt. Zion Church on Jefferson Street. Jihadists next traveling to Mt. Zion at the Jefferson Street location, they are trying out a new weapon at their event, they despise us they are dying to attack us in the United States, and in Western Europe, and around the world forces of darkness are at work everywhere looking at you everywhere. The Apostle, I'M telling you me the JESUS CHRIST, be not deceived many will have a heart attack when they are not covered at their Churches, and at your Churches and other Churches like yours where huge congregations are gathering for services. Nothing can stop them they are viewing your house; they now they are hid everywhere. So cover your face. You need a covering there in Nashville, they view all of Mt. Zion Church all the time and other Churches as well. And at the Mt. Zion Church you will need the Winans, a lot of funerals to cover at your Church death everywhere. The nation views your work and what you are doing. View their topic: there are lying spirits everywhere their group believe me, say oh Lord we thank you, and they view lower Manhattan as well did you not know that Pastor? Amazing I view them a couple of weeks ago; a storm is coming your way that's the difference your battleground is nothing new. Don't sweep it under the rug your people are limited on how to handle this sort of violence. Bless God; and your intercessor there is praying for you already. This violence: you all's Church be prepared you will be mourning. *View a reality: deliver them rebuke a bad habit, say keep away from me at our church, they are at your church and others as well drug dealers. They scheme all of the time; they view the work and the ministry as a territory—but not divine. They ride on yall's backside all the time, get that? You have to get that seeking for cash; they are walking the streets all the time that is their journey. They rubble for cash everywhere these drug dealers, these drug dealers are everywhere especially near Meharry. They travel as loners; they work alone reducing their expense. They view God as an answer to a prayer these young men. Many of them will be in the grave before they are 30 years old White as well, they use White congregations to peddle dope everywhere; they're always seeking for cash. And they have a new language for your neighbors seeking. I've got proof. I AM a witness says me JESUS CHRIST. They love deep in the valley the Apostle of God, it's for this information free and they love the Jefferson Street location as well. The agency breaking the ice on you the apostle, I'M going to overhaul you desperately needed keeping it straight. Meantime, I told you that you get on my nerves. I AM unconscious; I AM designing a breakup Bishop. I'M not criticizing. Apology accepted. Say you don't want me to break you up, so that you can get on with your life? Draw back look like feet washing could do you some good, I know you don't like foot washing, I'M telling you observing from above. Michael, judgment pour it on him political advantage these two witnesses. The distinction turn this out Uh-huh you're arrested. Call me anytime for prayer; I'll hold your hand your secret is out. I won't tell your secret. You would rather your Olympics Reverend. Say how does it feel, JESUS CHRIST has kept me even in restaurants? Say, glory hallelujah. I'M glad of that backwards if you think otherwise, then you need to get some spine for your churches everywhere. I view the cattle that you dance with. No university just honesty no offense, no invitro investment study. I saw that a couple of weeks ago no commercials it is your active duty. You bother me. You're not on probation tea cup from over spending on the web. Learn a lesson, the other option you're paying for it with what? Oh-my-gosh, we are having a conference, a little emotion you posted it. Say praise the Lord; the game is up. Here is a big announcement: restaurant curb your appetite. Say, wait a minute restaurant like Channel Four News. *One more thing open your value shut Jefferson Street down. I cover you no more. You're lukewarm water filthy like turnip greens from the country, before they are picked and clean. *A smart move go to the altar Barabbas, the right way—a smart move. Optional services see how it affects me. I wash my hands anytime I want to. Dangerous you look like a broom. You're no tomcat. The blueprint the other optional next your duty, say it out loud GOD loves me avoid the web, eating in restaurants pairing alone. Say, JESUS will fix it Nashville. Kindle a little fire no fire under General Jackson, no fire on the shore. Improve your relationship with the Lord. Improved your home been confirmed keeper of the kingdom knows. Improve your option road block trinity. Pull everything out doesn't like you anyway. A new statement greed the experts a whole lot of business, for me that's a no brainer. Switch now that the damage is done, **ELDER BURNS** will show you how, a great spiritual leader. God bless this man. "They say he's not coming over here, he's on the run." Don't you all start anything pastors, weak pastors be an adult? I know all those blank pages exactly line the street smut. The answer to your call deaf ear, your entertainment you are a kill joy. The enemy bragged about him killing babies, how many times have you improved your duty, "I didn't kill babies" well congratulations pumpkin. Let's switch sides just the opposites make it reverse. Can we talk to you precious, a map need water got water anyone? Keeper of the kingdom knows your dirt. Well congratulations you can't join here, don't you all be like that distinguish a whole lot of you Whites are in on it. Your brother's friends zero hate chitterlings. Invite more colored in on your grounds pastors, you ought to be glad. Be thankful. I'M moving up North that is where the pantry is up there; they are pumping more adrenal last summer as well over for you down here. Well congratulations, you lost your honor White man. Mesmerized you are big stink is what you really are; you're no longer working for me, any way you cause pain everywhere. They are my friends.

## A New Article

Spread the word voter turnout high. Talk about an election year hollow we need good improvement. "Don't bring those people here." Celebrate God the incumbent, friends of God your friend.

FROM UP ABOVE: A NEW SPEECH, A NEW MOUT ZION CHURCH HAVE YOUR CAKE AND EAT IT TOO, AND YOU ARE PROTECTED. SPEECHLES SOME WILL BE. FOLLOW PERCEPT STANDING UP YOU ARE A FAMILY MEMBER, I PICK MEMBERS. YOUR SOURCE IS JESUS CHRIST, NOT WHO YOU FOLLOW AFTER. I KEEP THE KEYS TO MY KINGDOM NOT THIS ORGANIZATION, THAT IS WHY THEY ARE NOT FAVORABLE ANYMORE FACE INSURGENT. THIS IS THE MEANING THIS WAY THE BIBLE TELLS DIFFERENT HAVE A DIFFERENCE ASK ME JESUS. YOUR HOME PEOPLE FAINT BLANK FOR HELP, YOU UNDERSTAND? YOU HAVE ANOTHER INVESTIGATION, NEGLIGENCE ON YOUR PART YOU SHOULD HAVE PEPARED EARLY PUBLISHERS YOUR IDEA SAFE. THESE INDIANS UNDERSTAND? TAKE A LOOK BETTER BEFORE IT'S TOO LATE. IT'S HEATING UP. YOU NEED TO RESIGN. WOE, THERE IS SMOKING BEHIND YOU VIEW IT ON CAMERA IN THE PAPERS.

THUS SAITH THE LORD JESUS CHRIST; thirsty get your special Mt Zion Church the Congregation. From above hypocrites finance the way you operate. I don't like the way that you operate. You may think I'M crazy says the One and only JESUS CHRIST, action from above but you need HOLY GHOST FIRE says the number One from above. Get that that is plain poured on your building that you cannot put out? Tear this equipment down the way it needs to be.  FATHER GOD, you have all power in your hands in Nashville, the Baptist their equipment they think they own it. Get some more air good for your kidneys; even in Atlanta prove your strength to me. You don't look much like me, with no regret your advertising view Black and White you should look like me the Brick Mason, the Keeper of all.  Set the alarm that is how I feel. How about that honestly okay it is difficult.  Is that merely your battle a wannabe church, that is cultural typically a thought thinking rich in society?  Open those doors. Say, that again.  Is that merely your battle your conceit that is the other difference? That is my point your thought a wannabe church with fellowship happy in love with conceit true.  Politicians save a lot of time using your equipment. You are their hero; you are made in their image.  March do that one time in the streets, a dangerous street violence guns everywhere. Churches with a staff in their hands, armed with a pin vocabulary time this is an emergency. See how much that is, that you agreed stop stalling. Does he agree traders in Nashville? Equivalent outline pantry made a promise. We have access BMW.  I view your reproach. Don't get subtle with me, two gallons of water and you're gone. You will have to forgive me. Quit bouncing around your activity agree? Read your Bible. You're forgetting something my service. Thank you, JESUS. We love Him. Take me to Him, not another preacher now no arguing tendency.  I will explain my friend, you are my friend.  My aide Democratic Party further announcement, the Son listens. We love you. Give Him high esteem grown people principle. Bottom line your equipment lip-sync Black folks.  Paint the line. Nigger talk racist's authorship a created look fresh Jim Crow cake. They are unruly.  Oprah, this is outrageous. How would you like to take a look at it now? Look up the gangsters backwards you are racists, bully, uppity, full of conceit Jim Crow bigots caring weapons, some are even billionaires my people are limited open the doors. The extension on Capitol Hill law be careful the faithful till the end; Johnny come lately featuring this generation wants us to forget the whole thing, and wants us to go hungry for education. "The niggers" "grocery mops their families the negative." Let me tell you racists, you Southern Baptists, pillow of the community think we're not equal. People center our GOD. Can you imagine that my friend, get it the question? The LORD said unto me; and to others a long time ago no excuses. I didn't break cheeses your character. I AM the author of this life, your defense. Are you listening? Don't fight with me, beheaded you will be your cheese. No volunteers just an expression in Nashville Republicans. Your houses are falling do you understand? Timeline soon no revocable, you need counseling yes you do. Immigrants the thread irreparable toward me, technically can you imagine that? Read the book now don't be afraid; the skin you cannot fix that problem. *Read the book the Bible that a real reality. A real reality check Africans my friends in Nashville, TN my friends JESUS Prince of Peace said; audible we know are you listening? I know you've got problems. Come on. God dear JESUS, hallelujah holy are you. Say it is our season. Move Baptist Churches, Methodist move out of the way. You are going backwards. JESUS will fix it. Amen. Oh give Him praise. Can you imagine that foolish, ignorant? Grown up at last on your pew your fellow Republicans even those democrats, black people celebrate me your change your moment. The conclusion, say God can deliver me out of this mess we're in hear that Ms. Oprah Winfrey? What about the next election pass me, I'm not a woman councilman agreed? A change in the next election, I don't have much agreement look here evidence. A total wash out. Threaten me intelligence blinded review a new concept. Do your duty to me next election that is if you are running, that is if you're running? Are you serious epitaph view it in plain sight for the rest of the world, you are making a speckle of yourself? Never give up America. Courtesy that's the point the right way your incumbent agreed people? God's knows before every election, even Democrats Republicans. The jokes on them, I'll watch you fall downstairs. I'M on the battlefield with them no joke. Whatever you feel save it. Mercy is the only way out of this mess. I AM a civil person. I AM upset don't do that to me, don't you dare I'M up here watching your every move. I view racial indecency this incident. Don't argue with me about it, I know you done it. Factor my God. He is the insertion from heaven, our mighty redemption. The Lamb's book of life, I'm positive a sure sign. I'll tell you all about it. Simple sure I'm positive my God hears me every day. He expresses it to me wonderful is my God. He can change the situation our God. I'm on my own; believe me my walk with God just like the rest of you. He leads me don't be a quitter Black people, don't give up. I know there's trouble you can't give up. It's just an expression we often use. Thank you, Lord JESUS CHRIST. I don't let a day go by without thinking you, for all your blessing that is the beauty of serving Him. Thank you, Father. People here is the measurement of a revelation, amazement no info let that be a lesson. Looking at my people no judgment an autograph signed. Look at me the original be aware of that don't be a stranger. At some point common error on most individual's part. Here's the answer looking to JESUS CHRIST, the author and finisher of all things-miracles *HEBREWS* 12:2 (The KJV). Beware it's a jungle out there. *HEBREWS* 12:2 Looking unto JESUS the author and finisher of our faith; who for the joy that was set before him endured the cross, despising the shame, and is set down at the right hand of the throne of God (The KJV). / A bit of turmoil He set on the throne, even the angelic adore Him. He will clean house.

    THE HOT SPOT YOU REPUBLICANS EVERYWHERE GO AND DEAL WITH IT THE REGULAR NODE.

*The Original Barbara Payne*

THUS SAITH THE LORD; JFK saw it they called it the Cuban Missile Crisis: October, 1962 at the height of the cold war another catastrophe event literally. Bombs were rolling in like rockets at our back door. The poor man was unprotected against such evil in society an event, and open event that is the proof. Thanks, to JESUS CHRIST it was resolved. We had to arm wrestle him Kosher style; angry Commander in Chief at the White House during the missile crisis get it, with the Russian Premier? Hoodlums they were. We hit a home run no backing up. Thank you, JESUS CHRIST. I did say my prayer. Strong arm with weapons legally on our side; I will give you the low-down it made a difference. The Cold War Republicans, no one turned him down including Johnson, our Commander in Chief, powerful he was ready to kick ass. Fate eluded him once, we have it in black and white spies they were everywhere. Hear that Murfreesboro, get the message. We were headed for dooms day, but God killed their plans. I'll tell you a secret Pentecost, no risk he was good for the country no damage done. Pentecost he was good for Europe, the space program, ethnic environment, a strong defense for our nation. He was a weapon like dynamite your servant Kennedy; thank him for his valiant leadership. Vehicular homicide was he under the umbrella, for the people of America. Black people loved him many Whites the same, but a number of whites rebels, I'm talking about hated him, wherever they are out there boosting worrying individuals not caring for justice, and equality for blacks. The purpose their idea blacks serve, while losing their identity understand racists that kind of stuff? We carry the torch for life. The tape we follow their program, their movement they have issues narrowly escaping unemployment. The purpose ticks politically blocking the way, no freedom left, for democracy we need a change. They are rebels caring flags keeping us hostage. That is what motivates them satisfies them. They were always grazing everywhere, where there is sunshine in the air. DR. MARTIN LUTHER KING JR., pure acceptance helped all individuals so follow his struggles. The charge against struggle the thing about it peace came without their help the wannabe's. PRESIDENT KENNEDY: for America, a strong dose of medicine was he kept us healthy hear that Republicans; Saturday, I see you playing games before the election on Barak. Everything came together under John F. Kennedy no ground war for him Republicans, injuring his own people. He would have blown them off the map. I AM a witness; believe me people everywhere no stretch of the imagination. Believe people everywhere a friend. He had good credit. His concern it was pure dedication against opposite, evil, even if he had to kill them all was his concern for our well being. Can you explain that? We were lucky to have him as President. We all ought to thank him; God referred to him in a time of crisis. Thank you, JESUS how we all made it over, our self-defense we made it. Thank God, his openness electric, he rubbed it in their faces, everyday a dream it had come to that. We love a dream a person. For example, he was just a servant no mess dream, he didn't carry a weapon he fought battles, George Washington the same we were wounded, and known's-African Americans like a door knob far too often. Turn that door knob it is legal to turn, tear drops wipe them away can you erase since you took office this election what has been done to us hear the cry. God surely can and there is nothing you can do about it read the papers. You count us as zero Middle America. View Pentecostal wipe the tears away republicans. You think we are litter backwards that's in Brentwood. Tear drops wipe them away we've been imposed upon enough. Can you erase what has been done to us hear the cry? Pitiful how black people been treated in this nation, they are a strong people. God give us hope. God can create more money for them to get an education. Capitol Hill, view the tax records gubernatorial knows he wants to protect them. View the budget the other budget, uh—governor. Can you be honest? Kennedy protected the poor kept our government a cool head like under President Obama, achieved! HOORAY CHRIST JESUS! YOU ALWAYS KNOW CHANGE, NOW STEPPING IN FOR

*The Original Barbara Payne*

MR. OBAMA. JESUS SAID; THE NEXT PRESIDENT OF THE UNITED STATES, DEFINITELY MY FRIEND LEAVE HIM ALONE POLITICANS. YOU'RE NOT A MONARCH I'M TELLING YOU. JESUS; CUTTHOART THEY ARE POLITICANS THE RICH BOTHER HIM NO MORE, UNLESS YOU WANT ME TO PUT A STUMBLING BLOCK IN YOUR WAY; 1:00 O'CLOCK A.M. COMING. Don't touch him in this Olympics of climate change veterans, alright? Not a hypnosis degree baffled, just think and no flu shot either not enough room anybody understand? Read my lips daddy "you say you can't talk about him" Register, remember the hopefully? The Keeper knows more well. Bulletin, look at me a discrete public ass belching. Watch this; let me show you something locally the hunted, the children, evidence. OUR PORTION: Clinton would have took a bat, and literally done away with it fiscally without the Congress. He knew the struggles. Clean hands was his for the people against the rich, like Obama has tried to do, before this next general election honor for the American people. Acquired is his new stand in this new calendar year's coming up new election. I am republicans no legal expert, the beating they have had enough. You have to think about others in this next election Mitt Romney: including seniors the nation is full of them, okay? Can you believe that Mitt Romney, they need protection? Given the facts trouble a new season we can rebound a new stand for this new season, change for families for the entire future. A workout for many stumped your worst nightmare, the plan tell them to hold it back the economy. Hooray, for Mr. Obama, the latest attack on him the candidate and our President. Mitt Romney, an espresso on him in the United States we are moving from scratch, the politicians with a fly criminal intent to get him out of office. We know the heavy weights political gangs they are, with a carrot field deep against the people. We offer it to you Mitt Romney collect. Contact the Chariot. Our President we are linked. *The people never give up; because of the economy they are going through hell these days. I've told them wrong situation suffering are a lot of people going through many difficult times. They are suffering caring their situations around. They never chose this route you politicians. Here's surveillance: they are good people with no food, their outdoors eating out of dumpsters for foods sake until they can do better. They are looking for food don't want to look for food anymore, participate they want breakfast. People are struggling that can't do any better. Politicians come on give oats, give a little more. They've got the gun come on give people a break. We can win all you've got to do is do right. Wives supplement they want you to give them plenty more. PROOF FROM DIVINE: There are many challenges eat breakfast is all some kids have for food nourishment to eat, they are poor. Go save them. We ought to be shaking our heads. We maybe all facing it with no stretch of the imagination. Sunshine, they're not working they are hungry; I've got proof. They're not deadbeats they are looking for sunshine. LORD have mercy, we could all be like that, be a friend sunshine institutions! JESUS we are out of bounds. It is a travesty. "LORD, help, help me" these people. I know you are hungry. I view them Black and White. I know principality taking strength. Finally, caring emotions around the messengers of God, a figure of burden for them we are shoveling. Control management, they will obey longer caring the blood of the people on their shoulders. You say, "don't go there don't kick that bull." Why not single one? Bottom half second ending, the practice no one knows the news been an awful day second heap. They are running ahead the republicans are running up stream warm it up. Flipping my government, the running for the next president of the United States, politics making a documentary this is the way it is final statics be nice to see nice. I've got the evidence poor Romney overpowered everything, draw closer to Mr. Obama white people in a year. He took a chance the next president. The running for the next guess what the President, tried it impossible? The dam leaked who's now running against Obama, tell the White people they woke up; tell the Democrats they

*The Original Barbara Payne*

are defeated. *Hillary Clinton won before and after. The next election couldn't keep up with him in a million years, if you wanted to run a side race jumping not one bit hear that? Who do I run for? Another icon you can believe it let's talk about BILL CLINTON: here's the point, now Bill Clinton my other friend, Bill Clinton an icon no arrangements. I remember the tall nonchalant man he had lot of people running, definitely. Who's a friend Bill Clinton, just look at the map go look it up? He crossed difficulty, and he passed the test about my age when he started every mission accomplished. In case you missed let me tell you something, alright? *They do worship him in a crowd understand? He lead Republicans a purpose, noble is his wife the same she is just warming up and she will be on the national scene. Get that? He had so much time on his hand, but he didn't waste it. There comes a time in your life you have to face the truth. What's He talking about? My friend nonpartisan offspring point new production point of view, his accomplishments no gossip exchange. Not narrow minded no wasted vanity my friend no exploits, I'M telling you. Strong bearing his own cross single handed, for the service both sides actually imagine that? *That is why we care so much about him Bill Clinton, White people of Alabama. The case his own point of view not for pleasure, not caring about money monetary corruption tree, caring with virtue give him an A-Plus future down payment caring his book a measurement for payment. He has written many books. He had a whole lot to do before the next new president, used virtue for the poor and workers middle class. Honor always a veteran for American politics. Give the man a drum roll for the cause. People expect more Mr. Lieberman. It's not your traditional wealth Lieberman renew your account. You think that losing will break you your affluent around the world. For our defense our savior field attack rollout funding. He knew citizens; he never capitalized deceiving politically politicians. That is the beauty of his improvement. Heaven knew that while he had the job. No patsy was Bill Clinton politically the former President. Exactly, see that Republicans knew his job slapped some hands in the kingdom. A giant no exclusion as President raised the bar to a new level Democrats, a veteran his own guy; that is Wall Street what you should look for in a President, fair minded doing his duty every day. You Democrats it's time to raise the bar for Mr. Obama's Presidency. ON THE PRESIDENT BILL CLINTON: he shifted reality for the people right away then he got recovery how about that, hear that Murfreesboro TN, he knew his job brought peace to my kingdom as well? A giant equipped on his hip a *double edge sword for the country, irrelevant to the doctrine. The whole matter 77° degrees a new doctrine middle age Upper Room experience, what to do following that day after. *Let the Ace' out. I AM not their book head Christians. I rule the kingdom, doctrine today JESUS CHRIST and His doctrine independent. He's our super friend, He sees everything God don't you know? Kingship kingdom enlarge me. Oh help me legally God. What; got a burden enlarge my border be on my side remember that? No more politics Republicans. Tell them He's ALPHA and OMEGA, isn't He Pentecost the man no out of bounds? Follow the best "I approve of this message people" give it to the Ace, He is watching you. Got a burden take it to God Mr. President, when all hope is gone unbelievable. I AM ALPHA and OMEGA, from the beginning and the ending: I see new faces every avenue. We've got a new avenue. Hallelujah, soothes nerves can't any do better. Please set us free real quickly. Nashville hear that? Cheer up my bother. You saw what I did to Wall Street flatten their platform. They were hiding their calamity hit also Wall Street. Incredible an Upper Room experience what really matters most; they did their homework, President Ronald Reagan the same. See Obama people, I view him the same an ambassador of GOD. Don't be alarmed. Guess what a new direction for the Government everyone is flipping. He didn't have to run the race for Democrats late night; a Negro. Be thankful! Clinton, I view him every night stickler late night, a stickler for contract. His agency he had suffered. So don't mind suffering do it anyway, I know the pros and the cons say I don't mind if I do it will make a difference. Take this don't mind a risk give it everything you got. It will give you strength equip you for the better, risky though. Legally a top notch lawyer in JESUS name on every avenue, a good kind of guy he had the energy to keep him there for justice, the Federal for the public good for the country. A good kind of guy a new political avenue he had God understand? Force like a book his ethics to do the right thing Pentecost, a made up mind politicians traveling his own self defense. TOUCH ME JESUS! He made a difference politically thinks to JESUS CHRIST. The issues politically thinking point of view, in the body no rubber bands viewed the White House as fellowship; hear that knew his way around in the world just a thought, the occasion engagement return a preventative medicine protestant, look at the poles. His optimism put many on the run. Engaging he was on taxes with the best of them, Chocolate knew that. A kipper flavor their boss no mercy Bill Clinton, rough on the rich their tax revenue. I saw all those people needed defending. Indicative play Bill Clinton was. Eyeballing his attitude wanted to know what it was all about. He had intelligence milked both moral Democrats, and Republicans, they heard him those Republicans. I remember the new President 1994, high bar he set for the next administration and others. *Bill Clinton served with class definitely he beat the rich man Mr. ugly, he knew about how we are and how they are racists. Bill Clinton, took a couple of judgments made a mistake fooled around with a visit Monica Lewinsky, judgment later. Here's a check with a reality. In the pass reality and for the new one President Obama, checked and broadening perfect cheese and event. Matter of fact both Presidents I knew their benefit, and their operation both of them knew how to keep it together how to handle it. Courtesy no political flimflam courtesy not like Watergate. No blow up on camera Bill Clinton, Obama either the difference. Even the President Clinton kept every avenue opened yes, he did learned how to engage that simple, and the new President needs to do the same. Tough on Obama racists block him right now. When running for office a lawyer huge success equipped wife also. His return traveling around a lot made him a complete success, knew how to network convinced people he could get the job done right knew networking showed people the way. Hey MICHAEL BLOOMBERG; I'M pointing a finger missed opportunity how cold you are your ideals misdirected. Get help quite being a control freak needs to learn that he's a control freak, not responsive. How about him his household well kept looks and sees how important that is, don't conduct says that all the time a waste of time a grocery segment. I see a mess all around him. Look at the republicans a disaster their having a collision. In your home could say, I was the chief disaster bottle strike got people watching three or four days a week fumbling, and messing around sending notes sounds good, but just clowning their destiny a performance Jim Crow activists barely getting buy. Look around trouble is everywhere all around him, even in the police department need improvement. Good luck Mayor Bloomberg, got "all spice" filled with sour cream no secret. Don't repeat dangerous here's where you go wrong rubber bands. I hear your lobbyists you're not a free agent. You talk too much. If you want to save money repeat after me need a new filling, typical sing a new song every day typical. Loss got chicken pox. Indicative Clinton learned to capitalize on his opponents his policy nothing proven available at the last minute, no second guessing with President Clinton, and no mud slanging he moved the nation forward, even with his opponents Georgia, obstruction he used wisdom. I never heard any bad news from the military. Under his watch President Clinton big time had his people together for national security. RONALD REAGAN: did the same identical. Leaned on me, he was a Christian no argument there right, and he loved the family when he left no excuse proven. Let's celebrate him together alright. Time to upgrade we need more of that complete including Democrats of faithful America, united in your destiny. The reason for this book you don't stand out like a sore thumb with your critics. If you ask me done the job right didn't he. Truth significance read the newspapers can you believe him republicans, dealt with the economy the annual budget? People were struggling. People had a problem; he knew where to start zero budget deficits unconditionally the deficit. Good for him! Before he left office Republicans served his office, people were getting along, showing they were Americans without the difference were open with dignity? Things can work in politics. Negligence they did he wanted to balance a budget, he took a hit no pass throw away; they wanted him thrown out of office, he had become a super star effectively. They pounced on him real unusual their favors, then later they pretended like nothing was going on, Europe the same a bummer they wanted blood, that is experiences. That is not unusual, before a big breakthrough single event spread the word. He was use to it he piped up. Some wanted him kicked out of office; exclusion. He took a big hit. Never rolled over and played dead for nobody, (a laughing party) too protect us to keep us from the lion's king. That's them any monkey, alligator. "Wait a minute I'm going to get to the bottom of this" was Bill Clinton, kept us from harm's way Bill Clinton and our allies no racists. Bill Clinton no racists, no apron strings behind him just be assured of that. Just like PRESIDENT OBAMA, is making a wave served our country well a good ambassador abroad as well. *Heave President Barack Obama the scope of him he made a sacrifice, and Vice President Joe Biden the same complete heave him as well no pencil head. God knows their impact for the good of the Country. President Obama his honor and his achievements and they are many then why do we not hug them? Why do we stash his events all of his merits, his achievements put them on vacation, and the President Bill Clinton and that his honor as well? Election year, for the service this event my Boss JESUS CHRIST can handle it for him this next election year to be continued alright? No chicken pox and no egg. He did well distinguish for this country and the next one, definitely his fellowship no sleepover anywhere. I'M telling you didn't act greedy believe me. Come on people need a recount people, innocent for sure the man Obama, no coincidence anointed people absolutely. Crooked individuals weigh him down like water; drag him through the mud. I'M telling you Pentecost, definitely. He is a real man. What's wrong with the world, we need guidance. We need a change in the weather in Washington. We need modification in Washington, D.C. in JESUS name, oh absolutely. Grassland super unemployment people in the hood big time, people merely a stop an echo those who haven't found jobs, misery their only other resource. Really you ought to take a look at this situation; they stay in the bathroom with their feet propped up wondering what to do frequently. They don't have jobs literally that they can't find work. They are fine decent people in the neighborhoods out of work; a lot of them are out of work and these are poor people get up off your duff and do something about this situation the group. Don't block them from working let them work put people back to work. Unemployment, block unemployment create jobs massive unemployment true. I AM talking to you. Black people you haven't heard, they are looking for employment back into the work force. They are not all in jail you bullies; they are screaming create more jobs. Help Black people, definitely curb unemployment create jobs be creative please help them? Businesses I mean business their getting help from elsewhere. They know how to treat them at charitable food pantry organizations; they feed all that are in need everywhere the U. S. Federal Government, and it is not complex people are eating a lot less many are going hungry every day. Oh JESUS! Black people worried about eating many of them are homeless, paying for college, paying for their rent, can't get a job to pay for their mortgage, they are in unemployment doesn't cover enough nowhere, they can go Whites it's your responsibility get a vision be a blessings. Help the children, children are non-elective and help the elderly. It's amazing how many of them that are out of work; they are hungry done lost their job, yes they are angry, they are out of work; many of them are living on the streets they have the blues—their weather, they can't find work.  It's not romantic. Fix it! You didn't know about that their struggles. No wonder they are giving up, they can't find work unemployment high-looking for work.  The price of milk keeps getting higher. What about them in the back of the bus operating on very little—and there are Whites across America, be at the fore front these are dangerous times their out of food? Say something wealthy, say it on "Meet the Press on Sunday's," a network politics aggressive people all over the land and Country clear the house. We need to clean house with no mercy then we can see again new programs, and then after that arm and hammer. Thank you, JESUS. More and more self defense people our man President Obama, discipline grass roots defense and Michelle Obama the First Lady. Give them a hand; my-my-my praise God a good Christian man, a friend of mine.  Better travel with that people. My friend, know that God is able he is my friend. He made news a new President, and a new fellowship.  Dear God, distinguished for this Country praise God. The turn of the century let's hear what he has to say no particular's let me tell you no accident.  Gratitude, the policy he made for this country, and around the rest of the world.  He had and aim with motivation, and he meant to fulfill it heavily while he was in the White House. Rise to the occasion if you want to be like him. Find your reputation. Doctor JESUS CHRIST what do you say, Agree with it? Arrest the Republicans they are anti-christ against the people, they block with double standards; throw away physically from GOD this century as well as all the earth boasting.  Our new purpose a new policy right now our National Security first, there are demons everywhere we just barely made it. Unemployment is high in this country no debate about it. Everybody the moment of truth the storm is passing.  From *GENESIS* to the book of *REVELATION*: listen to me shake GOD'S hand to the black man, I see Him everywhere. Wear GOD'S grace His favor his coat with you wherever you go take your Bible that is your meat no doubt about it. Say, now satan get thee behind me, true America. I fear GOD. You love GOD in this way then go after him; he will meet you there wherever you are. You like love him the way I do don't pretend, some people pretend then don't that is your answer, me I'm a princess we dote on each other, dote on JESUS CHRIST, hallelujah. That is your record in the kingdom of GOD. I'll be honest I'm glad I found him JESUS. Praise the Lord! Make a difference just an injection. We can promote Him go tell everybody. I see GOD everywhere powerful! He can prevent Joe Lieberman from leaving a permit a mistake yes, he can "Don't rely on God," one of the long legged investigators, one of the effect criminals demonstrating from standing up climbing the ladder raiding God's people completing of earth. Be of encouragement host and event for the government in your own backyard; see your pack summit wise. 150 or more Democrat's needed Senator. JESUS been a "Hot Spot" a long time one of the coon's raped us another one on the way. *Roll over pay attention to that Lieberman. You are my friend, I'll be yours later top that. The number one *Kennedy he made the difference for families. *Bush threw it all away your tax revenue, leading up to that he saw down the road. People been sausage if he had not, absolutely we would have been roughened it for years to come people. We serve and awesome God. Hallelujah. Deliverer and awesome God, my God mighty is he JESUS CHRIST. Most agree. Worthy is he in your neighborhoods reach out and touch Him, sometime give Him a hand. You may think crazy am I not flipping. Hallelujah JESUS, a good friend of mine. Currently talk to Him. A breakthrough separation we get to sort things out, the other side a slap on the wrist significant on his watch. Croissant the other element, the military boxing from afar that is the way everybody does it followed the law to the letter, during the Cuban Missile Crisis. The mid-range we focused our defense our attention on our military; the main thing we struck a blow during the missile crisis. The problem strike by numbers, Kennedy avoided a generation crisis. Repeat that again. GEO no overhead the same significant while on his watch; responsive the Cold War ongoing an agreement with a slap on the wrist of NIKITA KHRUSHCHE: the Premier of the SOVIET UNION during the Cuban Missile Crisis. We were in a Hot Spot rather every day. Things were harrying on both sides till this day. Defend off: pushed we won legally. Are we excited! Legally yeah, we won against the government. They won't give us our place Mr. President, the whole group whole lot of them rich folks. Thank GOD! We won that one! I'M a firm believer in that proven. We were on the brink of a disaster. Where would we all be without you JESUS CHRIST? Where would we all be folks united? We couldn't do nothing without you. Praise the Lord. You are the road map to heaven. Take my hand you are my friend you rescued me. You delivered me I was down in the dump, and you came and brought me back. What would we do without you cling to Him? It is no fairytale. I am focused on Him that is the remainder. First impression believe me hear our God, get it for free wonderful is our redemption, it's for free you can get it for free no longer wait. We have access. Say, we can do it. We can change things go vote down the street, you walking the street. Republican dignitaries, feel the weight of our redemption look out servicemen. Thank you, JESUS. We love Him Christians. Jim Crow law litigate, you are world class citizens tell them meatloaf no more. What about the department? They see vouchers wants Black people to starve to go hungry for education, go somewhere in reference anywhere these White racists people that they are, the next election any direction narrow minded they are to me. And this major event thus saith the LORD; I'M dropping a bomb. We are equal. Don't argue with me about it. I know your ways. I know how you are legally, even in Nolensville. Give me a tab in the middle your severance is coming. What a mighty giant you are. Your currency has folded truly, that is the essence of the whole thing. You are robbers.

## A New Article

You were very successful. There is an arrest going to take place for Black people. I'M getting them free finally. You are robbers. The rest has been known like olive oil in the Senate, the office big boss man keen possibility. I'M telling you three, I'M the CEO. Got that? There are no exchanges, no exceptions donuts zero. I'M in the middle. I'M telling you don't argue with me about it. Black people are equal, you pack of thieves. I know you done it. Look we don't want to boycott Nashville. People everywhere know you are racists all over the nation. Just say line me up white people. They know you are prejudice. You ostracize with your racists attitude, bad combination white people upon Capitol Hill. The one wash with control the black man's hand. They are racists; look out the one wash the other it's basically a run off. Principle, they cut raw deals you understand, given their opportunity many white people do that don't forget it? It happens to a lot of people their deals. They do it to stay in business. I AM an observer a lot of people are watching? I AM A KEEN OBSERVER OF EVERYTHING JESUS CHRIST. AMEN. Do you want me to repeat that, or dismiss it your fate? Controversy you know—the handle; the under guy and the victim the one on Capitol Hill the one you seem to dismissed completely. Let me tell you young White man, remember me your Limited Edition Stopper right now. Reversal shocking you are lost, Kosher as well my people Jews, and Mormons, they take advantage of Black people the race their motives, they aren't taking up issues politically. That ain't (isn't) no way to act all you pastors get that, then get honor take the buckler? Preparing for a homecoming are Black people they are screaming for a homecoming their race, discussing it while they are gathering. Scattering under the arm 80% of the population suffer to pay rent a practice often to keep households running, you thought of that a must their culture rolling are their people? They are barely getting by. Look what they are teaching them in the books, look up don't believe in investment the messages, have a heart simple that on your big paper Speaker of the House the U. S. Senate, and the

*The Original Barbara Payne*

Oval Office. The automatic groups are Republicans, and your last administration, there is evidence to support this document proving how racists they are journalist as well, Black people use your common sense. Listen let me tell you something, you ought to know your situation. I the Stopper of you get right everyone of you-simple. Keep practicing first impression, agree? Dirt, don't talk about him he is my friend, the former President George W. Bush did it, very successful young man standing with you lately Administrative. Someone knows your Executive Branch—you got a big mouth. Someone know them. You think of yourself. You bench press coward. You know Obama; mind if I talk about him you've got issues with the President in the White House now? Racism you're in love with that every one of you. You are nearing your group end TV commercials. For instance, specialist's senate Donald Trump and his brand hard at work to overpower the rule. *Wanna* go flipping burgers? Opportunity check this out Donald, remember Marla Maples your sweetheart nothing? You do the math it's not yet confirmed. I'll bet a thousand dollars your math you flunk; you owe me much JESUS CHRIST. Sure your hands are dirty. It could have been prevented. Base wheel will stop you. They have your face wherever you may go. Hey Donald, maintain brotherly love kin to my Father. SEE THE HOLY GHOST WINS EVERY TIME UNKNOWN TOO MANY, GOD IS ON HIS SIDE. Let's show the big shot be bold stand up Mr. Obama. Messenger defense with Obama White House, the campaign trail isn't over knock a big blow key to majority statement. The lineage Senate review things are a mess, help people. Raw Jim Crow days are over. For example, it takes an army to bring them down. I hate them you say Clan sulfur and ash. This is exciting tell us about it. Full proof no more your Lawmakers, your Executive Branch evil. Remember Watergate? That is what I think about you. Remember Watergate? Politicians they will turn your world upside down your agency. View them already 144,000 watching from the sky. Are you ready? Make a deal now. It has begun the offering. Have an opinion? I can give a clue and I think you get to think. I have your numbers. Get that monkey off your back. My chemistry one gallon probability knowing I'M dealing with it, Uh Dr. Registrar every day rigorously. Need a breakthrough Dr. Registrar, I AM upset, whipping fair game you broke the rule no paradox in Nashville, and in Washington. I'll tell you what they need kids need a paradigm. No regret believe me the one who can handle your reins tightly supervision advance. You should have been on top of this. JESUS CHRIST BIG SHOT MY GOD HAS THE ANSWER MARK IT DOWN, DO YOU HEAR THAT? IT GOES AGAINST PRINCIPLE. EVERYTHING IS DRAMATIC. The house is crumbling Dr. Registrar. I'M thrown in the middle. I am afraid. I see fair justice probability people want it everywhere the department. The end we are walking a tight rope one sided point of view. *This epistle by me, was recorded not for the entrance Civil Servants Republicans, but for the business of JESUS CHRIST our Lord; our development your service your way. Federal Marshalls evidence your Executive Branch for the building FBI, flipping Mr. Public Defenders legal proven investment, legal edge the building, the capitol investment your arrangement. Are you listening? They are going to catch you lawmakers, and in Rutherford County the cannon Mr. Public Defenders. Say, I would be honored. Chief your Executive Branch three people for the picking, for the building you are doomed. This is God's own business all alone legally nothing premature. We are running out of time at your mercy just for the picking. I see vengeance. YOU THOUGHT WE WERE THEIR PIMP IN METRO NASHVILLE GOVERNMENT. Save their video don't worry about it no questions asked. For Nashville Schools get books big time. I'M coming to your rescue for Public Schools in Metro-Nashville literally. I'M their rescue their development, and their benefit you can't leave people behind. We've got the paper. You'll see greener pastures people. You're not by yourselves; I know every funding avenue in Metro big time. I'M talking about the deal for our schools literally; I know their agency the people's money benefit incorrectly in Metro-Nashville Schools, you're about to get an injection. The people's money 50% here's what happened operating we were innocent; big mistake. Drinking champagne the all American lobbyists for the general public, asking for their request on a regular basis and that includes property taxes when it wasn't even necessary and the General Revenue knew that all alone. This is their forklift, their balancing a budget. People of color it's a White merger a group of them, I'M talking about the top dogs, the big dog people. Definitely they are the experts, know that I AM GOD attacking those people a witness, definitely fraud charlatans are those people in so many ways. What am I going to do about it? Okay here is the answer, independent tell the White House, the Government Congress, you understand? Recipe for a moral redemption no restraints bad budget fiscally block it, politics their request. Be a diplomat. No budget cut backs there in Nashville, Tennessee. I have real proof on demand. I view them a thousand times. Case uncertainty no more, I know the difference. *Their acknowledgement what'll I do with their funding we took on paper; secondary their action the group in Davidson County? They had it their way with understanding. Grip you give them license every day event their group. I've been looking at them. The way they act on Capitol Hill embarrassment it is. By the way lobbyists the building, you wannabe's legally on Capitol Hill, you're under arrest trading your measurement running their business the underdog. Your lobbyists on occasion blood money legally, your friend's lawmakers and the etc., the incident technical advantage serving their piece of the pie everyday to lawmakers. We need to give more scholarships to those people, the critics the foundation with pleasure. *I'M sending a message: they have performed abortion legally on Davidson County Metro-Public Schools. I'll tell you all about it they are doing it electronically their way using our public equipment they are, and no one lifted a finger. There are whistle blowers in Nashville, Davidson

County in Metro Government in Tennessee. Can we count on you this incident turn them in Davidson County? Pentecost it is no big secret what they are doing in Metro-Nashville, to our Public Schools. They have trained cookies according to their word (watch dogs they are). I see the leverage coming our way in poor Metro-Schools that is a fact. I categorize. Staffers they all know. Quick devotion throughout the State, the whole town knows cheap devotion politicians. Build a foundation disaster we have become. TESTING MAIN EVENT 9:00 O'CLOCK P.M. ....SECOND WATCH... MIDNIGHT - ITS JEWISH TRADITION. 8:00 O'CLOCK P.M., I KNOW WHO THAT YOU ARE...ON THE CALENDAR: IT'S JEWISH TRADITION. I KNOW WHO YOU ARE. I KNOW WHO MADE YOU ALL AROUND AT A DISTANCE YOU CAN'T ESCAPE FROM ME. I KNOW WHO YOU ARE EXACTLY. I KNOW WHERE YOU ARE. I KNOW WHO THAT YOU ARE CAPITOL. Literally the upper room, literally commence, keep watching about to come down literal, and fix everything for the people no alternative. I see everything deep rooted. Can't keep up with them big box robbed you friends we need separation. It's embarrassing. Amen. NOTE: cultural the army. Please read the following events urgency arm yourselves. We are running out of time at your mercy just for the picking. We have to overcome. Acknowledge scholarship plan a new scholarship plan, the final plan. We still have a rough road ahead of us. I see vengeance. We can overcome. We have big accomplishments. Internal a shift the velocity gage a wake, definitely a whole new complete announcement their medicine for Black people everywhere and all the races underprivileged and their children redeemed their policy, and they need new books. Georgia, see how far can we go Newt Gingrich. I'M talking to you the gap. View others too. View and uprising see who that permits it, view those republicans an uprising see who the winner is. I feel an earthquake coming your way, running over you total loss reality. We are changing shifts a whole lot of new decorating. Freezer open start taking inventory, I view thousands individually. Hooray, for black people everywhere. Say that again, hooray for black people everywhere. Say, final word open the back door. What is going on refilling? Mission accomplished young people. Learn another lesson stress has been removed. By removing bragging we are uplifted flying in the air the right way. The right way cleansing the porches independent, the truth now imagine that a new breakthrough. Total you young people merchandise given to them driver's total access. We were in a prison in the system countless uplifting. Company, I'M standing over you get the message? Say, we are saved. We were legally blind. Intelligence left the land Public Schools, without a compass let that be a lesson to you. Catastrophe: that is why we're so down in the dumps, we're in a mess. Controversy a blanket it's a mess couldn't find its way back home. Weakness not only that the building: (The Governor, new development and other sources hand over the bill Governor. The damage has already been done—like looking for a needle in a haystack. Hey you've made a mistake. You had a chance to do what is right.), later paid thousands from the fund, payback other arrangements special interest groups and their salary. You know who gave them the money Metro did it. Then all of a sudden they want tax payers to fund it. After that we are coping legally right up to date. They confused the land. Flipping they are now. A new document Metro Services poor Metro. Question: a document Washington changes the situation why don't you? Grassland in the ball park internal it has become both extremes in the dark. Eye opener oblivion for us *Studebaker diplomacy* so out with them. Say, listen this big event team for us. Help us GOD ALMIGHTY; dog and African American in the game. Everyone must fight for their equal rights, if we want to win. We see your passion. Stay in the game, yeah they are cruising your buddies. Massive layoffs will occur if this mess is not fixed. Uh view hesitation. I AM in balance with you Newt Gingrich, left you messages before, before you left Newt Gingrich. Speaker Gingrich, we're not following them anymore, Republicans. The Republican Party Mr. Speaker in America, your debt big political machine outrage you have become. Thought you had the best definitely. Metropolitan people we're not charity. Metropolitan Nashville Public Schools like a stick crippled. Defect politics I view you here in Nashville, be thankful for that. Anyway look at this, "This battle is not yours" (you cross your fingers and then say GOD help me; I AM Master of the universe. I'M telling you, you people better get ready. I AM a thorough witness we all agree, agreed? Your representative the true branch not the Hollywood bunch to Los Angeles, you have twelve months you have fought me long enough, even in the city say, it with confidence. I AM no dummy like you. I AM the Master. No one can handle me JESUS CHRIST, it would be dangerous. I AM GOD, THE ALPHA THE OMEGA, angles bow before me, and all of mankind. I AM the Supervisor confident even in the valley where the rocks hide don't you ever forget it. We all agreed. Remember dumbwaiter, I AM not. No excuse I will give you proof of what I AM saying. Another thing you all are pitiful now live with it), but the LORD'S; event read *II CHRONICLES* 20:15....The KJV. / Then we will win so arm yourselves Republicans, you seem out of touch with the people. All Powerful Washington! I mean powerful! Thank you, JESUS our savior for that. This is the one thing we've got going for us it *ain't* ours. Watch out blues we have become. Take it to the bank. If you ask me not cheap, definitely you think we are second grade your sponsors. I know your impact, understand? We are not cheap. "The battle is the Lord's," I've already told him to cover my back. We can over overcome. Thus saith the LORD; racism I know the pain. Heaven help us. Be fair to Black people that is enough, what is their accomplishment, see their accomplishment complete lately? We are not dirt think about it. We are worth it been like that all alone, even if they don't think so. A block our families we Black people. This race durable race they are black people proven. Mangled can't erase it, I viewed it a long time ago. I view everything trust me that I know. Use your wisdom before God, quickly make a mends the outcome will be better. We see red. Freedom comes with a price. Freedom does not come cheap believe me you got that? Woe I see your make up. You think we are cheap. They are hungry, I see the world, and definitely I see everything sacrilegious if you think otherwise the development. I know the passion their accomplishment. Hey, ACLU are you watching? I view you in Atlanta. Strike get off your duff, and do something.

YOUR ACCOMPLISHMENT LET THERE BE LIGHT; WE'RE COMMITTED THE DEVIL MUST BE REMOVED. MITT ROMNEY, REMOVE YOUR INTEREST RATE ENDORSEMENT ALRIGHT? ONE VAGABOND TO ANOTHER FOR THE RECORD, AN EVENT YOUR ACCESS COST TOO MUCH. SEE THE CONCLUSION YOUR HOUSE. TAKE IT UP A NOTCH.

Thus saith LORD; Conclusion I AM a strong witness. We have equal access we the people, main stopper JESUS CHRIST. I AM your blessing. See the mess we're in political. Crippled their intent from the beginning we are doomed. Now listen to me, a dog bag they will need. Bring it on Obama wrestle with it. Come on **PRESIDENT OBAMA**; the President you haven't block a thing. I'M paying you a complement. The conclusion: Washington we need you a serious crisis. Are you listening? No more politics. Are you getting it? For the record this time a new development overnight by me. I'M telling you set a record straight your evil activities. We all know what is happening frozen no more. You are dangerous Republicans. Set the record straight the development, the way it should be. Giving advice: to the Government a triple-A rating for keeping us down. We get the message play competition keep playing a vacuum cleaner people, for the record the pulpit relationship "I had a dream" was DR. MARTIN LUTHER KING JR., his address. Now Dr. King thoroughly would have done his duty, right voiced his opinion nightly through preaching to the nation. Dr. King would have never forgotten it. On notice purchasing take me to dinner your gab. Don't be saying that you want the White man to thoroughly wash this place, and arrest me for not paying taxes? Demonstrate through the streets go to court. Oh-my-gosh a whole new reason, churches close the gap like in your neighborhoods. For the service no more focus. It's a jungle out there. I see the notebook. People I know all the tricks, the reason a vacuum cleaner for the future construction a gravel opportunity. I know my authority. Recently it has been done, definitely. Are you laughing at me now? Careful for the service, now do better it's a jungle out there. GOD is watching you all the time police action next. You aren't that great a shooter your equipment, your gun, for the intended me a sacrifice. I smell your smoking gun. A vacuum cleaner for the future a gravel opportunity, I smell your fragrance your divers are a ton away. For the benefit the service it's a jungle out there instruments careful for me. Thank you, JESUS a vacuum cleaner for the future digging people out of the ditches, a new revolution a gravel opportunity. I smell a vacuum cleaner. You need a house cleaning, a gravel opportunity for the record. *In Nashville, I smell your fragrance every time you hiccup. Knock on wood. Your divers are a ton away. Are you listening? You have no real hole to hide in. This afternoon they are prejudice a group of them, they will put you in the real tank. I see the evidence. You're not the victim. Remember no child left behind—the devil the winner? Want to hear more? We are weighing in the balance young blacks in Nashville gifted. For a black man it is hard to get by just that simple. That is that simple. Say *We, We,* dear friend's duty waits absolutely. I thank you, FATHER. I view it on camera especially crooks panic has set in. I see it on TV my vengeance. I haven't forgotten their labor of love, their integrity the parents producing scholars. Don't hate I know things were difficult. Let me do the rest, I dare you. Just like a giant coming out

*The Original Barbara Payne*

of the woods their grave influences in their face, the results let someone else do it on top of their heads. You republicans don't say it's too late. You like that trough. You are so pertinent dope. A new prescription on black folks, I AM a witness cut to the chase. I view your appetite. Buckle up I will blow the whistle. I will make up the defense in general the requirement. The reason why framing it, because it is your epic. What are you talking about? Notice disclosure JESUS CHRIST. Introduction the entity also, because I don't need nobody else I AM JESUS CHRIST, and I don't need anyone else. And you need a facelift backwards if you think otherwise churches. I AM putting you on final notice, definitely. The thread is my own your make up agreed? Have mercy JESUS CHRIST against your anger. Available, I have grace for Republicans in love intermediate even in New Hampshire, most agree would you agree? Give me the evidence children then we agree. The case bath them Christians legally, true most would agree. Give them the shower none negotiable our race deserve better. Say, Republicans, I changed my mind. *Remember Dr. Martin Luther King Jr.? I remember his service, his program the essence history, the man a balance of his service for a Black man, a man of color favor like concrete this is his messages not arrogant. Hallelujah. A complement: he went all the way ethics that was his plan politics all the way. His station in life never give up you have the right. It's just like a cycle. It will work just plans add restrictions delay some. Get the big picture, if you plan God knows your battle? A new adventure uplifting let me teach you. People are watching don't be afraid of people and their words, or their staunch (strong ability) carry on anyway. Look at Dr. King; Dr. King did that that is your answer it's not a mystery believe me. A balance go all the way believe me. Trade up his plan, you will see a difference. His politics political a lot of people do go all the way the message. On the battlefield I shook his hand; thoroughly we were impacted connected a long time Israel, while he was running; his advantage Dr.

King he never forgot to look me up on the battlefield of life; traveling he was because of certain racial intolerance issues you all have; run away laughing at the event was y'all bigots. So much was going on Dr. King did his homework every night. Thank you, for my brother. God protect me on this battle please. No story a daunting task people a must have in racial intolerance; and un-forgiveness backlash in this world, the arm muscle your bitterness knowing no boundaries. Hear the *Gospel* that's your job and your defense. Host, I AM watching you the whole time. *Know Dr. King's plan a very staple he did a wonderful job Pentecost. His plan was God's plan help any human, and you can make it, we have come to that. Glory hallelujah! You hear that down in Mississippi? Adopted that is the theme help any man good nursery your responsible. Nothing frivolous about that see you are the salt in your community, a true foundation you and your families now there is nothing unusual about that. Are you the clan usual your optional? Improve race relations. Dr. King had the greatest plan: help these people been standing in line waiting for your help no tunnel view there. They are desperate white palomino. Shock you need a police dispatch getting the message? You've got trained officers going your way. Hold your breath. You say "Move out of our line get out of line." They are desperate for your food. You've got more food than you can waste, hear that? They really need it. Why tackle it, why bother, your infrastructure many of them are homeless. Lack of physical evidence current witnesses get the cue enough view, the average later they will be coming after you with legal weapons? The clan the white grace you're not fooling anybody, you're in trouble with the State Department. You've been borrowing too much new equipment. *The *clan* in Ashland City, help the poor many of them are miserable. I recently took a trip down there. I AM in hot pursuit of you, your grade. If you ask me, White people you are dirt your pleasure. Clean up the town. Now clean up this mess. It smells all over town. Thank you, JESUS CHRIST it is

*The Original Barbara Payne*

needed. *Now here is some more things that are difficult, I view you back so many years you get over with subsidies, you're on Federal subsidies help from the Federal Government you all look it up, and from the Federal Government and keep the rent on dollars supplies. We are paying for it your grant. I bear your subsidies legally. Give me my play equipment: and from the Federal Government they are grants already. Make that news get things build up. Subsidies enough your partial payment rural play fixed up, then the African Americans the other income try—stop looking at them, definitely your dollars paying the rent, they are servants part of the deal your play. Now look at them, they are on living on the edge, I AM a witness. No *ping-pong* swing there, they've got ulcers hoping somebody will come to their rescue. And another thing now post an arm backwards, your subsidies your leaders. *Now Dr. King, listen to this his arm a trailblazer seeing to the needs of others his task till death. Move over Israeli's be more like him—a compass. Copy me, JESUS CHRIST? See Dr. Martin Luther King him a great reality, he went all the way Israel, benefit showed me GOD. Martin Luther all the time around his neck just a servant justified very difficult for him a sermon on his neck. "He got up with healing in his wings," this is true. Later a witness against terrible that is what he stood for; wearing a great benefit around his neck, benefit my daughter! What was that before GOD? Tied around his neck with clarity he had a great epitaph; his grave marker in the kingdom of GOD was no romance. He was a servant, a good servant to the people he served everywhere. Awesome! What a grave marker. What about you? They didn't care can you imagine that? I gave him a new revelation, he didn't bounce with it. You all are extremes to the left of reality—your equipment. You will not make the kingdom of GOD. Cannon, I heard his voice a reality, my reality. I gave condolences to his wife; I comfort her, his children as well. *Copy Dr. King. Hooray Dr. King, the message and your pinnacle address a servant of GOD was Dr. Martin Luther King Jr., and let us not forget his wife as well. He and his wife they sacrificed look it up. They were a true big success in life with no stigma exceptions; they carried their weight all the way to their grave, a true written epitaph for them both. And Dr. King he carried it all the way enduring persecution all the way, passing his eternal legacy to his own their benefit. He carried the weight on his shoulders a long time, and many others they saw grace follow them as well, the movement against White supremacy till this day. You have to be equipped with favor that is the point, and have a good attitude, do an exit church people if you don't. Get by people, where were your group stumbling old people? Be like Dr. Martin Luther King Jr., justice for all every night even in Dickson County. You need a blood transfusion you grow like your fathers. You got the big head. Place unforgiveable. *View Rev. Jessie Jackson, and Mrs. Rosa Parks: of the original believable, and they viewed God Almighty the church everywhere. I have a friend now Rev. Jesse Jackson the man remember no usual, no apple in the neck. Remember the rule of etiquette no hesitation. LORD, help him. View Dickson County, I've got news. Let me tell you all something, a milestone his epic, the friend independent, Washington. Turn it around. I had charge over him Republicans, believe me now buck that you racists, and then meditate. Listen to me; see the evidence this book where the evidence is found the purpose what is happening, the book of evidence everyone a normal procedure. Hear a breakthrough. The Bible a beautiful thing celebrate it your pinnacle "Super Bowl." Baptist you know my friend, a friend of the Super Bowl. A G-Summit: you all have a G-Summit you all's initiation do a group participation success, a spiritual success. You all spend money doing everything else. Leave no doubt you all are not going to take it anymore. Get new books plant them the right way you all's children. All you young people compromise where is our Super Bowl legally? Hallelujah. Cut out the confusion. Jacob you know legally you've

## The Original Barbara Payne

been renting it out a lot lately by invitation all the time. You haven't dropped the ball everyone thought that. What about it the bible? Well it's a matter of opinion everyone's classic acceptable. It's just a statute an established rule some say maybe. Keep the seat belt strong evidence heavy evidence against you. I know things that happened to black people. How do you explain that? Follow the kennel. First of all don't dare me, don't laugh at me. One thing I would like you to understand, I view you from heaven be careful. I AM the bread of life. Do your part. Urban you can do better, and urban oasis investment crippling discouragement their staff. I AM a witness. Function I view their training every day. I'll tell you who they are Republicans. They are very rich, Mitt Romney. They are rich crazy those Republicans, Democrats as well. Thank you, JESUS. Sour note before God everything. Say, hallelujah. Defense, things can get rough don't hold back, I know who they are, humble yourselves you pretend like nothing hasn't happened. Enabler, they stand out that's their testimony. They are crooks major development and others. *"I'm backwards say, the kids." New data white people know that, they view it directly. We've been strapped legally for a very long time. Save it for the kids. The degradation: fooled the whole world planted the evidence against colored folks, President Obama spit it out, they are undermining. Let's face it for the kid's things are bad here in Metro, liquid equipment their equipment. Too many things are done on the sly. Their pet peeves, their reaction. Thimble under the table outside interference, they brought this trouble on their predictable. Messes they are entertainers in their own right. Their impact, pour anything on the ground resources. Nasty they are these white people toward black people, definitely on anything meaningful toward black people. On anything you wear the focus is on them that break youth in your neighborhood, it's a sacrifice. It's a wonder they survive at all. They aren't going to help. SOS help it's an emergency. From Above the wannabes' have their way gay rights.

## A New Article

They have their own convention, stench they are. Constant battle we are in. Why don't you plug them with the norm a gift? Admission we see the yard your cycle against young people. Pardon me being the Shepherd your friend. Read *ROMANS* Chapter One (KJV) the difference. And engagement induction no elevator up without Him, completely thinking of JESUS his kingdom a force of JESUS CHRIST telegraph to us make it your defense around the world. CHRIST JESUS said; I view you everywhere that is how you look at it, definitely the centimeter and official on both sides of the fence. View the solid rock that is me JESUS CHRIST. I the husband AM with thee. Let me tell you something, they need to get a hold of God. God is their judge. Boss that my friend. He gives everything even your neighbors a gun He is JESUS CHRIST now take that. He bosses everything that is the difference. Now look ask Him for forgiveness for everything looking toward God. A wake we view next. Teachable don't need wannabes, Jewry hear that? Pentecost, seek God that is your answer. Hear that Jewry, Pentecost as well? You need backup this includes Baptist. Data representatives are the Baptist, their custom purchased approval. Wasted I will skin them things aren't settle, Catholics as well. You say, let by gone be forgiven without the paper work follow me in Tennessee quickly. Say all due respect say we haven't bothered, we are backwards too for not bothering contenders of faith in Nashville, you haven't bothered. Underline Nashville, remember your upbringing. Yes, JESUS CHRIST loves me you say. I view the contest you think you are rich. That is your crime, your virtue, your island, Pentecost your examination, your steroids, your make up shots, your drone's continuous sound. A whole lot of loving going around benefit you. Fog up this is the main hour, a new freeze treatment around your boarders centrally located. Benefit me get it? You know your GPS antennas mushroom legally. Here is the latest news don't threaten me don't bother. Check this out, I view you every day. I'M looking over your debt natural your filter. Bull your debt. You've lost your home, your lively hood two incomes gone. Quit crying wrestle with it go use the bathroom. I don't see how you stand up. You've got a problem emergency. I get tired of working with dollar people their paperwork. Sorry say you don't have insurance, you started it your debt. Count your debt even on Facebook. You know how to make a difference. Give Black people, and poor people another chance to keep their home, I see their effort. You represent God. *And at the Jewish Synagogues your wealth you can recover with no restraints, Trinity you the same and others it's a shame the way Black people have been done. Group payment alone could help. You Jews have fared well substantially well benefit. Money crumbles all the time. Your finances may not always be available. I'M launching a new policy fundamentalist last forty eight hours. Want a way out? What direction, your help is coming from see the Boss GOP. You're afraid your thoughts defined. I define you. Remember I AM the Supervisor. I view this madness. Just stick around Republican eager beavers least of your worries. Their time is limited no clouds there, definitely. Say that real quick their time is almost up, definitely they show offense even in Memphis the Government. We remember what they did to Dr. Martin Luther king, Jr., no excuse we held nothing. Bishop hateful trade up more chicken feed gizzard our autograph. Dr. Registrar we were behind our children, were afflicted and more and people didn't know it accepted it. We took a pill Representative, no virtue in that fantasy pie. Battled Jim Crow and the brown secured our freedom. He put his life on the line. Look at where we are now. *Mr. Clint Eastwood, yes Mr. Clint Eastwood ugly their thing, they were ugly against us the Negros. For the way they acted low down just brutish the White man were, just review it at the news papers. A new President bragging, definitely Jews and Christians against Christians coming we're screaming *déjà vu*; you'd think that he was a criminal Obama. Listen to JESUS CHRIST; I've got shelter for him tell Telemundo Houston, a new legal address to the White

House November's election. I've got something to say about that fact—simple no fascination vapor come and hear a puppy alright? You allow another charlatan (false expert), President in the White House to keep the office by the million, the extreme no blueprint for us, no blueprint Whites you idiot. You can choose someone better idiot. I'M building another system. I've got news, ringing your deposit lawsuit big thrill. You're out of your mind. That is bad news you didn't think of it toppling. Battling *déjà vu* hollowing it is time to stop it the violence and the hate, or it will be *déjà vu* all over again when broken got to stop it now, or *déjà vu* a script. They keep holding us back. Do something about it, or it will be *déjà vu* all over again crippling this nation, and around the world. *Many are in houses they are depressed. *France knows handling it a missed opportunity survival their house, their element and ours; we still got the same problem among your people no solution to the problem. That is some reality there. How about freedom? Thank you, JESUS the co-pilot. A lesson take, a demonstration to I always demonstrate a closure. Welcome to the club the more mighty African American club. What club we are the victim? That mess what a vacuum. That will end it no more drinking champagne for goodness our destiny right off now quickly. Come forth religion it's an embarrassment. I know their address. On alert demons are destroying America, and there are demons out there their acts text books pivot their resources. Private resources a new resolution these are demons for souls in America, homeowners the same. You say, "I can't pay off my debt," Economic turmoil, I will block them says JESUS CHRIST unto me, at that very moment. You're talking about the Government. They are demons (devils) and in the Muslim community as well full of hate; my response to these Republican chains. JESUS! Be on watch Black people in America, the people he's your friend President Obama. Pray for President Obama! President Obama, the management reason politically they borough the grain, I have their number. The unique case issues they enable everybody. Look around you. Behold blue and watch, he died for everything. We love him very much Martin Luther King Jr. .... Honor him. LORD, I am the agent you are their match no mercy their ethics have no mercy. Thus saith the LORD at that very moment, Israel I remember the crime, and who pulled the trigger he did not pull the trigger believe me. The new President: President Barack Obama, you're the man covering the Federal Government for National Security over this, White man you cannot avoid it. It will come out you have the evidence heaven help us, slowly bits and pieces here and there bits and pieces. Oliver North, typical the Federal Government mixing up things their jig is up. Look at the White man in America, tremendous, move this mountain. I AM going to move this mountain that is why they want desert private-sector in America. They are turning the knob for the Middle Class, and the African Americans, economics a new bill will be passed soon it will be on the news their jig is up.

## WE BATTLE THEIR NEW LEVEL NASHVILLE, NOTHING VERTICAL

THUS SAITH THE LORD; those Republicans and some Democrats here is what they want Government class structure control, their big shots mobile accounts with State premium, their premium Priceline, a bonus preferably at the State level for their convenience. They control the bank. A fluke let me make that clear they made a deal. So Evil! Hear that Dr. Registrar? No big that is how they feel. They need a tongue lashing. Where are the political analysts? White man take the elevator up to JESUS CHRIST, focus on your solution. Confusion, Oliver North him they skewed. We were in the dark Nashville, Tennessee. Their created offense typically our region, and in our neighborhoods we view them in the camp; we've got to make up somebody else their debt people that is ridiculous. The offense that is what they think of the majority in Middle Tennessee. In my opinion it's a blurred

## A New Article

vision in other words, physically to distort from range all over Nashville, Williamson County, and in Rutherford County, fundamentally they are criminals later on to distort from a true value or a symmetrical form. We were the target. I swear to God. They think we're garbage White traffic exactly. Conduct over the rail they did it on purpose. Asymmetrical not merit symmetrical concrete, public that is the way they think of the majority understanding? Your goal Whites to devalue. The Oprah Winfrey show: they battle Jim Crow everywhere, they hide their feeling, he did not do it his crime either Oliver North he was doing what he was told. Evidence need it, I have the evidence. The people and JESUS CHRIST, the agent already know it, they are bundling it everywhere some prosecutors. Let God be your guide, your conscious understanding? Then do right. Shout it from the roof top, I will tell them Saint Peter gangs. They killed the leader unofficially of the African American Community recorded. Thank you, JESUS CHRIST. Strong is your defense against those gangs their intolerance for Black people everywhere. It is a shame! A new job war will take its place no yellow there. See, these Republicans. Thank you, JESUS. Their plot, their game, and their dirty deal production no brains, the people will love it their exit annually soon to follow. People billions of dollars spent with the Republicans, spent on their races. Republicans Houses wasted campaign what they market Democrats. Hear that Alabama? Trust me the races how about that politically frozen emphasis their big exit, and unusual circumstance? Nip it in the bud was your answer atypical. You're looking at a grain of fox come to our rescue; we're going to take that to the table legally. I feel so embarrassed fundamentally. A free gift do it man, a free gift historically not a broken promise on your life piece of luggage; don't behave like that bite the bullet, don't let it come to that. Your places you can hardly make it see folks struggling this day a piece cheese and macaroni their dream. I see your devotion, I know it hurts flavor. You can't make another house payment. I'll be honest it's a different train coming here it comes Christmas. Shed some light on it you bit off more than you can chew in the wallet, you and your new company. You're under judgment, I'M telling you. Sad the original are flipping, people are watching you. Mayor Bloomberg, are you alright you get zero? The recourse the next election your insurgent, the next election very heavy turnout customer approved. Cable your licensee common decency. I see you Mayor Bloomberg; first fruit a moral tendency you draft overseas. Are you listening to me Mr. Mayor? I've got some good answers, the tendency your feelings radios as well your game guiding your boat. Showboating you have become. Civil rights development is not your quest. Your TV networks audiences are listening to your threats people from around the world. Theatrics you have become part of that number. Sad it is. At the start people are going to vote you out quickly your boo-boo. I have a lot of friends. Can you take me down? I AM here on the ground. Legally I reserve that right. You people are in trouble, and so are the House Democrats. Show me the reason. Candidates you will find out virtue coming next. Upper Room, get in your place near Vanderbilt, and in Madison. Kick off nobody left out. CHURCH MOVEMENT: Churches we have to tell them for the young people. Some of you already know like parents, keepers of JESUS CHRIST. Oh magnify God at last. *No weapon formed against us shall none merit, because of the supervisor the honorable JESUS CHRIST. View him shortly I said it a long time ago TBN. Watch your ratings don't go up in Nashville, just ask me. You are feeding public graffiti on the front line, and the pulpit as well. You have said a mouth full nationally. The crime your revenue think it is amazing. Come on clean up this house are you listening? *View your neighbors you could help Grand Old Opry people, I'M telling you I view you every day. Your television networks view master 5:00 o'clock shadow falling, actually in Los Angeles there are clouds. View the clouds across North America your ultimate reality. What a coward it's like an old drew (draw) key art, the system exactly just a balloon. We're ready to identify it your equipment ready to be torched. Nashville music industry you are in hot water ask little Jimmy Dickens, beneficial. 12:00 O'CLOCK: CLOCK STRIKES MID-NIGHT ON YOUR NETWORK Little Jimmy Dickens. Watch your languages. It will keep coming every year absolutely controversy. Oh Hallelujah. Young singers, bragging, young singers you watch say abracadabra your craft performers; your birthplace gets that endorsement, and small endorsement, I watch you use that craft. You say, go get'em. I view you. I view one on one Los Angles. You use it knocking a home run every day using your equipment network performers as well, thousands of hopeful young people I know your evaluation and your purpose, and technicians Cumberland Valley Tennessee, people everywhere, they are dangerous because of that. 11:30 P.M. the interlude your actions, your entertainment read the book songwriters not upside down. Read the book. Your bath it's coming. You say, "I ain't (am not) hurting nobody but myself—dangerous. You entertainers with your witchcraft practices terrible! I'M onto you go on with it your country. Sing "Rescue Me" I know the value of it. I view the Nation's. Thank you, JESUS. New version for their entertaining like slaves in a coliseum (like Barak Obama), your special interest group dismissed him basically. Put those people back in an abolition society. "We can't afford them moving forward." We cannot go backwards politicians, and yes you are racists in that society the at large veteran organizations of those groups. Heaven help us all. I know the root of all of that, this junk that you're saying about him Republicans behavior. Just like turnip greens you view him when you speak of him, and them— Black folks everywhere, the other White people running loose with their feelings of gang hate just celebrating your bigotry. Dr. Martin Luther King Jr. would have called your hand. "Try the spirit and see if they are of God," (The case viewing read: 1ˢᵗ JOHN

4:1; The KJV). Have a good attitude. That disturbs me yes JESUS CHRIST. Post your arrest now From Above the kingdom is watching you, your every move on the face of the world. You cannot do wrong and blame other people, let me help you. "Heaven and earth shall pass away, but not one word of my word shall stumble" (Read *MATTHEW* 24:35; The KJV). / I AM the shield. I know your crowd. Look at the bridegroom. Do you know how that sounds to the rest of the world, your white infrastructure? God is angry. Courtesy constructions: join me Macy's that universal function, and that functions come on T. J. Maxx. *I bring new weapons. Macy's you try to be smart, that is your answer alright? I will be on top of your head in a couple of minutes, let me tell you, the HOLY GHOST publicly. Macy's some of the originals understand, I'M going to give it to your family litigation with a fist? It will ruin your business then you'll have zero, then you'll be singing the James Brown commercials anywhere, and at any time the usual, oh-my-gosh people; we're public relative Nordstrom's as well. I'M going to get the racism out of you White folks, all your kin folk's young ones as well—face judgment. NOTE: FROM THE ONE AND ONLY JESUS CHRIST; follow me you all overlook it every one of you, that is all that you care about noted politically this entire next election candidate, November, political restitution choices governing the market against President Obama, the argument agreed? You all think President Obama's Administration it is a big joke. Good at last think him for his service; I don't think it is a joke. Sad news key vote major turnout in election—people electives they obviously vote Republicans. You believe? Hey Krystal stone crush, I've been watching you from Memphis being on TV infrastructure. Pure intelligence Redeemer this November, absolutely watch the battleground States coming with fire for Obama in every State. What a blow! Local papers recorded President Obama awkward right now. Understanding the election level a unique opportunity the clock is ticking. All the resources I have and all the aces fixing you know what, extreme long your fix. Typical, here goes your punishment some maybe arrested; Government cover up damage has already been done. Thought I'd forgotten did it on purpose. We were overwhelmed. No need of crying Democrats waited a long time. Strictly politically remarks straight tongue from the Lord, hopeful in the United States hear that? My- gosh, women as well a revolution better come again this hand. My-gosh, women as well they play football for democracy hear an echo for Republican values; Republican Congress they will stab you in the back for the President Obama. A lot of people feel that way about Obama, their kin to the President. You are in the fight for your life. I recommend JESUS CHRIST, to all those Republicans. A lot of them in institutions were sent to prisons. They are Americans. Go and make bond get them out on cross bail, Martin Luther King did. Review *GENESIS*; your house The Keeper. See what you are up against The Tea Party people? Democrats and Republican key players Republican friends of mine, those major U.S. key players, all elected officials and other players elected officials; I'M pointing a finger up and like your Lake View politicians understand? You offend me won't see you in those bars anymore. Say, politicians you look like guinea pigs you politicians (a dirty pig in a group) end of your game. Say uh Mr. Public-Officials Nashville, I hear you every day Mr. Cactus Officials friends you abhor capitalism, naughty I know every single one of you. Typical your freefall political view tired of it your jingle at THE GRAND OLD OPRY: you know how you are. Are you listening? I'M tired of it. Get comfortable. You practice Pentecostals based on music people love to hear, and your accompanied measurement stringing people singing those songs. AND ANNOUNCEMENT: this is true you can't help it practicing that old school racism. Lay down that burden under a rock. Put it under me my cloak all that pressure. I will be standing up for you. I AM the ambassador of all regardless what the world thinks about it conservatives country, exactly. Stop, your real conclusion let it go racists. I'M tired of it go after me, even racists you understand Republicans? All people White people, even Black people-the African Americans, Jews and Blacks, Asians, Latinos, Caucasians, practicing racism are you listening? You're in trouble Blacks the African Americans; even the Latinos against Blacks promoting their fare share in the Country like White people with their attitude times are dangerous violence is everywhere. I view the situation. Your children are practicing racism. And Pentecost dating back to slavery both sides, I AM familiar with that. I've got your phone number; I keep good records this I know. And in both Houses of Government you hear me get along with that, you are lukewarm keeping that up I hear it being practice every day on the radio. Looking back I know your adversary, even the Arabs are watching your portfolio, your pinnacle they are talking about you a whole bunch of them, they've got agents everywhere in this country. The difference their velocity is climbing soon share-croppers advantage will be gone 80%. Now take a look at that, half of them are over here illegal I'M watching their increase. The NAACP you should be keeping up with that, and their attitude you go figure that out, it's because they want them over here these politicians and the groups. Now look at what is going on in Paris, France and in other Countries around the world they practice the wrong attitude, they will topple France, they will topple the results. President Clinton would have controlled their atmosphere, go ahead turn them in they are here illegally. Mistake if you don't many are here illegally, they think this is a football field pilot wherever you want to go, and nobody will find out where you are, and who that you are dangerous are these people. People everywhere these are gangs with known methods, and those events with no substitute they use women as well in those practices, those are their practice these are giants. Finally, also remember the "*Stars and Stripes Forever*" well it won't be, if they keep coming here illegally. Out of bounds you know better your propagation, you'll regret it on Capitol Hill, view the census a big mistake it can't be ignored not healthy for us here in America, and around the world I view the whole thing. Let me break it down Jew and White, Gentile alike every racist dangerous. Age appropriate dissolve the conflict engage me. Settlement, go after me I AM much more than that put it under me JESUS CHRIST. I dare you. Be my guest. You're not in disrespect; I AM the pilot I drive all. *"Beulah land"* your traffic fond of it, Opryland you are having fun White people that are actively involved for putting slavery back together. I know your pass, your landing, your will even church people everywhere from the pulpit. I know your quest. The region we are distress. This very evening you add racial insults against my people, Black people and other colored people. Let me tell you something, you are offensive it is no game insult upon insult. You are kidding if you think racists practices are going to continue in this nation, and in the rest of the world. People are suffering you are ignorant. JESUS CHRIST KOSHER PRACTICE I DO! You think that is racists? Evidence your celebration by professionals out selling for gathering by individuals, and their network group Heraldic racists extreme just so you would know for non-profit Masons primarily they are dangerous, what's happening of their group bone naked they are racists. Bringing charges what do you think about that? Touch me JESUS CHRIST super knowledge; backwards if you think otherwise, as if you didn't know your interest pointing a finger the knowing, you need a check up your gang at that gathering at different places your politics? LORD JESUS; KEEP THEM AWAY FROM ME, AND MY FAMILY THIS WATCH-KEEPER; THEY ARE PICKING THEM OUT, ME AND MY FAMILY KEEP SAFE WHILE THEY ARE SLEEPING, AND ALL THE REST OF THE BLACK PEOPLE AS THEY SLUMBER I WOULD BE DELIGHTED. GOD HAS SEALED YOU. I HEARD IT ON LINE, I HEARD IT ON LINE A COUPON AWAY. I HAVE A BACKUP YOUR PLACE

*The Original Barbara Payne*

NOW; YOU'RE ON THE WEB-PAGE INDIVIDUALS WHO TALK BLOW UP HOUSES. Anyhow check out the list, I'll tell you all about it hayride, your urban are increasing they seem ragged; Spanish speaking people don't tell that are active individuals in the country. Come on Spanish speaking people; look away turn over a new lease make the difference. Turn to newer version written by popular individuals Fontella Bass, Raynard Miner, and Carl William Smith, in 1965, at your entertainment it's just confusion not "*Beulah Land*" well known Negro Spiritual written by Edgar Page Stites in 1875 or1876, music by John R. Sweney, or "*My Anchor Belongs To God*" while on location, while you're on the stage it's an embarrassment even Apostolics, the bad news low-down this 21$^{st}$ century. Get your Bible and read it now. At least we can sing "*The bye and bye*" our exodus your effort. Prophet you'll mess it up using the interjection, it is coming anyway revival is main event. GOD you are awesome, literally directly on our galaxy, on our planet of vibrant illumination of your entertainment Hollywood. Night has fallen quickly on Nashville, on your performance, your entertainment, the Country Music Industry world the family White people. You are drunk, I AM a witness. Your ethnics technically gravitation this is how I feel. I view your measurement The Country Music Industry other artists as well buckle up; you have a rough road ahead of you believe God in this matter. Arm themselves are you making fun of me, remember me? Where are you going? No sense of relief. To be frank, I see the little faces saying help me. Low down are you White people destroying children the Clan group they are. Taxi help the kids in the inner city it's not tough on you. I have your directory. Help the inner city kids, help God. Some just need structure in their lives. Be a mentor, be a nomination, help the kids it maybe your change for a new life. Your responsibility inner city children that is the major solution; my agent they need your help the White people. Utilize your brain. I need an apology send help be a friend. Now you get to feel like other people that are not in show business, in the entertainment field. View this article complete. You heard me you can't walk away your interest. I hear a knock at the door answer real quick. I know who you are, and that what you are just gathering noise your balloon politicians entertainers. Tell them who you are, how unspeakable it is not a beacon of light, you need a lantern. Oh say, be thankful. Model Japanese as well, you want clean air again before the ice hits your television networks, and Mr. Fox as well? Then surrender. I'll tell you all about it. I'M not bullying new episode. Junks of ice will fall everywhere injuring TV stations, then where is your revenue even in Mississippi. Low, Mississippi do you hear me? Poverty crosses the line everywhere, and you do nothing about it. Clean up your mess. I'M talking to Mississippi. Food network a giant your industry, do you think I'M crazy for hitting your networks? Call the Mayor Bloomberg and see if he can fix it the junk you all's junk news network all across America; you'll see it on Halloween your new network watch it everywhere. Christian Networks somebody draw near—Trinity. And in East Nashville, in Tennessee rainfall will fall faster than you can blink your eye. *The Deliver, Keeper of the kingdom will hit you with disastrous amounts of rain fall so long North Carolina, the Deliverer. I've got rains tremendous amount. They will hit you so hard it will be like putting bullets into a tank. Then you will listen. You can't hold back ice or rain, when it is falling from the sky. *You were trying to take it down the U. S. citizenship for African Americans. I agree says JESUS CHRIST unto me. GOD, is ahead of you, GOD is in every corner of the world. The comforter is coming to take your place. A change is coming. The whoremongering days are over for network satellite television, Opry Network as well total investment in the U.S., no outlet you got nowhere to go. Hit the economy where it hurts. You say, "We were an embarrassment." We have a battleground. This is grave illness. Where is the moral? Preach it brothers review your wakeup call your team.   Biggest offense you are just fools total the equipment now From Above on that "The Dodgers" in the outfield your offense. P.M., eventually you are rebels passing your responsibilities public response. Outfielders are you on the mounds okay? You are dodgers they are screaming negative response your own local government, and Federal Government hit the ball staggering, microfiche. Mounds get in your place. Kick off ready for the kick off? Reason both parties will experience it—big turnout. Like Jack and Jill children.

CREATED MOMENT ENGRAVED BY THE MOMENT
    THUS SAITH THE LORD; Mayor Bloomberg big pillow management, you draw a double flare elected official against the people. Mayor Bloomberg big city operation everybody knows you television. Know who you are dealing with who you are referring with right away Mayor Bloomberg; you have a dump in the hood your nuclear waste is its way so prepared. Say God is on my side. A lot of nuclear waste is coming your way to be dumped on that town 24/7. Your shift left that very city you call home, the rail system more pollution, and killing than you can ever stand it is air pollution. It is concrete complete. It will be the worst thing ever happened to New York, that City.  H-m-m-m—these apartments' people were racing to back streets no way out. Let me explain, no elevator, no cab waiting, you are going to fold and the violence can't drive anywhere, people stopped moving no privacy on the rush. You were choking. "Clear the tunnel," the tunnel no exit so have a good time pushing your way out of the city. Essentially I know the root of evil. Gridlock in Nashville, Tennessee people common everyday man their effort your U. S. Federal Dollars used in Metro Government. Hey your development hundreds of people went down in the river, thrown wet in the east river. No more dope dealers. Save New Jersey, heeded the warning. People were laughing. Arrangements the middle man leaked it out. They were riding the buses company buses and inferno. No revenue powerful

jolt. Take me to Florida. How did they serve it? I'M serving you yes, you elected official now listen to this, be upbeat to this big market, Black people they come in all different races; Mayor Bloomberg, dangerous the beginning the other Sherriff hold for ransom uh—Mayor Bloomberg? Now leave a ransom we recommend all the King's men, the Doctor Domino effect. We'll explain, your makeup you are filthy rich. Thank you, JESUS. We have work to do, the war hear that equipment in a couple of years Mexicans the people, and the Cabinet to the spot light? Thanks to those rich Republicans, White people filthy rich all of them all business group, obedient all Mexicans until they took it away. I'M telling you, I have the revenue evidence Black people, they are responsible White people, know that GOD is able. Lost jobs nearly five million or more people affected, the auto industry here in the United States of America, in this Country people lose jobs in this Country. You have got to be kidding? Can you imagine that? You count zero can you believe that? It's like telling another age old Christmas story those Republicans again, the way they practice dragging us through debt. Look at them the lizards members of their own local society, a network you can't define them, White trash every little town has them in them can you imagine? LOOKING BACK: their chief of their little images network the forces these are a *rude Baron* are these people, white people who know the difference literati are becoming just white trash all the time in Ashland City, they are prejudice bigots organized, loath that community black list him all the time, and they did that to Melvin said JESUS unto me that morning. NOTE: FROM JESUS CHRIST; now your *"Papa Bear"* was no ordinary man, he was not the usual; looking ahead was a great friend of mine JESUS CHRIST saying a good degree. They ruined your Papa Bear, and his image those White folks they did, they talked a lot about Black folks except Walker and a few others, they cast a lot of stones at his image, I'M talking about your Papa Bear. *I love him Mr. Melvin said God

*The Original Barbara Payne*

JESUS CHRIST unto me on that day; now on that morning and here after. There's not a shadow walking after him down there on the earth being it preferred by me, The Almighty God, to me from above. Draw your own conclusions the White man some of they are reptiles with question. I loved him till his death your Papa Bear. *Very important my young man (my son) no stumping ground behind him, Holy Ghost get that? I've got telephone records; they got him eating out of their hands. He's safe now doesn't live their anymore gone South, but he won't listen like a *Jango* Williams touring in that Nashville. Don't be afraid. *Now don't cry. I'll tell you something else; you don't know he won't quit disliking you, okay? Like a rabbit with an arm in his left hands, I view him everyday waste. Bango you are a rabbit (their pet)? Do me a favor now don't cry Barbara! There's help for that you know better, you are above that their pet not pleasing God. You must believe God when I tell you, he will move away from all of them. I desire him for myself use in my kingdom, him and Camille and your other daughter too. They won't do like Camille, keep themselves away from the world and all it has to offer. They all need to know the responsibility you have on your shoulders. *I'll make him leave them alone Ms. Barbara, knowing it's a jungle out there thinking Santa Claus (their effort with your son), window clearing with no regrets know that I AM able. I've been observing him for a long time. He doesn't know that you've suffered legally because of them, the Whites the effect those two. This happened to you. You are my colleague in any event. They have been working against you for a very long time using politics, wolves they are. You know the kind Black people, they are hateful wanting freedom desperate tonight chiefly eating out of their hands, now relaxing my son enemy of mine a red brick against you, don't know the middle blossomed backwards youth. I have observed cankered like whip cream too lose verbally against you real smooth, he can't help it his mouth. *GOD! Save him don't leave him out. He's hurt you, rubbed him the wrong way a long time ago, still know that GOD is able to bring him back again. He doesn't know what you know chiefly how they work, feelings in that he can find solace in that won't rely on GOD. Better get the Bible credit to discern his return, he can't interpret the way we can, doesn't have the advantage. Weak in his flesh, causes him to be backwards like Cheatham County. Stomach politics and real loud offensive, he's wrapped up in himself no joke, and there is a lot of Black families like that too. I view them everyday better be careful, and some are in a cul-de-sac across the street. No joking some of the people they are dangerous, compass exactly. *Finally young people here in Nashville, you don't know evil Ashland City as well, Yes, Pentecost I view Ashland City as well. *JESUS looked at me and then he said to me; your root if you ask me it's in your home danger for you, he's messing around needs improvement. Don't be rude my friend Pentecost okay, imagine that? You are in danger in this house, the scum a whole lot of people know that he's messing around. I'M getting you out of here be not afraid. Barbara, you need a lot of fellowship it can cheer you up. So trust me making your way. I will escort you out of there. The root clipped it (my husband), I have the advantage, people don't know that now use your wisdom, your fellowship lost behind your back the answer Pentecost watching with his eyes always focused on you, spiritually wanting more fellowship the opponent. Pentecost your look heavy, you've suffered for him and needing a friend are you, I view you downstairs all the time. *Knowing the young people your son and the young Black people terrible, hateful they are to their ancestors. They know the wrong kind automatically. Canvas appeal (no compass the things people say) a boxer Republican Studebaker (driven obsolete) your kid and them, they rob God, they aren't your friend. Yes, JESUS. I think you. JESUS CHRIST; make him your shield and other people culturally whenever they need it. It breaks my heart young people; you don't know what kind of animals they are inside, when they attack another human being. They don't really know GOD, you can't mess with darkness. *A lot for Marco, he doesn't know that can you imagine, I will build a fence don't you worry about that wolves they are in a pack? Now swallow that crooks. Typically they generally know young people. Now don't be afraid of that evil mess. Evil never take your eyes off of them when helping me, for a split second. Like a microwave they are when approaching people. They are ugly and in restaurants they look pretentious, they are dirty never take your eyes off of them, big mistake if you do. *They surround him and build him up, weak class they are the youth of those generation's young Black people. Wearing a coat-offering, they look like a duck (like a sitting duck for their advantage all youth not use too much), if you ask me they need help. Don't look like a pigeon in their kingdom, let me repeat that a couple of times. *Be careful not like your son, and be thick when they are with you never address them turning your back on them, they walk a different mile. *Had people beat up in that County where you use to live (in Cheatham County, TN) fueling their revenue fuel it up plug it up, they put on a tremendous front of facial wainscoting wanted you to know that—double-wainscoting You're on to them now and their message of friendship. You have written a book. All of them are backwards in their society. Basis multiple middle have been run off the road, their equipment swinging left usually in a pickup tailored to suit them, just observing, just laughing when they are doing it the average wainscoting, an alert if you don't mind industrial in my book, and your family as well they are all going a little bit crazy. Quit badgering us their grave ability group social class trash they are determined going after wealth, I don't like their trash, even though some are expensive in their groups accumulating wealth going upper class they are. The veterans they get along a little better with other people, but harmful just the same. The all White Gangs they are, they loot while others get by even in peoples home. And they loot a lot. They are a mess.

## A New Article

They really know how to perform mean folks they are. I eat rally with them. Everybody sees them as the messenger go between business success stories, rotten they are! They are dirty human beings crooked they are, physically they are as well, believe me like Oklahoma Ranchers. Don't hang around them. Agree. I agree? I love you very much JESUS CHRIST. Thank you. That's their movement I'll kick butt. They've lost their home. Robbery they are their trail, they are the queen of it those White people, and their advantage they rob GOD, and good people never walking straight. I don't like them anytime. I understand daughter. Listen, apple of mine eye with affection like a real success story, are you alright? I know him your son a mess gambling on Whites. Stop putting him on your check list, you've got a problem with him people already know the Whites and others. They think you are trifling and no good, hopeless, they often think they know for sure my daughter and my friend. You are best my friend. I AM the jury you let me handle it. I view their audience every Sunday. Like a ripple I have already fixed it. It is a real possibility they will bite his hand for sure. He walked right into it muck (filth), they will attack him on a Saturday for sure, any day during any month. He had better leave town, and quit rubbing elbows with them. Daughter up above Third Degree they don't like him. LORD, please build a fence in my house a wall all around me most definitely, exactly this week crisis. One day I'll be there and I'll give you presents, The Keeper no doubt about it your friend. No scapegoat no more. Like a ripple effect, I view their Three Third Degree Pastor, he watches out for them. Trifling they are looking for an easy way out. Gambling their society, gambling they are run by Barons, they disgust me no more secret society. They keep people in chains. Sorry they are he needs to separate himself. *Cry on my shoulders this is America, he can accomplish success; he has a career now his social security don't need them. They are members of their own network, a secret society of politicians controlling us that is what they stand for. It's about time we let those men have it our culture. Disney they are, think about it. We are our own success story; Thou kingdom come this century due to the eternal. Shame on us read the census pick up a packet. I got the numbers a different kind of view. Get this? Politicians the facts read the ratio, the odds Black inferior. Soon my friend waiting for something to happen that is what it is all about even here in Metro Nashville, a hot button I've got the data. See the task force. Now you go figure. I will save your children from above. Don't be concerned, don't panic, believe me they woke up. They got away with it read it at Vanderbilt. Plus the Federal Government with the evidence so political, ruined politically those Republicans our economy those people, and for Democrats to the rest of the world in Middle Tennessee, truth to that rustle jobs away from Black people brought into this Country, typically their moral defense Government Agency. People need to know due to economic times. Mayor Bloomberg, go back to a deal. Go back to work your fidelity in exchange your market Bloomberg. It's like catching some things on fire with a bucket Mayor Bloomberg. Give it a couple I see your loyalty Republican, me JESUS CHRIST. We score 400, 000 the average missile attack. Thank you, JESUS for being our defender against the Republican corrupt Government. No more wrestling true armor standing at your deal. I'M pointing a finger your accomplishments "Triple A," I know your address from the foundation up above. A new foundation God gives power at this point. The opposite you better not say anything your revenue republicans, the democrats legally the same. Opening letter see I will be all over you real fix judgment, and at the Democrats. Straight from the engine hold accountable. Get out of this house. You cannot deny it any longer. They reviewed your blank weapons (opportunities). The people came out even The Church of Christ, no reason a desperate reason for the schools in Metro. We need NAACP help the pro's, the veterans, The Churches of Christ as well coming together returning the favor, a staple we're all coming together. Ask President Obama, see Nashville. In other words, Obama we clubbed zero out please put it on top of your agenda. Describe it showers not Metro Schools closing in Tennessee, we demand it. A big over throw the Government in both houses. No need for lawyers in Tennessee, a new prescription please afflicted enough. Now we need wood burning outlet: not and lobbyists' 80 million dollars new endorsement. Keep it simple arithmetic you do the math, and we will do just fine. We're tainted enough. I'M tracking you, definitely Government pains about to explode in both Houses simple. I'M telling you you've wasted enough time doing nothing face it. I see the packaging. See those Republicans and those Independent politically in Tennessee, after the election the special interest groups join the conference. I view you the same group, a lot of times many have oppression in Tennessee. See the poll a hundred percent, and amazing story in this Country's system, The Tea Party Republicans I view you a long time, I view you one hundred times. I make my way. You've got to make the payment give me a break your revenue income. Boy this Country is sour. How do you do your boundaries? That is the way you treat other people famous. You've shed a drain of fear, Pentecostal don't laugh. Say it is time to worship, it is time to synthesized hold on. Amen. Make and armor from the deep freeze. Low standings treat other alliances well, treat them like you would want to be treated. In additional, you think God is crazy regular view. I view your company. You think God is playing your whipping. Angry God is Pentecost, your house danger alternative. We need a revolution. We have to instruct that is what it means. We have open discussion the world, thank you, JESUS. We have to go back true alternative the average. The river God gives to all that is your blessing. Big blessing people Black and White not hate burdensome Pentecost, and you Republicans in the Senate. Shame on you the average; we know the whole thing giving the Government lead way like that. GOD frowns upon it Pentecost no joke. "We see four kinds," that is what you were raised on people are equal White people. I make you a better offer no distinction. People everywhere are going to be saved just look at me. I make a difference. Show some respect Indian people, Black people, and White people, Pentecost individuals in your neighborhoods White groups and other ethnic groups. Be a blessing, save your blessing wrong way. I don't like that. And young adults we'll be dancing in the street. Tell the people everywhere fantastic now put yourselves in their shoes, stop running away with it, your blessing and other people of other races and different nationalities everywhere. They are your brother's equal everywhere. Many are headed your way Pastors. JESUS CHRIST the river flows for everybody; this is true people everywhere coast to coast. Give me the stick Pentecost Holiness heritage landing our redemption, our root canal is about to come out it is coming out. Archaeology, I AM in front of you White people life's journey JESUS CHRIST, typical your way of thinking. Incidentally, color you have to acknowledge it quickly. I AM not salmon color, my color like Black individuals me JESUS CHRIST; yes the White that is right. Now spew that out my color individuals of White society. Factor in that. I AM GOD. Your part be thankful for that. The issues due unto others as you would have them do unto you. Strengthened your order Pentecost, get along on the highway grow up and behave. Be wise as you travel this life's journey, people are suffering along the way life's journey. I see a supervision Pentecost. One day Pentecost, the freak show will be over down here. One day the learning will be over, and then where will you be? A new formation in heaven Pentecost, JESUS CHRIST the head, and everyone else follows suit no more trash talking idiots. No trash talking up there not even the notion, surrender always will be all the time way back to the beginning of time. Thank you, Lord JESUS. You copy Mayor Bloomberg, do you copy? The project, I measure above underdevelopment quite a ways.  Say, when are we all going to get together, and build the building talking about church folks, those who accept a dark head Black man no competition.  Flipping, overlook me all the time in one of their services due to their racism that is that.  I AM the new avenue Mr. Republican.  I AM window watching up there no excuse, you got some nerve that is how I feel about it.  You've got all possibilities that is how I feel about it, if you ask me.  See the attachment I'M not going to have it.  View the plans I AM coming racism.  View, your race should have a long time ago then fool yourself.  Racism the barrier I hope you enjoy it build your own race?  We are ground breaking.  When are you going to think about me, and let some other people in so other people can be free? You are putting on makeup. That is your norm, your straight, amen your current condition.  But do you love?  Conquest look what you practice, you remember your race.  Are you listening? This is true Pentecost, you will be held accountable for all people all races.  You have a model.  I the sheriff see it rough especially on the little ones.  Reminder I AM your friend. Who is your friend, the one and only JESUS CHRIST?  That is exactly right in plain view people everywhere lift up those hands for me, and praise God.  I view his presence, He is awesome.  *People, the body of believer's Christians everywhere seek God's grace. Let me repeat, this is an eye opener God's eyes is full of wrath!  With all due respect, Christians everywhere need to seek God's grace night and day.  View the heavenly Father.  I am a witness.  Let me say one more thing, hallelujah, JESUS.  GOD is awesome.  God will meet the need.  Hallelujah.  God knows our ability.  Shout hallelujah! Just fall on your face and repent.  View my presence.  I inspect people everywhere.  That is not even the half young people.  We are friends. I AM their voice, those who are broken hearted devastated over this situation.  Something needs to be done about it over this trouble spot.  Did anyone ever tell you Baptist ask anybody, I AM your friend a good thing the intercessor your friend?

Dial 911. I pray for everybody. I AM the sheriff of this department everyone knows. It would profit you to abase yourselves to realize that. Furthermore, I AM the gateway your entrance. Evidently you don't take me at my word. Have you heard me? Take a look at your standings now, whether you are in good standings. Your policy of self-centeredness needs an alert, a face lift Democrats as well. You're lucky (favorable) you have me Pentecost; Baptist as well you offend me.

A NEW PROGRAM DEVELOPMENT SOME ARE FASCINATED WITH IT, THE NEW INVENTION. SAY, GOD I'M EXCITED EVEN IN ATLANTA. WOE! TO GREAT BRITAIN WATCH YOUR NUCLEAR WASTE; EVEN IN THE PALACE A GREAT MELT DOWN IMAGINE THAT? THERE ARE OTHER OPITIONS. PEOPLE ARE RACING FOR THE PALACE TO ATTACK THE PALACE IN GREAT BRITIAN; THIS IS AN EMERGENCY OCEANS AWAY. IT'S LIKE THEY ARE PROSTITUTION NUCLEAR WASTE.

Thus saith the LORD; Listen young people move away from that even in America, the whole land is like a sickle an abomination, even if it costs you a pound. Time to get together in our Country as well these are serious times, the issues one drop of nuclear waste a bomb in a pillow *of nuclear waste* in the United States, and around the world a prescription custom made no more island the island people, and in Europe it's like a cancer it wouldn't exist anymore in the airport even in Canada their own messengers. *The veterans liquid waste airborne all the time even on the ground, and in Great Britain calling it jet fuel. Looking at the assessment total liquid, total limit, looking at reality even in the United States of America, its coming here be careful. Island even in the city over there like a homemade bomb dump it, some even look forward to it you follow me? Remain reassessment people and their game politically. Even in Great Britain, and in Europe, because of the economy Great Britain. England we found similarities in other people across in the United States of America, in Europe similarities let me tell you a thing about it, because of the economy a tragedy. Let me explain, their economy everybody knows though what economy, The House of Windsor total value our economy. *Peoples in the South of France, and here in the United States, their network past and present resistance a reason for creating it via Chicago. Us they're on top of the mountain tipping none their economy. I know your Blair your low-down. Let me inform you messenger, you need a staff a butler go right on over there. I know your game and your intelligence brewing they're at the door, then a nuclear bomb total emission their waste radon in the cloud. It will kill a lot of people. By the way, in Nashville, Tennessee they bring it in from everywhere, they bring causalities copy that? Their nuclear waste the ball is in your court, they're already testing their weapons. New experience it's an emergency even in Nashville, Tennessee. Oh JESUS CHRIST! They bring equipment here every day into Nashville, to toll America. It's an embarrassment I've been observing says JESUS CHRIST; a lot of deaths will occur.

## PEOPLE TALKING FOLLOW ME JESUS CHRIST, AND NEVER GIVE UP.

Thus saith the LORD; Bee quick! Unbelievable I know them don't be afraid of them daughter. I know you are afraid-baffled by their looks, I know you are afraid. I put in place; I know you are ridiculed in Nashville, I view your grandchildren and their parents, and they won't turn on me. Some of you get off the stage you are just liquid. I'M very proud of you. I know where I'M coming from don't fight back you're in the middle, their gossip secret address. Don't be afraid of the people. I know their reality, a reality gangs. Justly most significant they bother me friend of mine, their smoking guns looking at Ms. Barbara all business, definitely my friend your situation spiritually. They should bear "*the fruit of the spirit*" (found in the book of *GALATIANS* 5:22) of GOD, cornerstone of God. They see ridiculous and attempt. I see the gangs their performance friend of mine, their customs, yearly every year. You know the thing to do Ms. Barbara Payne? Hear me, low down they are. OH GREAT JEHOVAH GOD! They are out to get you depart from class structure, your reality. Onions they are. You have reached a milestone. They are after you. JESUS CHRIST, come to the rescue of me! I view an opening your defense. Check never come back your defense, they are out to get you. They really are out to get you Ms. Barbara. I'll help brag on you. Behind me the police, GOD you're awesome! Situation I deal with it no other recourse. Come on Ms. Barbara Payne, I give you confidence don't be like that, you're too emotional don't be emotional arguing with them "*try the spirit*" that's satan (another passage). Don't do that you're telling them how you feel that is the way they operate. I see their faces. Evidence they are after you; view *NEHEMIAH*; the book the complete text then you will know how to behave around them, read the text for complete instruction when around them and in their actions; junk too you are them all. Are you alright? Defense the people never turn your back on them ever. I talk to you, be thankful. Come on Ms. Barbara, I know you are broken. Don't let them see your face, your reaction just a blade simple stuff; sad a whole lot of them. Be calm anyhow my friend. I see you when you go to the bathroom it hurt, your calamity outstanding they crossing you. Do you understand? Hollow you feel inside go to the Doctor. Tell your family immediately when you are losing it, white people don't care. I declare in the kingdom, their assessment it's just who you are that matters. Be honest clinical studies I see your life. African American your black brothers are jealous crossed up-politics. Be wise. I see their encore delighted design against the LAMB, because of you. Enough with them, you'll get over it come be with me. Your brothers and sisters thimble for breakfast get over it, your credit backbone. I'M watching you. You'll be okay stop mourning wipe your nose clean. Keep it that way. The Keeper, you are my friend a dear friend. And analyses remember God covers your back, understanding my friend the Shepherd is looking out for you. How long have you been like this? You are trembling you are a child of God, look up don't be afraid anymore. You need more oxygen providence. Living next door stereotypical stop before I settle this mess, they are laughing at you from the back extreme, just crazy they are. You are rich I'M talking to you, I know who you are. I know your attitude good I proclaim friend of mine. I don't like the middle in society. Number one ring leader, I'M watching you as well. The ring leader talking about you against whites, donating nothing their attitude you know better. CASE IN POINT: I know your station. Tell somebody I know you've got feelings, and I'M looking out for you. I know you are losing it. Come on Bishops, you can do better than that. Big mistake get off the stage now don't forget I view you constantly, and your family only a course of time. You are murderous class; you are backward given over to disputing one another. You the person, I see a whole lot of blood rushing to your face making you piercing inside, making you go inside. I see your blood pressure, for the record whaling yourself from the outside. I see the symptoms making you nervous, that is why you can't get up I'M watching. Enough is enough. Charges, your husband aiding against you, your house you are loose cannon aiding that is your husband. Conclusion, be ready I have the evidence let me start telling their dynamite hang ups across the board, let me tell you a few even last year; alright by me. View the camp front and center there will be whaling in the department. Shepherds are you listening? I have the evidence a beautiful thing pastors. I know their number. No more brushing things aside like you use too. Say it now deliverance, praise the whole bunch it's now in alphabetical order you are in trouble. Just a moment I will fix it. I want to think you. Are you listening? Fear God, fear me JESUS CHRIST. Oh thank you, JESUS very much. Don't mess with me I'll give you a whipping, the gang your pocket, your hemisphere just a concern. SECOND ANNOUNCEMENT: Commandment alright, leave the anointing alone. Your weak shares I see. I know you are hurt publicly. Don't fight them others this hemisphere. Are you okay? Say, your final place GOD'S heaven deliverance. Your personal attacks will end the accuser all by himself. Say, rescue me Barbara Payne look pass him their agency. Say, sticks and stones may underwire, but for you talk will never bother you, congratulations to that! Keep cutthroat away. Blindfold they are. They are your kinsman. Come sit by me. I know you've never view your estate, but look at me one day you will be there with me an event. You are weak. I view you all the time keep fighting, I know you've been fighting a long time. Come sit by me, JESUS CHRIST. Testimony of your past mourning red while everybody else is. I will put some sunshine on them stay away from them. I've been eye balling it for a very long time. Go to the bathroom, strengthen, I know you've been weary your common thread me JESUS CHRIST. I know you are losing it. GOD makes a difference never give up. I touch you. I have a difference open the door let some fresh air in. Dynamite your blessing is on its way, and then you will be a show off agreed? The only other option view my power. The lonesome side they keep ganging up on you keep trying just for a second. Yes JESUS. Oh I smell JESUS in the upper room! Yes daughter. Difficult I smell their root their accomplice. Daughter view the upper room your window of success, your new season is on the way the option. The emphasis, your success tell them to move over are you alright my daughter? I've been telling you listening pay attention hear enough don't give up you never give up? Mockery nobody is on your side you are a joke, you are a friend of mine in season you are a winner. Remember the season smog there in Nashville, near Vanderbilt their campus public viewing soon. Don't be afraid be strong. Don't you worry wipe your tears GOD will win, we will win across the gate. Cross the finish line a window of opportunity.

THE MOVEMENT COME AND SEE A REALITY

Thus saith the LORD; A new storm. I see visiting cleric from on high no artificial (watermelon) men, they are cleric from God, their mission a reality; They are top Senior Men ready to do battle like you, nothing superficial viewing your neighbors. Please don't take this personal carrying their own reality. I've waited a long time individuals seeing a reality ahead of time. Simple question about me pressure about the nature, do you understand talking about God, not a political thing? Whoa! How did you find it? Eyeing it viewing your individual situation, we smell a rat. Make sure there is room for me CHRIST, woman caring papers joining with you the movement your Jim Crow days are over the message. Let's get things shook up here in Nashville. They have new ideas. Coming to your services, in your services coming to Nashville, a prayer meeting a rally, and in Hendersonville new born officer's clients favorite sons, helping to stamp out the pollution in the air with new equipment totally on me, and near Vanderbilt looking out. *Daughter, says JESUS CHRIST at that time unto me, we will win every one of them caring Bachelors of Science Degree, and their Doctorate Degree looking at the best doctorate, and it is earned under their arm to fight this battle legally. Thanks, for this day. It is their battle a third unit common forces no romance. Ms. Barbara, I've been waiting a long time for this to commence for you, you were the one who thinks like them. "Trouble in my way" the song in my hair, whoa CHRIST! JESUS CHRIST, will always fix it. You want some protection; I will give you protection, absolutely your defense. Did you hear me? Get your Doctorate Degree now, even if you are solo. I guess you are right. Thank you, JESUS CHRIST, my protector. They are losing it, definitely. Pentecost, we may somewhat start a civil war that is your accomplishment.

## The Original Barbara Payne

God is angry! You keep putting it off let the ball fall where it may revenue. Let me give you some advice, their camp they are rebels. Their reality as it appears whole lot of faults, brothers jokingly literally. You can do better. Their test you need to get over it colored people. "You say it's nobody's business other people." White people, "I can make fun just as much as I want," you want to bet says JESUS CHRIST unto me, in that moment. Quit calling them names; you didn't think I heard you in your region. I know your address, and your affair. I see how ugly they are like high school just a service, definitely. They look different but common no advancement flap in the end, I'M trying to tell you. The other direction let me give you a tip, set the record strait a mirror their bonuses, their measurement, their captain talking about you a freeze away and their members. It's a trap. On their track limited edition cruising. Thus saith the LORD; chuckle GOD will be the announcement: *PROVERBS* 1:26; (The KJV to that). Amen. Use a calculator be my guest it won't bother me legally. I see this new program a meltdown. In Nashville, lost do you hear me? Wives you are not even potty trained all shapes and sizes. I can throw you off a cliff, and you will never hit bottom, yet small ones your wives. I know your sun roof do you hear me? I know their places. Their Pentecost donations are in big trouble women as well. Who's watching their pretty living expenses now, imagine that. I view it on camera the record payback come and badger me. Another different story dig it up damage to the core, you will get another belt whipping old cases out of the boxes. You can't sneak one in on me. Too bad they are already pressing charges now duck prescription. Like a snake they have been watching you. "You say impossible," and another thing, they have viewed you a long time a whole new ball game. I have the evidence. They need a whipping remember I grew up with you *big gun*. I hear you screaming I AM a block away. Their conversation Federal Government mandate the FBI when they say, "What happened to me, they are coming for me."

## A New Article

"I'm arrested" and they will be judges as well in that old town of yours for letting this story of yours go on for so long. I know you are angry. I view your life, your accomplishments every day. Wrestle with it no longer okay friend? You can't give up goodbye with it now. Feel comfortable you are not along. You are decent my friend. GOD measures you at 2:00 a.m., and before 4:00 a.m., you're up focus on me daily your credit imagine that. Promise me you'll listen. I'll give them jobs after a while you will go back to bed, they will grow up. Your equipment economic survival situation viewed. Pentecost the people cottage cheese eggshell wasteland that you are, forgive them Lord. Ms. Barbara, SOS learn how to do things right, alright the day their mountain valley payment crushed? The mountain valley the industry crush your neighborhoods high jacked every day no reason. You need and appointment, you need a withdrawal. Understanding your view with your GOD, open up their eyes never give up daughter. Christian folks sensational to show off they mock you, their company arrogant, implement you all the time forget you are in adversity. They are racists. I AM a witness. I mock racists tell them racism looked on you, spread the word independent. The pilot ashamed of favor where is the flag? The men ordained are going along with it? They are disciples. Let me tell you a bigger story. Pentecostal I have knowledge. Here is the knowledge your donation the excuse. The management the whole house your agency underground, like against Black people and other races. You need more discipline in that society, that is a good argument there special grace a balance. Now here is a thought, biblically Abednego drained. In the beginning belittle on the gas that is your condition upper arrogance you receive high remarks. The number one condition arrogance is your neighborhoods. Your needless I AM going to tackle that with a coupon that is available; adjustment your interest the other one your approach. A coupon adjustment on the race: just considering a brand new real estate agent can you imagine that a difference? Don't tackle with me in your operation, your all around cleaning get that, don't mess with JESUS CHRIST. Read the book. That's true subject.   On top of that, you need Purex or Clorox covered deep disinfectant a treatment it's very chilling; From Above. You need a breakthrough saving in His word. Thank you, JESUS CHRIST.   Christians cleaning legally: a word document cleanser; all of God's children his people everywhere a reality from the beginning no weapon Pentecost dangerous in the house;   favorite sons on you are backwards, and others you serve a lot of people all races you serve a packed house.   I'M a believer in that Pentecost. Read *AMOS*; the book and then *JOEL*; the book talking about modern day your defense, your generation against a packed house and against President Obama.  This is true.  Believe me a lesson. Amen. How do you do that know all these things big pastors, the HOLY SPIRIT; put a damper on it your generation just like in *AMOS* the book; big preachers everywhere their doctrine disguised?  They've already done it Pentecost, we heard the grumbling by way of radio and TV—object able people, December. We feel disgusted.  You want me to set in on your meetings?  Have courage just say no, and sound the alarm.  The royal kingdom hears it all the time. Just like Bush serving up other people double your whammy.  We wrestle demons in the church house; we are in the middle quit pointing a finger.  We both love God move the private fence. Quit your wrestling people are equal everywhere: a debate, a challenge extended at your kiosk, or you will split the unity in the body.   See *EPHESIANS* 4: 4-5-6; our doctrine (The KJV). White people you say, "Ridiculous you're not by yourself." Quit your gripping and your belly aching, and let's get back together.  You say, "Don't talk about me," it's not like you haven't done it even Church of Christ. Stop chopping on words a debate. Then we'll have a great time. Oh my God; a mistake that you have made legally the theme guilty in this place church that is the icing deal with that in the tabernacle.  Your settlement along nothing you can do. You don't serve me. Our destiny no joke send them a message public welfare, and those Democrats in my diary your own ability. Don't look down just yet further words United Pentecost, UBS-Fluff, your play a plus absolutely. Quote now do you need a nurse? No kidding believe me, I'M tired of your arrogance. You rattle me. Give it your blessing I know a number of you. Here's your windfall a breakthrough before your barbecue, a red flag. *And Pentecost woman of God, to these women don't you bother me. Take two or three deep breaths, and some of you will get it even the notorious. You have bad breath. Women it's a shame Pentecost, you need a catcher's mitt From Above the announcement, okay? Let me explain it, you say "Don't bother Jim Grow your advocate, we belong here against Obama," those White women their defense. Amen. Are you scratching your heads Pentecost? Blacks, settle your groups let that be a lesson! Dressing your word document signature by His authority trouble this Country haughty lunatic, your heritage gets your smell of your arrogance against Obama, the decision out properly 95% of you this percentage-The Keeper. A NOTE: on that your cleanser welcome to the Doctor's cleaning His house. A new development rinse Pentecost people everywhere yall's rinse, and no action taken yet against your house. Clean your house. Tell the plumber you legally have access, the damage has been done before there is violence against Black people everywhere. Better draw closer and stop being hateful and ridiculing. How do you like that good soldiers of mine, give me your heart in a new way established? From above I'M pointing a finger. Heaven and earth may pass away, but not my word. Read everywhere *MATTHEW* 24:35 (The KJV). Scream exactly as you are. Now do better no other resource can be found. You give me a headache trying God. Your measurement: we have observed. I'M withholding dividends, a blessing from heaven JESUS CHRIST, and even Apostolics across the board in their closet, ladies first take your place destroying images just neat as a pin gradually graduated its awesome. What year is that? Sweep on my friend the oxen this is an emergency you are in the dirt like savages, you need a buffer. We have the evidence. Politically you know what you are doing, destroying images just neat as a pin. Local in the city of Nashville, their images are in the waves against the African American community. They are waves in the church get out of the pool Pentecost; think you're wonderful how about a little thanksgiving and trying the waves snacking off of junk food? I'M keeping their blessing. Your gift a good recipe your duty and your character devotion just crooked, up with the mess. Amen. Begin with that I AM a witness. Just cheaters draw closer to God. Walk away you're blind. I can give you an infection both of you, it will hair lip you extreme until you tickle Pentecost this place. The problem the whole gang in the house they are his servants, Black people are to other people in their services to God, ridiculous your agent. You run a trap against people of other races, let me solve the problem, I'M telling you now cease it. Listen we have a pin, a spiritual kingpin in your camp. Dangerous is your operation better get it all together for your family. Stumped different people act like grownups, I'M not fooled your charges stays with you. Let me tear these things right down. Let me repeat that again, better get it together it's true. You ruin traffic. People everywhere are very hungry for God; a member of society to make that difference in their lives. It kills me how you view eternity; you are evasive to others that are not *pure Puritan color*, not so evasive by yourself to those who wear no smoke screen. Y'all are judging count the numbers. Make me free. Say, Lord make me free. I don't want to be turned away make me free. Crimson is coming one day, and others I don't want to be outside of this church locally His services when He comes. I know God is my real redemption. I view my homeland. At the roots you wear a dirty mask blooming. Veteran, the easy way out and your grandchildren the easy way out come and visit a little time left, when you hear them falling away from me, view their dying no joke lost favor hope no transparency, your department different arrangements. View your well, your equity, I don't want it anymore. THE ARGUMENT: Hear me, your fuel tank a microwave for a fuel pump. Shave it Murfreesboro, your entire wealth gone without making a scene, I recommend. I see the garage door opening on that town, watch grace is the factor ahead of you view the universe it is legal. Do good put the African Council first? Aim higher Pentecost please there is no more scrape food left believe me. Look at the bigger picture your willingness is blind. Or the next bath will be yours. I've made an announcement. Good question Pentecost, I'M talking about you this is significant in this house, the issues they are enormous straight forward, and they are incredible for no reason astronomical about people. I've told you a number of times bottom line your character, you need salvation. A new framework for the Country be a good citizen okay. You are offensive you say "ah bologna to that," you don't understand? Thank you, JESUS CHRIST. I've got the message you are mean. You in the military someone is watching you, I've been watching you. I watched you all grow up dancing with demons just like a toothpick; like another's toothpaste squeezed cargo you to death. You are infected. Hear that? Population you are driven stained, your activity benefiting *big-ones*, except JESUS CHRIST. Gentlemen counting even the Church of Christ, you're upper kingpin in the sand licensed to preach those are the issues, a New Jersey (descriptive, out of place). Now squirm from that a new washing 90% of you Tennessee. Would you like a hot bath this morning legally? They want a two part series being busy picking up demons along the way, hovering around heaters eating ice cream. You think I didn't notice now get out, ridiculous. You're eaten up with digestion all the time. You're going the wrong way the message follow me JESUS CHRIST, get the picture? Spoil they are like politicians rubbing shoulders with Black people, like politicians pretending their not racists. NEWS FLASH: people

*The Original Barbara Payne*

don't back them up. How they dress low grade. Infrastructure is JESUS CHRIST; pained I know the mileage fast and furious; they are the hunted that is the scope of them. This is their complexion their color rough pink mixed. "They aren't our people many Mexican immigrants" we want them out of here. Oh thank you, JESUS CHRIST. They want and investment. You heard me. Help for us today call 911 now. I would agree. They come in this country illegally. They are filthy rich guess who brought them in here; it will be like a domino effect? Call me now I AM available people of God. Listen to me, you missed it white folks typical shot up American gangs, they are complete. Three thousand people in this country witness alone on Sunday. No argument they are soon to carry out their lethal destruction on black people. Speech their message they know their value. Dangerous they are lethal organization. You can buy guns anywhere. Help us JESUS CHRIST. Ban them across the city, semi-automatic weapons. Are they legal about 80% of them got them now Latino's as well? They are making a lot of noise, they are devils all of them. I view them on the other side porch screaming, and they are yelling for help. Come on stay out of the woods practicing. A Burrell Night (accent spoken like that), followers among you Nashville, I see Bluetooth basics with lethal weapons white people low intelligence they are, you can't change them. Epic you are underground low life, your kindred with an accent. You are offensive with your weapons, English accent icing they are in pursuit Tea-Party automatic carrying guns people. They are management buccaneers; they carry guns on their way to hell. They snuck in here lately, crazy people armed and dangerous. I will see many of you in the hospital. Lord! Be thankful, they are about to be arrested. You'll hear about it on NBC News—big production. Both candidates ought to listen their lives are on the line contributed. Welcome to the Tea Party people. Straight being offensive you are warming up riveting, you are dangerous divorce them all of you. Stay away from them, there are prostitutes prostituting the Federal Government and its riches, sizable regular this group intelligence. You heard me. English spoken with an accent for sentimental reason as though ya'll were speaking Spanish your den. Company they I'M finger pointing everyday talking them in America, they are illegal understand? Arrest them fooled the whole house you are a loser. Make up your mind view intelligence, just read the reports look and see. Yes they are crafty these individuals sweeping Nashville, these Republicans. Black people do me a favor, now don't patronize their places they hate Black people, they watch you all the time. You lose your place, your campaign, you are racists. *The President he acts nice trying to listen to you. Let me explain something, the objection colored people their angle they have no respect for America, its ice to them. View their restaurants, they bring their own agenda like these Republicans giving it away even The Middle East they don't care for America, they want their own way success story, not contributing to our way of life our success story Black people including Hispanics, they much about tradition not our way of life. View the Constitution of the United States of America, and our Statute of Liberty a true success story. It's all about them and their way of life not the people as a whole. They don't want our way of life in the United States, separate but equal is their way. Incidentally they've wanted our way of life for a very long time now, a blank sheet of paper to erase the American heritage, and American values; although they will never admit it President Obama should know that. They will burn the American Flag a new residue for them. ^Don't keep your mouth closed on them a new revelation. Exit is the next big battle between them and a lot of Americans, just take a pole and see if they are acceptable or not. A lot of rounds is coming about their group. Trying to fix it is not the real answer to our immigration problem. We need to purge our system get rid of them, let them find jobs elsewhere, it will improve our economy for working Americans, who are becoming weaker because of their success living here. Move quick and take a value of their wealth many are here illegal, and we are flipping trying to keep up with them wanting more and more because of them working in the system. Go back to our heritage and let people come here the right way. Get all of those people out of here, and let them come in our nation the right way. You will be surprised what will happen to them not a true success story anymore. *Watch them singling them out our Federal Government interference can't do enough for them, Republicans keep supplying them food on welfare. A lot of them belong in the penitentiary Mexicans as well believe me JESUS CHRIST, true helpers they are not Republicans and Democrats. People don't want to offend them you'll be wishing you had not reached for them more are coming. Watch the neighborhoods and just see, definitely who they are moving in your neighborhood. They are not all Hispanics, and the Latinos, anymore wanting to come to America for a better way of life, they are handpicked by drug lords, they are baron's those criminals just planted here. Here is their blue print run every one of them out of the nation America, America will be overrun with them. A hundred thousand more know they are extremes, they are racists, they are terrorists, part animal running around underground living right next door. The big aftermath they will be ruling America, the patriot spirit will be gone, and we get the perception, they are here illegal more and more of them are coming here illegal. You need to turn it around before we can't find them. You will hear more and more of them ^are committing crimes of illegal entry on U. S. soil, and then what will that be. Their dream soon they will be running the White House with their tradition, running the White House with their way of life; we've already got them running our well being. In the evening I've heard enough with racist's extreme; the crew know who that they are. Particulars join them these folks coming from abroad, and from above dealing with particulars during any time don't join them the White race, or any other race these individuals are extremes. They are extremes backwards people like Tea Party people, and their candidates. On the WEB they are offensive. Get them out, you hear me off of television. Hateful are these groups. Dancing with them you are dancing with them. I know the ABC's. I watched you ten thousand times pointing a finger, you are offensive sour note before the break of day your Christmas, Merry Christmas. Say, Merry Christmas and goodnight to your blessing, and your Capital generally the Stars Spangle Banner our welfare and our well being. YOUR REPRESENTATIVES: don't look the other way. It's important to remember what has been said, the principles don't look the other way, the bunch you've adopted. A lot of them are here illegal, definitely. Give black people a chance to work with you more, and some of your white friends. You have best friends who graduated with you needing work all the time, who just happen to be legal citizens of America. ^Don't look at their cute wives and their relatives, just a jester in that furnace of hatred against us. BY THE THROAT AMERICA: a lot of them are relaxed feeling comfortable, and real relaxed now that they are here feeling very comfortable, you got a mix of them everywhere, looking over here with no passports anywhere to be found. They are here to promote drugs everywhere, sales are really up for them and their members baron's they are, they come over here every day with no expense to them. Strong arming Americans with nowhere to go, they get on welfare; they use the system to their own advantages and privileges these illegals. Run them down in Nashville, and get them off of welfare, they are cleaning up living off the system people won't die from this, they have money leaking it in from somewhere else those agents and those groups, Intelligence know this already. This is an emergency get them off that river. Incidentally they are crossing the river all the time near Farmers Market; they have loyal fans watching for them this group. *Hear that Kenneth Copeland, the Baptist who like them so well.

## The Original Barbara Payne

A lot of people go that way, and now we're heavily populated with them in Nashville, and surrounding counties. *These are ISIS people with a corral look walking around every day, and they are well kept doing their adventure in the middle class America, did you hear that the American family, they are among you. Put them under arrest by the Federal Government. And they are heavily populated in Canada as well, don't you understand they are evil get them out these criminals out of the United States of America, these people will attack you, they will attack each other—lucrative for their business, they are like ISIS, they are not Spanish run inns, no-peek-a-boo Americans desiring a better way of life, these wannabe Americans, they are just here illegal to disrupt our way of life, just ask South Americans. NO MORE CONTENTION THIS GO AROUND: I'M talking about I see an unusual tornado in Tennessee hitting Nashville, and in West Tennessee Memphis, Tennessee, and in Middle Tennessee as well, about the path hitting power lines, even ripping underground as well grab your home and hold it by the hand. Traveling your way breaking up racism that army of racism, do I make myself clear? Make it fast and quick, and in Goodlettsville, marching forward definitely they are white, using country music all the way. Traveling don't go along with it you're on the cutting edge of dirty. Pentecost anointed in Nashville, don't be backwards like the Ku Klux Klan members know that you are moving backwards mind your manners you have to talk to me. Listen ethnic job offer, the journey yall's people in the kingdom being bias racially let it freeze. Typically your welfare in the kingdom so that the next generation Pentecost won't become secular due to suffering, I see the thinning out now they will be cutting up bible verse after you; go ahead and get along with the African Americans, even your wife in the services. I'M telling you have courage be an independent vessel in the kingdom of God, and you'll gain that is no accident, your lamp. Have a great attitude. And your answer right now let me give you some advice additive in

Davidson County with scripture give them scripture, I'm a crusader for God, alright? Don't be in the middle. Thank you, JESUS CHRIST. I know what I'M talking about. It's a shame going along with it; definitely you stick out like a bird going along with it. I know all about it you can hang them your branch, an attack have courage don't go along with it they are bad people, walk away the habit don't go along with it. God loves all people be independent children it is healthy, my answer. Now what do you think my people? It is an embarrassment going along with it, betrayal for them to have acted like that no moral reason your region. Now clean up the mess junk just a habit, now stay sweet erase the habit believe that. You can depend on me. I know how you feel who they are how they step on you not acceptable, right hand your covering having been there their mint, their machine stand up to them other races. Pentecost now don't run out on them, make a difference for black folks you're the servant. You want to take a peek, the Upper Room someone looks up to you? They're not going to get any better, finger pointing. They've got the power you are under attack the women not your friend, be brave when you're under attack. The women carry it on they are the judges, they have no manners. They have shaved skinned my friend. I have their phone number their spanking is coming. Stop running from them look at them the video. We're putting it all together. I paint you a picture. It will be viewed by other people they are desperate. Their university their focus obvious on black people and their race, instead of white people main story; they don't hurt them their race to tear them down they are a mess. I'M like a yellow rocket tinting no second guessing. I know how they view you, I view their video a harvest attacks against you busy, and you they are so low these women. I view them their behavior against you Pentecost attractive. Sleeveless open when they want to be. Unusual situation that is the way it is criticism makes them feel good. Their service their like journalists snobs, viewing you burning investigation against you Pentecost

## The Original Barbara Payne

white people, you Mother. I see the underwear they wear shameless skirts held high. Why do they bother drunkard industry carried on everywhere exactly? I see them in the powder room, captioned not to mention just a rumor whispering about things they know nothing about. They aren't friend's wasteland they have become. I've got their backup. They aren't immortal. *I view their video looking at you and at your people; news battle top of the news White people building their case, their equipment what they said about you. Celebrities they are. They should apologize to you right away that is a fact. And incredible reality you are defenseless. I will stand with you. I will back you up. They hate my children despite all their giving. I'M coming full swing. I AM a great witness don't never give up. Oh my God! They are dead tuna fish hateful their entertainment their network, blaspheme on the phone. I know what I'M talking about. The video camera I'm sick of acting practicing. You're in the middle watching an unusual situation. These ladies they are in trouble despite their effort. Just keep smiling no one is talking to you captioned you are, picking on you using their weapon playing fake politics in additional, while you rob the people of everything. Bring everything you own. Another teachable moment together my friend, for the record I know all your pain this is just another teachable moment. I AM anointed, the rule I AM available. I will give them a bathe extremely openly. I will pour out my validation proven Republicans, a letter this is their pay back now hiccup. Don't never say we can't win Republicans people need to know we're changing the country. We will win; we have it available to us. I viewed it a long time ago, their principles 2007 amazing. I see the press representation, your victory. Thank you, JESUS your equipment. Unfortunately many are going to jail, they are white people. My friend, we dearly love you completely. Thank you, JESUS CHRIST. A new weapon a new reality, you will destroy the yoke every time, definitely absolutely. You're welcome. Meet you on the other side. Ugliness I know how you feel publicly viewing. Move closer to God. Pay attention to what God said, I know all about them I'M telling you. I see clearly they are caught up in a whitewash society. I know all your struggles don't struggle with that. A new development you are sending many of them mixed messages, give them a brief message the crew at their lighthouse company. I know you have been having difficulty. Turn around we have it all put together. Have a race card, and see many of them think they own their tradition. Many of them have multiple sclerosis like the American Government; late volunteers infected in their head excuses their mentality. They have no disciplined like your effort. That is an indication when their brain stopped working messed up in their mind. I know your sacrifice. Please buckle up for the past years your duty evidently wasted. Many of them are embarrass, are grateful you took a different stance just grateful for your work, the local Pastor himself your offense being a veteran. Many are just staying in their little group, and they are grateful. Your road winding breaks your confidence. I know you are hurt, but you will make it no more blocked up local media in the wilderness. Black folks walk out the door, hallelujah proud of you for doing the work. They are just locked up conflicted; they are traveling with them and they are afraid to leave the group because of you, the group busy they are their luxury. They are frigid. See them no more you found favor with God, most definitely. You are intelligent don't deal directly with them anymore. I'll be happy too. The benefit we're in it together your struggles. Here is the benefit and angel guards your door, while you sleep my friend. You are living a superficial life, I want to thank you. Here is where it is you want the truth? I see your worth. Their second engagement alright, definitely sometimes your ability in a sense sometimes knowing Omnipotent the person; no burden with everything that is their answer, the supervisor cares can you imagine? My dear friend, do we agree friends no offense? You are no problem to me, your advantage. How popular are you the cause insurgent, their secret strategy against you? That is what motivates them against you. Your real defense JESUS CHRIST, your Lord my friend the right way and the world. Avenger I AM your friend the CHRIST the witness. Remember me I can make a difference, if you let me. Crystal clear I AM a witness don't be afraid OMNISCIENT reserve church folks, and most of the people in this world children of God. I know those people what kind they are best friend. Unique kind I hope you make an objection. I know what you're made of your evil thoughts, brown at this time. But I'll survive. Your burden your way of thinking white people, I've got news for you, definitely people everywhere. I know you are anxious. Thank you, JESUS. United States of America let's validate view the bum- a cancer, let's get him out of here. Navigate what would the teacher say people of God, be correct a novel not a course, a new decoration an unusual way of looking at things don't be distressed. Look beyond get me my daughter, I'M telling you leave no doubt God has your best interest, you are a pilot don't be distressed? Say, Lord help me the workman. Documentary you are a success hundreds of people know that already. You are near the cross. Don't be afraid. Never give up. Don't be distressed. Do your duty look away at distress back away from it there is always hope and Vanderbilt to? People of God just don't give up never lose hope. You'll get your blessing in the end documented understand? I AM available my daughter, I'M at the door. So annoying I know it has been rough on you. I know you have sobbed you are writing a book, challenges legal I give her credit, I give you credit woman of God, one more thing but you can take it no joke look at it my friend count it as a free fall special action. They are threatening you. I have viewed you since you were nine years old. You are one friend of mine; to you about their operation against you have no anxiety a threat. View all before God. We're in the middle here, backwards. We're getting stepped on. Know the difference it was no accident imagine that? A unique possibility black folks see how funny we look. Praise God, I view them a whole lot their practice on people. Make up the hedge somebody we made it, if we ever get out of this jungle this bull pen that we are in. Praise God, it is worth our sacrifice we all have made black people, people everywhere having to deal with this, it's distressing business. They were conscious knowing a Bangkok infectious virtuous (an addiction), they are double feet otherwise a musty odor red white and blue decorating universal, they have become their own decision, their dignity persuasion telegram. I view them a hundred times as a thorn group. They are on the internet facing the internet with their problems for entertainment many of them are just hilarious. To us you'd better get comfortable facing the internet just net. And other groups' let me make it crystal clear they are keeping individuals, down seeking jobs. "I love them Wal-Mart, be with them okay?" They view Wal-Mart as family as their town, their good friend "I have been with them for over 30 years racists, they go after me for no good reason have you uncovered." Review the backlash. They need mercy in their package middle class America, positive. A bunch of the people and their family has posted on Facebook. Things are very problematic. "These people are ruining the Country," we view them every day big time talk conclusion on Facebook: bankrupt you. They are problematic put you on a ledge, and they are on the internet complaining executives on Facebook lately and their wives. I know who they are. I AM going to shift gears nightmares after that, the wheels already turning. You are going to hear screaming against them, these people. Their identity the damage has been done. It's a topical situation I AM going to shift gears. I know their ability they will be institutionalized. I would rather be six feet under. Charges cameras are everywhere essentially almost unbelievable, a visit major retailer a break down from the U. S. Justice Department internal audit, disturbed are you the impact on you. Can't argue with the impact your losses will be great, when one consumer collects data for them. I know who that I AM, you need an adjustment hope you are listening. Let's talk about nature fair enough, my nature the superintendent target your benefits targeted your racism, it is amazing? I AM the landlord of all neighborhoods, JESUS CHRIST. Fifty percent of your officers do not frequently discriminate, thank God, a good investment. Hallelujah. What exactly do you do public officials? You say all those things do not matter. Do you know who you are talking too? Follow me in your business practices, when gathering employment in your company ridiculous otherwise. I carry a difference and I AM warning, the difference there is no future in ethnic discrimination. Tell the executives I know your worth. I do not discriminate racism, and religious freedom. I view around the clock. Churches I do not discriminate, that is your plan that is discrimination. You practice racism against individuals thinking you are entitled, and the middle man Republican stiff neck white man always with your head in the air messed up. They are underneath a white cloud pushing people off a cliff. I've had enough of you. You are under arrest right now. You turn in thousands of dollars a month in revenue to collect, think I didn't know about that didn't you for individuals? What about you? Some of you are laughing just view your intelligence your way out of bounds 90% of you. I give you an account 100% with no more change it's like looking in a mirror. *You had a nickname on the market legally The Tenet. That is who you are get comfortable. Face off a habit: poor black people many people view you all the time racists. Down in the valley unique a subscription poor people black looking at *ISAIAH*; that is who you are a redneck specialists saying you would die for them their cause. You want me to transport more saying JESUS CHRIST; a coupon of fifty to white a subscription to the clan there in Atlanta. That is who you are obvious belonging to their clan imagine that; an addiction a yellow redneck? I get you breakfast every day over the years. Say, JESUS CHRIST our savior, the savior of the whole world a lot of people think that; I give you free range in honor of Him people no lounging; I give you that medicines bully yellow redneck for your loyalty. Let me encourage you the kiosk Government, I hurt you believe me; gap in Tennessee like a silver bullet your racism a brat every day, Atlanta and in Arkansas. Thank you, JESUS CHRIST. Better duck I see the finish. Thus saith the LORD; I know who your company a big slick diversion just one man is responsible for it SAM WALTON, the obvious then pitiful black people. Amen, dirty Republicans. I make fun of you *Sam Walton the Tenet Mr. Hollywood. A REALITY: "ya'll better watch you're not street wise like those" (niggers) whites just a suggestion. Just being a big fool around the Country traveling with a different accent, just riff-raff people everywhere know who, certain of them they are claiming they are true real Americans. "They are free just pure a reality." I've been listening to them, Whites wherever you are. You will be howling. Incidentally, haste I know your name check, Pentecost give a flip. Romantic you are in college. Who is JESUS CHRIST? Give you the shirt off of His back. Are you ready for it believe me a unique finish JESUS CHRIST, more powerful? How powerful, helicopter team effort ultimately no more smoking Pentecost your brand weak, when it comes to the Lord? Shot heard around the world, the same unique endorsement Republicans. And then later on, the Democrats old grinding at this table wasting put something on the table clean the atmosphere, we have poor access we're running out of strength believe me. I heard shots fired around the world everywhere, and angel talking. The latest justice women everywhere wrote in, nothing back fired for me. A new possibility demanded. A new referee we've got the evidence. I JESUS CHRIST; I'M upset about it. Barbara here in the United States of America, we will comfort you. Thank you, for your labor now headed your way secret legislation no more going it alone, a new referendum heard around the world. We're going to make it a group in your service. Better have a song book church folks just the icing on the cake, better wake up principles doing research. Anybody got any emotions left, loyalty the people in your neighborhood? I AM the referee, I measure it quickly all of racism, conclusion because other don't know how resolution loosely this is ridiculous. I AM the agent resident knowing in this city give it to the Doctor quick. I've got big news can we play the race card? Have a field day at it. Gentlemen, black folks get on the bus, I know who the bus driver is now you need improvement on behalf of the American people you need new seat covers._You've been driving colored people crazy, you are nuts in the south so congratulations. My first impression, we here in the south we don't think of you as a great disaster here in Nashville, running around using all your capital resources a predator from the top. For security purposes all your leaders moving checking all your resources, checking all your equipment including Jefferson, Davidson County, and Middle Tennessee. Did you hear that, absolutely? First, running around town using double standards honestly, we being the doorman by margin a wolf using legislation so political; sharks we voted for him the white man dangerous no accident in any election, wanting to control the country coming out of the woods anymore. Urban feel take an aspirin use your diaphragm. "So take that still-man driving that big pickup using all your resources in public degree Newton, all that waving politically—both black and white." You say, white people on character "those people we're fine niggers, but we've missed it your industrious thinking. Your advantage, taking advantage get a career get some papers get up off your duff and get a degree first, and not your church protection using any direction not using your tongue calling us crazy the government, then you can say we're lazy. Get up off of that your grave intention distraction. Your wrong impression flipping, this Jew I'M not turning it in anymore your vehicle, your servant. Get some principles on this note Republicans. "Stir the niggers up," they are greedy white people Ku Klux Klan they are; it's no excuse white people educate yourselves ingrate politicians. You say politicians, we're not suppose to say the word nigger ever, then perfect walk on over. I agree with your assault and battery. A joint effort people of color a prerequisite, I'm a southerner too facing it this end to all the people. Your shirt white people you old rattlesnake, take and abortion get that nigger out of here go to hell you drive me crazy. I marvel at that line of ignorance the group perform an abortion. Whiplash I'M looking at the film now you rascals, Washington, D.C. first. Then again your favorite people you know how you are courtesy. Your chief informant "you blacks going national is that what all the excitement is all about." The Republicans to those Democrats "You got you a new President gold teeth; wait till the next time around won't be in here." They are racists, but we are going to make it by the help of our captain white people. The Christ JESUS CHRIST, it's just not going to look like it anti-Semitic the same, they are under the umbrella testified in the United States with a new weapon.

## A TRUE INVESTMENT

Thus saith the LORD; see they are cleaver tempered. See you at the registrar, just see who you all are comfortable with in your stores 100% all the time sweet potatoes, and apples at the cash registrars no peacock. You feel comfortable know that more sweet potatoes and apples. That is how it works okay? *Blame me Einstein watch the JEW initiate; take no offense you can do better. Watch the program another program real life know the universe Jewish Man, no separation even keep the Sabbath, for the future event any event talking about Pentecost my friends petition those you want to hang out with no squares in Nashville, Pentecost they are God's friend, and the man they are Jewish His family from the beginning Pentecost organization they adore me real life; specialty if you want to go to heaven no chaos typical Jew a real Jew the man to watch JESUS CHRIST. For a good example, be it yet active to every

Jew, swell no offense taken medium, He cares for our family the nation people, and have for years as we rescind trade. Washington no fairness about it giving the land back to Mexico, Republican greed against this nation only a racists would do that; and we are in the middle of a deficit. Confess, no counter terrorists Mr. John Doe President you are racists George Bush, your camp you are all racists. Hold on people save some for me clipping West Hampton Mrs. Barbara Bush, low President Bush. You better know what I'M telling a direct debunking Barbara Bush, low President Bush, and treasury included another mess in your courtroom. Know this here is a fact prescription true prophecy. What happened President Bush, it should not have happened, alright your accomplishments a marriage on your job in Texas, your operation you failed this Nation tremendously. Put Seven-Up on it your dutiful freak show just meat loaf, you and your wife proven a quick decorating Republican operation. You want proof? Ask you know what you don't know the true meaning of worthy couldn't recognize it. You're full of *hoopla* at its best understand? A relieve circle counter a Facebook page no apologetic, over half the Country are in struggles a deep recession prepare for more, that your segment any consolations your accomplishments devilishness, J.R. of Dallas TV big crime network show saying jealousy, I'M stinking jealousy. On network shows you couldn't handle it. Sniff your parallel your own show not after you would run everybody off with the game. Could have had left over's not that much. You all look familiar couldn't have done it better attackers against America, truth to that. There's an opening for you soon with no return wisdom. I view you naked already, the aftermath not a single word both Bush Administrations. Watch you're changing your dialect. All the things you said, I pay you a visit. I'M head of the church and this administration the Obama Administration: Homeland Security as well. No teasing don't mess with me, law and order Chief Executive. Say, Honolulu walking around with a pillow on top of your head

## A New Article

on The Obama Administration, honest literally *Cupid* backwards to death Julius Caesar, your son's administration you all are racists. Like George, your father they made matters worse humility is your shame, and you are criminals against President Obama, and his administration literally. You boat handle saying, they aren't going to go anywhere his administration, his accomplishments, hoping he falls off a cliff. You are criminals independent, and the people know it. Go through the last lap no mercy. People are dying over there every day in the hot sun. First impression your administration, your equipment, that's the reason. Your son quit walking the floor your offense. I'll tell you the facts: READ *II CORINTHIANS*; I DARE YOU, AND THEN CALL IT A SHOT FOR NICENESS: YOU ALL NEED TO READ THE BOOK. I'M HOSTING THE BOOK. You know how it is your frequent deficit, I've got your answer we are in the middle your son's administration, I can hardly keep from crying, I've almost lost it given the fact all those boys in an Iraq operation never got back, now give me a hoopla. I'M telling you, you heard me. Cold hard facts some of you are going to be red hot inflate inflation, and Mexicans the illegal's *get'em* out of here. Hallelujah. ELEVENTH HOUR: glad to hear both sides night has already fallen. They've been pimping here long enough and that is a fact, most definitely. Thank you, that's telling them big time. Wicked they are going back to Kennebunkport. From America we made it legal, because of trade we cut a deal with no promises, The House of Representatives, even Obama Administration that watches the whole thing all you people. Let me explain, reminder I've had enough of a new episode against Jew, bother any Jew just ask Congress. Racists drumming I know who you are. Racists you bother another Jew, your regular practice you are a veteran. Let me tell you, net one third net racists. Hear that Vanderbilt, and Senate, accordingly view the first principle they keep to themselves, I back up the nation! Deduct, offend racism, I JESUS CHRIST am offended. I AM your man divine universe over time. All but a few reproofs' you don't know me I'M telling you a deliverer, a good testament, for your games messing with me assault all your life totally. Making a difference around this mess hit me, assault weapons no man can handle. I have the upper hand. Are you stage fright?

## VIEWING PROPERTY DAMAGE, VIEWING BACKWARDS IN NASHVILLE, TENNESSEE AND ELSEWHERE

Thus saith the LORD unto me; Listen to this everyone you're driving me crazy, I AM able Pentecost. Mighty you are. And get this Pentecost an expert you have my name. Pentecost are you ready Nashville, your service? Look on me. SOUR NOTE: Hey, Honey Boo-Boo, no Honey Boo-Boo distraction. You need a balance. Pentecost, please upper class for me your service, can you stay connected, *and stay away from Honey Boo-Boo; small town riff-raff. *They charm the devil with good intentions following their dirt dreams big time, they are the victim. You look like a fool. So you want be laughed at like on television you look like a fool, perfect. Good luck, Honey Boo-Boo. They are backwards trade on television you can't follow them. I AM fusing. I AM your friend. I have been connected for a very long time to the church, me The CHRIST your anchor. It is free my friendship, even to the middle class and above serving. Stop the distractions look on me I AM fool proof, choose your identity there can be no mistake about it believable. I agree. I AM the man hear that? Look at my record, the reality keep it real how I like it. You have no excuse, a definite. I view a puppet. You got cold feet? I can't stand racism. Pick up a toothpick you know they are free, reading numbers just listen to me, Upper Room Pentecost in the building in Nashville, TN. Here is the main point redeem your religious practices, I AM mad wiping tears away Pentecost your agent the lineage saying, God help me. Your integrity you are going to be mourning for JESUS CHRIST, saying fix it wiping tears away. JESUS CHRIST your shepherded Pentecost you've stopped your dedication. Legally not your coupon average friends of mine, modern due your amount it's free from me Pentecost, improve your relationship call me at anytime that you want me. Think about it legally you do realize don't you that I AM amazed; your secret ripples even across the ocean through the roof? In case you did not know call a detective. On your honor you're not afraid of me, look little Daniel you deserve it treat me like oblivion, the kitchen help, a lot of white some black people their little pigeon. I'M not your entertainment oblivion pigeon out of your predicament. Moveable I can help you out of your pain this jam, a messenger. People are listening it's free, your good friend right now. Just keep on listening a derange immigrant to me. You want me to demonstrate? No crouton read *MATTHEW*; your deposit I'M hosting, even the Government. I place value upon you. I know your value their value to me; you just mark my word I would be gone. News suggestion the truth, we can come together alright? Mock your friends independent every day, oh absolutely sweet potatoes they think they are. Black people hit the red button your appearances in their town Miss Williamson County, good old boys network "niggers we don't do drug like everybody else we productive." That is often heard. On their curb hear them saying, their leader ripping apart in their steak houses "we're old country boys" let me give you some advice, just dangling conservative they are. Politicians "Yes sir you're my kind of instant coffee no peppermint candy white, and all that stuff is made of." Listen to this, when bankers come in "take out the trash these women dumbbells forget it, who gave them permission white trash for colored people." What difference does it make? Ignorant, low down, better listen to this white people caring cap and gown and clinical records bucket, just like yester-year donkey typical can stop blowing your horn, be grateful your father's knew it. Want them to come to your town? We are still able we can picket your trash, and that music The Opry at different places. Say, rise up we can come after you racists. You think you are hot caring your picture your crosses. LAMAR ALEXANDER: don't cross the picket line. JESUS can fix it right away for black people everywhere, on yall's yard going to heaven spread out. Let me let you look at some of those brothers in your eye. They are white conservatives picking up phony doing low down, low down in the basement serving BURGER KING, eat ranch dressing, riff-raff dummies blowing snort out their ear in advance. Let me tell you, they eat at SHONEY'S; I can pick you a hand full. Let me tell you the rest of the story; ten thousand ready to blow your town away on the verge of it now. Where do they shop? You're missing my point on the verge Google it commercial free. They shop anywhere even at Thanksgiving, the whole nine yards they follow, "The Shoe Barn" for their feet where they buy their shoes, when not wearing thongs on their feet and they are sad put together trying to look *translucent* those are those rascals, Pentecost I view them all the time. Let me tell you; Southern backwards public packing trash mainly get out their guns free from commercials non-subsidized, and engine evil persons in the basement, a vain offering development from flip flops for their feet. Obliged to their race select from a crowd Republicans, they are the wannabes racist's trash *wannabes* in the grass needing arrest, for the many crimes they have already committed. *Let me explain, they are the Republican's nominee stimulus conservatives. They are not brick masons. And you see them out in public watching even the President talking morals, let me give you a big tip just watching their radius established it's amazing a difference making Mexicans look bad. NEWS FORECAST EMMANUEL'S WAY: Seriously the Temple, and Pentecost, God has their number. A new forecast listen, directly their group trust me hear me. Another bad habit don't get involved with them anymore the individuals. Here is a notion, their women for commercial in our city dangerous in Nashville, letting you know that is for real traffic is for real, definitely. Officially I'M not accusing them, brand indecent exposure being a real gentleman like

## A New Article

normal people, race that is the issue of the fact, even in Kentucky. They are flipping using a calculator being in trouble that is what is done. This is no electronic game. After the fact is known churches, that is what counts flipping drugs they will come and arrest you. Think about it some of you have been in jail, and turned around astonishing after the fact. There is no excuse for certain issues Pentecost, after the fact against race. Caution I Alabama Pentecost, cease I AM coming to arrest you Pentecost, and your children that have been watching that typical in your neighborhood, and in your town breaking news near Gatlinburg. You're going to see a turn around. You've been on the late news causing problems. You heard the news you're like a ping pong ball in your neighborhood a negative in your neighborhood, I can see you're talking on the telephone. Elevator up I AM watching you high, pitiful that is scary that I AM watching high accusers. You think you are riding high. You know me I AM doing a new thing hunting pornography at yall's racists church filming each other having sex with one another every afternoon, typical some of you have really cut down on it with it you are a coupon. GOD is angry about it with your church, an elephant your scripture dozens of you know it, so don't excuse it claiming they know nothing about it it's in your face. It's time I did a background check in your neighborhood, even in Nashville. Letting the local papers try you, uppity you even the local papers know about it, I'M dealing with that Pentecost as you wander and play. I view Parsons, Tennessee as well those people. Observed check the adult play as Christians, it's an epidemic it is exhausting the epidemic. Some of you are going to prison, spending the night behind bars where you don't want to belong. Public my advantage very immediate, I recommend it. However, some of you are going to have a heart attack saying, "wake me up from this dream" watch me those individuals, contributing you're getting away with it not even Black or White. You know who that you are, I'M talking to you. You know better than to live like that. Your thread in the closet, you need help idiot.

You come to church hoping God can do something about it. The next message these people cheat on their wives, from above thinking I AM nuts good luck to you the next time. Meantime you heard me a thread your last restitution, I'M getting there keeping flipping me off a show of hands Pentecost, even the Church of Christ you think the same thing, it's your entitlement wait until you get arrested. African Americans better quit hanging around them move closer to God, that's your destiny. Your proof you don't fool me JESUS CHRIST; I give you a sign the selling of drugs and the laundering of money, I see your gross you selling drugs out there, I view you from above and you're making the race a fragment look bad, and their wives. I see your resources and I know your involvement. Wait until I turn on you. Quit flirting with half white girls take a sticker shock actresses they are, it is no accident more of you will be found dead in a hotel room, guest house, hotel suite, or in their own room beaten to death. And artist they are an adulterous, you guys are mushrooms. You think I AM crazy, they are brought here illegally for trade just check their records, amazing they are your desert hope you have brain surgery. About the actresses, they aren't flirting for nothing view their doctrine; legally most black women they know better, they keep to their own race. They will put a bullet through your head keep messing with them the infidels, they are greedy people. They come in this country thinking they are of the White race, view their picture here they are illegally keep that in mind. I agreed. Those women are strange; muscle men are behind them this is true.

## LOOKING BACKWARDS A SHOCK I'M TELLING YOU UNBELIEVABLE

Thus saith the LORD; we all should set things right make things right among each other, agreed. I harbor no harm against them White people those that are nasty in our society doesn't sound like racism at all, I agree. They just need a bath before I take a stick,

## A New Article

and beat them with a double edge sword, exactly that me making a brand new fish. Let me explain from above says JESUS CHRIST unto me; we get weary their symptom musty, their appetite nasty and controlling. Just simple stuff nasty they are doubly. Future shock their like a boiling pot ready to boil over—flipping future shock. Be decent a breakthrough accountability garbage, we're declaring war on your roadway. Say God remove that mountain, even whites who mingle with them all people. I've tried to minister to them even whites, be careful they know your name and they know who you are. I wouldn't do that I'M telling you leave their house alone. Don't have anything to do with them. I'M trying to tell you this nation they are white supremacists that won't behave, down South racists they are in chains the lower class people and they are looking at you. Mean people they are like a snake backwards, and ignorant caring weapons. They hate all people even Mexicans, the Black man, and Latino everywhere that's the group they are White racists like the Ku Klux Klan they are. They are everywhere shameful they are crippling society. It is a sign of the time know the Black man people God is on our side, getting the message? It's a cancer they need to quit now their operation unbelievable. Good news a new moratorium on the cancer cell draining society right now. What a waste their activity. The Black man what about the black man show him no respect? I make my case they are thirsty for his blood, so don't feel comfortable your redeemer from above unbelievable their activity. You don't want to work with them they carry weapons all the time. If you mistreat them you may be found dead, they have been known to do that. Mr. Obama, they lean on President Obama they hold a grudge, and they are ignorant all the time I'M counting. Daughter of mine, face they know your face. Be brave the Federal Government is in hot pursuit and literally is going to prosecute. Red white and blue will prevail. Typically at Thanksgiving in Nashville, Tennessee avoiding long lines locals in Nashville, no doubt about it they keep themselves hidden. This is true. That is true they never use restrooms depending on how much gas they have had to drink, ninety eight percent don't use the public restrooms their access avoiding whites and black people, not to draw attention to themselves in their own little planet. They bump into you have a blank stare scream attackers could be detrimental. Know that I AM available for you at anytime.   MCDONALDS: at McDonalds have had enough of them scaring their customers away, and *it is documented. Say a prayer in JESUS name if you view them in a crowd and a public restroom. A news development for the public follow these to yall's church, can you imagine at you all's church. Christmas tree uplifting be playful youthful a mistake their on drugs, their like day and night when not there?   I have the evidence. Want to relive olden days, when Black people were really suffering it's their economic suffering those individuals. I view them every day. They eat a meal at McDonalds, Pentecostals they eat there quickly it's their place avoiding nice restaurants, apparently their eating restaurant harboring, and gathering around you can't get close to them. Believe me, they feel satisfied these defendants in their own hood.   I know what I'M talking about Blacks and Whites know who I'M talking about. A curious kind of locals not a buff teenager big fellow kind of development, and they like hand guns hidden under their belt legal weapons Pentecost, and they like hand guns in their possession be concerned.   I'M telling you Pentecost, these people are avoiding the Prince of Peace. They are dangerous let me tell you, champions going to gun shows heavy hunters. They like the cross-bow weapons, and they will steal your property. They smoke cigarettes keep awake at night they are distinct.   Let me tell you people something, and they live across the street from you so be careful, and any kind of gun ammunition rifle firing legal weapon these people will end up just crazy zap you, so never pick a fight with them approach them with a stick. They carry legal weapons never approach them they carry dangerous weapons, knives as well you will become scramble eggs in the ground, so be prepared keep out of trouble they will hurt you—*hasta-la-vista*. Anonymous within striking distance, we will catch them within striking distance. They carry legal weapons manufactured for violence highly successful they like guns, they carry guns everywhere. Anyway view the circumstance people after the fact: on your record all should be subject to too me JESUS CHRIST; they are nasty individuals roaming out there, they are individual racists. A matter of fact they are hillbillies, white men drunkards running around everywhere garbage ganisters after you. You are looking at them right now in America. There are racists everywhere out there looking at you wanting your money, even Obama looking at your back watching while you shuck and jive (kidding around) with them. Do you understand Black man, Black people stay away from them; you are threatened they are racists. There are so many of them people everywhere in America, militants they are marching, they are after you I'M telling you Black people even with guns, and Black people everywhere these are militants gone crazy they are after you, and some of you White folks Catholics as well and invasion in your Churches. Move them out of the way Catholics before there is activity, Catholics I view them all the time, and they are watching you many of them are packing, there will be trouble everywhere that is how it is in today's world. Play your banjo no more in the city enough is enough. People they need to be under arrest they are criminals, they commit every crime available, listen they are under watch now. They are nasty; they carry guns weapons wherever they are going. If they ask to come in do not be afraid. Acute unemployment has made it worst. Let's face it you can't run look them right in the eye, and give them what they want they are dangerous. There are many in small towns that is where they reside so don't be badgering them people, hating them, here's captain angel, they hate the government nothing their brand. Mr. Obama, be quick suicide mission they are on. We need to work with one another. Want more don't get near them battle ground be safe. So stay safe. "I am so under privileged, danger zone." Now whose going o pick up the pieces?" "Things are a mess," their argument no outlet hopeless they feel, that is one of our strongest and biggest problems. Our weakest members of Congress voting Democrats let's face it this system religiously shiftless stop complaining about everything, putting the blame on raising our taxes undocumented judgment hit the wind ego.   View negative. So we're bouncing officials vigorously up and down it's tarring us apart no secure budget and income tax, and we know our national security is at risk. For instance you're not safe if you are going to the grocery store lock your door. *Finally look out the window, before you let anybody in. So brace yourself be on the lookout, they commit violent crimes everywhere, Reagan / nomics (economics) put them there, very impressible they are all over the Country lately, and in Europe those are the people traveling put them there and drug abuse. You might wake up one morning and open up the door to find one in your living room, your kitchen, they are everywhere. Cooperate or you might find yourself dead. *You ought not to act like that be and adult among them, the people when you are with them they are a gun toting bullies everywhere. View their camp, welcome training in their camp rapid impulse with each other. These are little rulers. What kind, anything that will lie on the ground? These rednecks be (are) in hot pursuit after you. You're going to end up dead. They have a unique talent, and will use it on the Black man they want to kill him at random their notion. Extremes, racists are everywhere. They are even in Nashville, Tennessee somebody can get kill, absolutely. Here is a clue White America, nameless they are the Whites these people typically giving them their new revenue, apparently drinking coffee it's an offense if you don't, and their new revenue tipping plus leaving them a tip just like a dog a new puppy. You think they are strange.   Then they eat lunch there every day the whole nine yards. They never eat out at nice restaurants, better restaurants, typically exactly trying to avoid other people eating out at good restaurants trying to be canny, avoiding other people black people most people typically at other restaurants, their strange. Listen to this, it's free people ticket for free their whopper; they dine out at several places their restaurant to dine. How they foot the bill holding down side jobs? They eat at BURGER KING, their place to eat morning, noon, and night. The same thing Big-Mac off from work hit McDonalds, for the night the raff. Let me make it all clear, Channel Four News knows it they snub their nose like normal people at them. Constable network, they are truly amazing pimping armed ware wearing their guns some hanging from dashboards like the good old boy cops network system, they are cold. I'M telling you speaking to people, families in their flea markets, drinking sodas orange drinks, and other soft drinks pimping shoulder to shoulder wearing their symbols, they are a mess. *And here in Tennessee telling people backwards, defending their pimp agents in the entire world, that's the part that hurts the most despite all their efforts, and viewing racial harmony it will be on the ballot. Racists there in Springfield in Robertson County, in Cheatham County Pegram, Tennessee, and in Pleasant View, Tennessee and in Murfreesboro, and in Dickson County saying, "hay nigger" to people over that bridge. *They live in East Nashville, move to a more physical family oriented area. Dickson County racist's specialists have at it, and in Hickman County they love it *whip-a-la*, they set up check points numbness they carry it all. Would you believe Fairview as well they are extended. Off balance, yes they do exist even in Cheatham County emergency cold they are, and just as cold more in rural Robertson County; and in the end let me flip a coin thinking its guerrilla warfare in this country their country. CONCLUSION: as said citizens these are bonehead bullies—will rip you off garbage in the neighborhoods there is truth to that. TO: POLICE THE OFFICERS; do your duty. My friends you will see the contrast believe me, reason in Tennessee adversity urgency no joke these are backwards thinking grouped individuals, passersby on impact in a lot of places cornering the market, definitely replacing gun control legislation. Living their good life some have as many as 23 semi-automatic assault weapons, a vital. They pack a lot of guns if they get arrested, they have them with them no speculation about it for real. "This ain't (is not) real here in Nashville." We're the center of attention believe me there is abuse, a mole investment in every neighborhood these folks are dangerous. Black folks, these are shrewd individuals buying everything around them. Look at this, I'll tell you everything don't drop in on them; don't get to know these people. Let me tell you, I'll tell you their secret Armed Officers they are dangerous, these individuals acting like soldiers with a gun. Police Officers and Tobacco & Firearms Officers, we've had enough do something about these individuals. I view them all the time packing they are dangerous. You say, unbelievable just trust me. I'll tell you grouped for over a decade making up thousands in Nashville, TN. Do not approach them when you're walking these individuals. Open that door is their policy when soliciting, they are seeking individual's justice run their way hunting individuals, commandos using rifles, assault weapons, heroes, some have been in the guard starting to give up trying to survive. Unfortunately they were trying to become a soldier, these are trained individuals carrying legal weapons, thinking individuals wanting to survive they make me nervous. Local law enforcement knows who they are. Things are grave for some without a doubt, no opportunity for their success to manifest its self for their present. They work here in Nashville in packs, so give them what they want unhealthy if you don't, they think they deserve it. A new recipe let give you a warning quickly just to be safe. A pat on the back adjustments there are a lot of adjustments here in America we can make, before we get lock down practical solutions. NOTE: the rear end back to adjustments this operation

## A New Article

for this city, and Murfreesboro time for volunteering be sensitive for example, these people when they come to your home leave them along, don't hide give them what they want there are so many of them, I'M telling you many of them are common criminals, just bruise your ego—response just help them. You say, "You're just throwing money away." "We've got some shit going on in this country." They will put toys in your mouth they really do exist. When you go after them loosen up now—you will bleed to death they will watch you, I'M telling you Nashville. Don't make a big scene it will all be over very quickly just that quickly, don't try a standoff, don't follow them give them whatever they want. They are ace commandos. Hear me; don't stand in front of them like a detective. Do not block them your town, they are dangerous many are living off of crackers been really catching it just give them whatever they want. A good recipe give them what they want, no mistake. Qualify a definition, like a monkey a national convention just stupid, when available to Nashville, immediately they will be packing when they're on your street; so don't you play with them leave them along, sometimes they will hit you in the head. These people are extremely dangerous. But in Los Angles, Holy Boldness they have access, and in all small towns get to know you like a snake get to know you, local law enforcement. Their convention I'M telling you, smiling in your face walking there out on the street in a pack, view a pack of them, while you view television roaming around marking you. View no romance about them walking the neighborhoods drifters acting as officers. Tell them what they want to hear don't act stupid, you know what I'M talking about their not just passersby. Bye and bye just give them a donation. I AM a witness. They act like we are *serfs*, without a doubt. Help us JESUS CHRIST. On numerous occasion unbelievable their dialect, they are damaging goods harassing Mexicans. And in Cheatham County, they harass black people like they do in Dickson County; it is hard to get around them in those small towns. That's for sure. East

## The Original Barbara Payne

Tennessee they are the worst. Don't eat with them white folks; these folks are amazing without a doubt. Agreed! These folks have no vision its senseless talk in small towns, they are so rude benefiting the establishment, and they are behind them though illegal. Say Grace and Amen. Ya'll are going to need a lot of it when tornado's are behind you leaving nothing, when yall's homes are destroyed in each county. Ya'll hear that, and leave the Mexicans alone? Legally they think they are self-righteous people, keen people, females are the worst. Do you understand? Sad, they are here in Tennessee. People it's the worlds' best kept secret answering the call to duty—their religion. They are backwards thinking they are millionaires. Keep a sense of humor. Of it white racists in our society prancing with their temple, reservist declaring nigger look at that nigger eat'em up. Heaven help us all. Register dozens how they dress well done flattery following politicians dividing Presidency, white old timers many are atheist that is how they operate, their game shuffling around big friends of the NRA. They think they are filthy rich with successes local, they are here so shut your mouth. Right here at Spring Hill, southern plantation apathy horse play gentleman, wearing guns, practicing they practice a lot clinically. *They hunt a lot and not just ducks even Black people kill all, definitely if they weren't afraid of the FBI, alright? They are not comical. They are crazy one hundred percent, they are poison. Stay away from them. You got it? Audio accountability speak, running, don't you know it's like a cancer you going along with it your party saying, "come have a drink let me buy you something to drink" bringing in the new year New Year's day your apartment. You're going along with it the wrong thing it all makes me nervous. Identity stop it, I'M witnessing it you're going the wrong way black people. Records tale-tale pranks lately rubbing it in you can't pay any attention to those tales. Here are the results different subjects: "You know about Eddie George dating a white girl can you sleep on it a little while" backwards then "big tale?" Crossed the same; and watch your neighborhoods those places a lot of people do they just don't say nothing about it, definitely I'll tell you about it you're held accountable. Black people criminal justice membership saying, "everybody have a happy ending," with their video camera picture security "thank you, very much." The Titian family doss: this line direct to your family remain faceless in your industry as you're walking around in Nashville; you are at risk your general success, your consensus novelty. Everybody has been talking about your college athletics even the government; shut it down you heavy young players pestilence your temper. You're watched a lot, you're not perfect. Fact off the field not funny poor accountability the industry, you are and offense. Keep your accountability up out in the world, even if for a moment you are faking it good practice.

## ON THE CONCLUSION TO BACKWARDS WHO ARE DEMONSTRATING.

Thus saith the LORD; it's free. Say, God help me it's free. He has never failed me yet. You're walking on air. Keep going you will burn up that is your end. You stood up, and those events you are going to people pushed you out of the way. I've got a new revelation you can't give up fixed, a new revelation a weapon Pentecost let me talk to you your friend. We grew up together don't ignore me, I'M telling the truth a new revelation for black people. Its church we're not going to play I can't do nothing, without Him. He is my source of strength. Say, that against forces of wickedness. Sound an alarm; I've been in this church for a long time. I view your grand kids the usual, and they will be in the deep freeze blown up on their way to hell's kingdom. You cannot use that ball, I can lift a finger your troubles out the roof away not and impulse. Give your program just a junction saying, help me JESUS CHRIST; courtesy point out of this mess your entertainment totem pole, the totem pole championship Mr. Articulate. Manners, women are all after you all the time they are can't get enough of you. The way you are, decent evil feel like they are dancing with the stars, I'M not blind to that either the hotel. Let me tell you something, open your mouth say, LORD I want some help. Remember yours free anytime viewing you like wine, and pretty makeup and wine and women. Look give me that whiskey your etiquette. Your compass it is always free and available to me anytime, anyway they are valuable to me don't forget it, your treat your redeemer. I'M an avocado, then yall's treat you'd better believe it learn a lesson. You better stop messing with me your redeemer Pentecost; then are you listening blueprint clear? Their scapegoat just the opposite just feasible, be thankful, like Dr. Martin Luther King enjoy the host. Now take the exit. You need internal treatment tallied technically, and the U.S. Labor Department all due respect *adios*, I view them a thousand times. The employment trying to swim the necklace your ornament making a big difference, no more charismatic be big-time savings. "Plenty more the nest egg" the company "if you learn this business." Why don't you pay your bills, including your regular Federal Income Taxes? Then we would be free. The people with restraint, "don't knock them suffer okay." I've got their number, I will restrain them. "Baptist, listen definitely hit the savings hang on save some of your money, and be like me a fly on their wall be paradoxical son." "We know we have slaves their all sniffling around here the good old boys Nashville, the new President from top to bottom, definitely they are conservative. Wherever you're walking those Republicans STONECREST, they *gotcha* Black people checking their DNA oh absolutely, can you imagine at STONECREST be grateful? That is real life for you that shouldn't be allowed. Did she say a nuclear bomb, a group for the century black people in a tube left Memphis followed it all the way into rich neighborhoods, reflecting police near the stadium, I'M going to put my foot down? Next course of action, I will show documents. "Refrain from being hostile, we are the dark world. My system join a credit union, be like them you can live through this just beat the system big savings after a while. Open and account. Help put your kids through college-your bank account, and save some equity at this point your defense, never catch you off guard. Use your money wisely." The message, comparable don't cut no deals haven't been a scapegoat yet. Thank you, JESUS. Their system slippery hang on stay competitive. They all know what they are doing, exactly. Practice Jim Crow it will all be over after a while. We will get even, we know what we are dealing with Mac & Cheese still we are broke. God lift our spirits with every effort. No house guaranteed premium plus those are the steals super house your package. Tell the desert we have problems black people, while they finish shopping their investment new settlement with Mac & cheese. Get me the pinnacle your settlement the Mac & Cheese padding at their window your roof had you ever got a home zero down your baby, just a few extras now make a wish have your own bread, and charge it to me your monthly. We are millionaires' now on line. Know a reality know the outer banks people of God. VIEWING STONECREST: I watch you all the time. They are racists most of them the white people, kitchen help vaccinate yourself; have a prayer meeting let the Master help you, and your children from them early in the morning even before school, I know what I'M talking about. I guarantee you it will work your equipment. THE PASSAGE WAY: know the outer banks people of God, a broken assimilation a lesson learned. They are caring chemical warfare you hear me, definitely. They are dangerous with their weapons, they will use them on you they all are dangerous. God is praying for you, people everywhere. Bind it; put your trust in God. Black people don't give them your black vote, evil rest everywhere elected officials. Don't inoculate them anymore good written broken poor white trash followers. They are monsters in your neighborhoods caring papers shotgun ready. Southern assimilation over, Neo-Nazi groups backing them different places, cotton fields while you're picking cotton you're exactly right; we carry the injuries a long time don't get friendly with those groups. Republicans, they seek for violence Neo-Nazi's it is their food, their blueprint.

THAT IS ENOUGH

Thus saith the LORD; just as intense extreme these are the issues they post on the internet always in the family. "I would keep them; I'M talking to White people take some Pepto-Bismol." "You didn't want to have to clean it up Pentecost, jive turkey." "Let's not get personal." "Look after them look after his employees. "Come on man, Hey Dude!" the black fellow that hear the gospel preached every week, "you don't treat them right." "Where is your wisdom Pentecost, you've got sense you count none zero Pentecost Cracker." "Their wasting their time away how the company survives." "Come on man; give them a tongue lashing keep an open mind." "You want give them a chance even Black people please keep them; for a good reason you have no excuse having dismissed them." "Be concerned." Hallelujah. "You are saddling you White folks. They can't keep up those people." Black people, "what the inauguration hurt you?" "JESUS!" I know they are racists against Black people, those White people. "Every time I turn around I get knocked down in the work place, like a big wheel run over me." "Stop falling down." "You always take up for them making excuses poor excuse." "Shiftless they are." "You go to the Pentecostal Church, you are cold hearted." "Review their self-esteem help make it a habit." "We black folks were all thinking the same thing, a few been late a few times." "We know your program." "Exactly" "The white man they don't deserve it view the circumstance got to go to the doctor, we got the prescription." "Are you scientists White folks said?" "The black folks "GOD, get those people for colored people everywhere." *TIME TO GROW UP TAKE A LEGAL PILL: keeping racism and your racists efforts, you are string beans caring your own trains, and not anybody else. They don't deserve it. Black people legally guilty saying, "He's not hurting nobody." Creating your own pot behind the scenes, that's why people have been asking about the newspapers you're reading all the time. Things are going to shift for Black people legally. I know your bakery; I know your street Mr. Pentecost come get legally. Embarrassed you've got the IBM shuffling around thinking you are free, holding it trading it. I know where you are expenses controlling the operation. Say, it's a miracle I got any income coming in. They form middle class America they aren't in gangs. Internal Revenue, your pal you don't want to cut revenue holidays out White folks. Try and pay taxes your capital the right way, you'll have more capital income, and you'll have extras, your general pocket book big business. Leave the middle income families alone. Let me pay ya'll back. CHRIST JESUS SAID; the evidence people in your neighborhood. Let me do you a favor on location; have you looked recently do a background check on all people? So much so, you have a lot to think about got ex-criminals working in your stores, those other people rebels, definitely those other groups in the United States they are demonic. Who are they threatening demonic criminals gone astray? I view them all the time. Know some symptoms they love weapons, these symptoms they love money evil their intent; they tried it on Obama, and on Clinton. I AM concerned needless to say, keep them on watch don't take your eye off of them just don't panic. Underground they are people you don't want to vote for them their message. Stay out of that a lot of them have been arrested. Grass roots, well they have fallen underground driving middle class America these people. We're trying to handle it the best we can. Alarm! I have come to measure you, remember the MASTER. Don't do me like that, my business irritation. You're just settle in your own ways 98% your point of view individually; wise up politicians those Senators, for the record we're making it the answer threatening people. Talking about an agreement: you say, your own record a lot of people don't even know, I AM WALKING IN MY OWN STRENGTH IN THE CONTINENT OBEY ME. Remember Martin Luther King, publicly with accord your dynasty, he reasoned with me on the aftermath, your administration. I reason with thee a little bit, this is the business at hand, JESUS CHRIST. I COUNSEL: Republicans, people know what that means that includes Democrats. (*ISAIAH* 63:1 Who is this that cometh from Edom) Here are the specials: The Baptist; let me encourage you be scot-free. I'll tell you all about it. Scot-free they are worthy and other Baptist walking free give me a chance born naturals, pastors would you agree? Let's make a deal. Lighten up be a little free as an adult your last chance your redemption. Yes, it is free friend my redemption Catholic's as well. They are going to need it. Let me explain, just with respect take the elevator up vacant seats. With respect listen Catholic's not another angel. You've got return, but you always refuse typical you are waiting on another the unforgettable testified, and take you nowhere neon trash testified Saint-freak, not me coming to get you believe on me, for the elevator to take you up stairs to the entrance. Your elevator speaking of him your destiny, how is his condition, he will be known as hypnosis? You believe in disrespectful you are backwards encourage me; arrest me your major conflict. *JEREMIAH* the prophet, speaking of him back before the fall of Jerusalem, when the nation was one, back before the days of the house of Jacob, even before any prophet you got the blueprint know me. Speak of him the average blueprint the average living. Know that that is how important it is. Now what is the difference? Thank you, JESUS. You are the most stable group of people walking around, but you don't have mercy covering you. You value take a leap of faith with regards no magic exit view. Your exit view is not in the Old Testament. See dangerous your point of view handle that. Let me explain Pontiff, let me tell you about it from the foundation of the world not an offering on line; black people used front people, people everywhere, I CHRIST, will tend to you everybody. Marriage is equal thank you, JESUS Roman Catholic as well, under the whole umbrella of my safety. Constitution not a threat, but a new way not and opinion a blessing for your children no matter what their rank is in birth, Holy Matrimony consecrated. And amusement park with deductions have you become like a pool, The City of David, not newly discovered knows they are free. They have assurance, ONE, in their back pocket. The City of David knows it's free leaving the old behind, and putting forth the new contrary to the will of the living dead western civilization, they know they are free. They have paid off their debt by being free. Yes, they are free can you imagine that they are free, walking in His own strength give you the shirt off His back? Amen. He is worthy think of that give thanksgiving, amen. **Pentecost you're not along say, give me that house back; [with dyed garments from Bozrah? This that is glorious in his apparel, traveling in the greatness of his strength? I (this generation), that speak in righteousness, (Pentecost) mighty to save]. Thank you, JESUS CHRIST. Here are the results your administration. A brand new weapon *ISAIAH* 63:1 (KJV) people of God, traveling your way, your rhythm be grateful traveling your debt Pentecost totally accepted. New soldiers coming your way, and they are legally accepted by God. A new organization fingerprint morally accepted a new branch off of the big-shot old ones. Favor, not watching television preparing for the day: read Isaiah 63: 1 Who is this that cometh from Edom (democrats a new program setting us free. I will tell you all about it), with dyed garments from Bozrah? / In any event says JESUS CHRIST unto me know that I AM able; never give up you'll find out about it all the people. Snakes those Republicans, you think I'M stupid all the Federal Government. God help us. Oh thank you, JESUS CHRIST. Republicans no middle truth half the world knows this already. Hallelujah and amen, definitely your record in history digging us out the freeze Federal Government. *I'M confident let the world know rising from Bozrah cleaning, digging, us from the filth, [Isaiah 63: 1 this that is so glorious in his apparel,] JESUS, democrats coming again [traveling in nothing, but the greatness of his own strength?] / Yes, JESUS CHRIST we are free Pentecostal double whammy on you; these are the benefits, the instructions. I AM your king without a doubt no middle man, here are the instructions. We are free Pentecostals without a doubt yes, we are free, I that speak wisdom to Pastors, religion on this day Pentecost vengeance JESUS CHRIST. Come take another gamble, I know your ability [I that speak in righteousness, mighty to save.], this no golf course everybody is playing watch me, definitely. I'll help you out your mistake not honoring God your deliverer. You need a renovation say, oh my God you've got blood on your hands. Yes, Democrats as well a lot of people don't know this, I count everything you do wrong. Mercy you should cry! Individuals going ahead you should know JESUS CHRIST, you need therapy complaining blindfold taking out his own vengeance. Let me give you a clip a lot of people understand the issues, the Federal Government know that it's a different circumstance, agree? A lot of people are taking the heat they are trying to bring you down both Houses you are a broken window Republicans and both Democrats. House Democrats their agenda these liberal Democrats a lot of you, and those fiscal Republicans who rule Congress, Republicans the ones annually who want to pass laws against Republican spending getting out of hand for the fiscal year, against President Obama. President Obama, in gridlock with all the spending did what he had to do with federal tax revenue. That includes recent federal tax cut incentive to help lower the deficit, federal income payments after the Tax IRS Revenue is taken out. Savings, better be careful on your bills income your increase the deficit. Half of the Federal revenue the treasury no not half could be reconstructed. They are looking into that now. Banks and Republicans have an edge on Obama, just keep on looking at it Republicans keep an eye on them. Force them before November to do better watch them, and you'll find out what is missing that helped to increased the deficit, appreciate the initiative. Thank you, JESUS CHRIST. Earthquake development Congressman seized by a black man a friend of mine. I hear the trumpets sounding now. Edge yours for the taking a new development. And those Democrats House you voted them in this session, and Republican leaders the people. You still got time to pass legislation to help people up increase that notion—Ethics increase spending in both Houses. Take action against the Tea Party members, absolutely. Don't let them keep this up stop them anyway you can. Others can get their job take their place to protect middle class Americans, and lower income families. They are the enemy of the middle class. Cut the spending new revenue their revenue completely. A new production increase tax revenue on the wealthy, and those tight investors. New tax revenue will keep things from getting out of hand, you're battling over nothing. Tea Party they are Nashville people, say it good luck on the next election give yourself to JESUS CHRIST, and yall's those Senior Republican strategist a lesson. Bottom line you'll never get reelected know there're people all over this country are needy. Suggestion, there negligence used to create more wealth 80% more in this country against the people. Just said to all of that in this country all people are free that includes business. To the people notion: relieve any notion that it counts as good government, their ability the same against the people of God, people everywhere. I'M praying for you black people everywhere, a witness true evil anywhere. The fall view your compass you know you are crooked, I have the evidence a thousand times bigot. Don't get mad at me Jewry in Middle Tennessee, this is ridiculous your organization in Nashville. Have confidence hang that up physically give them up. JESUS! Take me back legally, I'll find you a place. I've been at this a long time. I know which way to turn. Hey Nashville, I'll secure your past understand, a defense a unique opportunity for free African

Americans, and your grandchildren for free Black America okay? It will be a trend I follow you. I know you are hungry for more. I AM divine, I love you very much. You break my heart rambling at the table defeated nowhere to grab, but to kindergarten, and church seeking more. Bologna they ought to do more. They help other people all the time needing help. People of Nashville, Black folks what are you waiting for in Middle Tennessee? Memphis ya'll spend way too much on frivolous things. Saying, "I want to go shopping" that is the way it has always has been. That is the reason you fall victim to things. Do you really want to know why you're bankrupt, where bankruptcy construction in the south specifics you know this address? You haven't heard yet from a politician's stand point, and black folks they accuse you this is an emergency do something about it. Come again, exactly people of Nashville "black folks backwards concerning Metro Schools," citizens say. African Americans "yes we are backwards can't get out of this kingdom of poverty. Welcome to our world Pentecost in Nashville, Tennessee." "Let it be known clean up our unit here in Nashville, a drop of blood everywhere," the old people in Nashville. Listen grotesque everywhere now." Young black people "in our camp their opinion right shouldn't be like that," confessing to me JESUS CHRIST saying, "JESUS move it out of the way." For example, the people "the racists as for me it's all over it's a jungle out there." White people say, "do me a favor move the blockage away Republicans. These days is anybody listening outside the community? We desire clean there has to be somebody listening? Exercise your right go and vote. Get this epic vulgar everywhere southern way of life and up north for colored people. Agree white folks I'M not pretending? But we've got our own weapon good luck needs a weapon. A new peninsular narrowing escape the infrastructure way of life microfiche, shear destitute we in America we are. No wonder we are weeping our average serving in America waiting for worms, the infrastructure to help us. Isthmus (narrow) from our neighbor's our style, our way of life, but we're waiting for our savior hungry for more can you help us out? We're honored our coat traveling watching the world go by us saying, we've missed it in our wallet for a very long time leaving sponges behind us many of us Christians. Mosquitoes this bunch same sex marriage gets better treatment. Say, keep that away from me. Finite we are in this country. "Dam them we've lost our business you can't imagine, while we eat their beans, and other vegetables struggling to pay taxes free welfare to others." White folks on Jefferson Street traveling bleak, even in the projects trending bleak, or somewhere else comes roasting white folks, white gentlemen, in the African American community battle racism this is a crisis. NOTED: in Tennessee, legislature serving presently from the south no accident in Tennessee legislators serving full time as mediators with nothing crap my opinion; they are from East Tennessee serving. Presently on our back damage done free rehearsal particular look out, there are racists minding legal business. There are racists everywhere Channel Four News. Friends those corrupt politicians Ku Klux Klan members racists count from house to house; but we manage. Just a witness I give details. Look at their record master thinkers of the prom; Catholics and Jews your style and amen. Hallelujah. Every sense you've been elected, and dirty white Jews you are racist's just white racist's Corporate Jews, whose specialist's against black people have blocked us thoroughly, The African American people. Improve our heritage stop being racists. Stop the racism! Settle Mr. Bush and senior chip off the old block filibuster uppity you offend me. Say, amen. You move people around, and then give them the axe, even Whites and Latinos of lower class. In Nashville there are plenty like you your camp. That is the way that you are. Your defense segregation "I don't see how people hardly get by," the African American people, terrifying for black people no mercy. The engine weak lentils for us main diet in the city, in the city we got a peninsula ownership a wall struggling to get by. Township, death few of us we are facing hard times, things suck around the block for us this Christian way of life in the beginning of this journey. We take it on our journey their open house laughing at us talking about the picture, thought things would change in my life totally wrong. Accept if, I did see a black President elected. Looking back facing us things were so discouraging ruined for us the dressing, food shortages; ruined housing everywhere HGTV. The country we've wrestled with for success in any event ruined housing America 100%, that's the authority civil power mostly whites Americans. Stay the same among black people in America these days, the Mexicans, Latino's any Latino's giants. Always been like this dogging us around know catastrophe 100%, don't give u. That's the way it's always been for us the poor, poor black people we count for something the African American Negro, Blacks and White people in the community. For example, authority's people of God this country that's the way trouble be for us a full tank. I'll show you something Mr. Obama, fought for it and other people. About that join in we're not on a suicide mission are we? Going with passion we are running this race, and most definitely blocked your third ratings of us. On this journey everyday prosecute. Conflict now consider this most definitely, politically your convenience. We the people of God, no accident you held us back from the beginning. Even if you had to beat us to death are you listening horse whipped us, get a printing get me? True people are equal be a friend. Though we've been beaten Executive Branch-The Federal Government just that simple, can you imagine that on a lower level here in the South? We tried to run this race. The case: their equipment, the foot battle they are foot soldiers that's the real story. Listen to me, now do the math in this country some have had heart attacks playing stupid jokes on people. *The whole cruise (journey) we think it's a bad idea everyone. It's not a mystery their thing ignorance and stealing in Tennessee, and race suspension annual their stamp, their daily routine. Jerking see we've lost the desire, the last election a lot of people don't know that yet, but the next election bring money equal to Tennessee. A part of it advantages just that simple talking about the conflict. Traders against blacks they are pitiful Democrats, them they are dangerous dozens of them, the whites are pitiful the outcome it's a shame against black folks. "We had a mission" both Houses. People taking advantage their daily routine. Say, that again Democrats control the city, and those Republicans control both Houses. Now remember that. The printing yes wow yes taking advantage, but grace gave us some backbone. You think we don't know how in Middle Tennessee in Nashville, TN too tear that political fence down even the custom. Here's another rerun next prescription-Keeper. We got backbone didn't you tell us our backbone. We have our ups and our downs, our bad feelings talking about the time people, the journey we're on. The election our effort unforgettable everyone knows this how about you? I see justice to deal with it this trouble, for any cause no matter what. Politics have ruined our lives, and the budget created just for you and your wealth, and this economy square people end of the discussion. Thank you, JESUS CHRIST, the difference early on we can become a success not one of those bipolar arm swinging gentlemen on Jefferson Street. Be thankful, I am grateful. White House wake up to this be friends. Listen to this choose a difference for black people. We are not deranged people don't you care America, people everywhere our case? Humanity we need a breakthrough we Christians, we are holding onto JESUS CHRIST, but we must hang onto JESUS CHRIST our Lord and our Savior, rather than money the way we look at it. Our fruitcake children, these are sensitive areas for black people everywhere everyday are mostly facing death make no seconds about it depending on where you live. This is an emergency. Things are difficult this is a desperate situation stop blaming us for our downfall. Consecration we need a breakthrough, we are on the verge. Republicans look at the seniors government they pay taxes, whose fault is it if they can't fill their bellies with decent food with integrity anymore? Depending on where we're born most of the African American community, the people colored peninsular Jim Crow activity can hit you hard. Making a legacy dying for few is a blessing that is their option. Now give them a hand black people. See a group of them measure till we rest, and beat them again the white man in Nashville. Trying a new foundation nothing—trying a new one sucking crumbs falling from the master's table battling here, dining room won't tell true African American. We need more cast iron to get through this needless opposition our President faces red tape is all it is. Scholarship Jim Crow practice hopeful downtown America, across this country the back hand help keep it new treasurer we'll hungry. Stop blaming us for all the petty horse play, goofing around in the House of Representatives both Federal and State affecting rough side of living. Wisdom more attributes JESUS CHRIST, we're backwards. "I help black people these people just won't work" the recipe. Your name, JESUS CHRIST sends you this; frankness with all due respect DR. MARTIN LUTHER KING JR., gentlemen the half has not been told, when he was shot in the face and in the head, you need and "OSCAR" for your reluctance, even this weekend running specials on Dr. King's message. You ought to be horse whip for all the things you claim you do for the Black man, you hate White man the African American community. Black History month, when ya'll chose to honor him. No dumping ground for yall's pitiful role you played in promoting slavery, your ancestors did. Dr. King, a trademark in a book can't donothing about it until Black History month. We know everything, but we're going to make it out of this mess we're in. Yall's trash— lost history of the civil war's past iniquities in the south. Let me tell you, your sins and spiritual wickedness against the black man in America repent now, say, LORD help this man. Critical just so you all can see that announcement important, before it's too late

## A New Article

and the major middle class are hit with disaster in lieu of tragedy. Understanding: "are your windows broken" look at it unbelievable with just bathtubs flying everywhere, and with police running everywhere that is how it is going to be watch? You don't believe me then learn a lesson? Now hitting the ground your business capital see pay for a rental car. Now take lesson footage, and you will understand people call it what you may. Strange battleground for the unbeliever's better give up and epiphany, better back off told you I have a revelation this is a revolution in this hand. For the record who knows better people of God, it doesn't make much sense their appearance it's an epiphany for lack of a better word. School districts keep watch even elementary schools they were hit their school district ugly their camp. I view their trash everywhere be conservative. Hateful they all are full conference racists, their little ones hit with a brick in North Nashville their neighborhood the worst, and even on Woodmont you are polluted. You are backwards setting a stage; I view you every day on Woodmont Boulevard. Woodmont Boulevard you are the victim the case. I'M telling you internally you're out of time there is pollution in the air your dumbness people playing innocence. *You're missing an opportunity ROSA PARKS did not; waiting your thing so get to it. Say, when we all get to heaven enough is enough. Anyway I've got a great idea Nashville, do better open up those gates, or I'M coming full swing even Vanderbilt their roots, I know your criminal record peopledone in Nashville. I think He's coming after you it's an emergency. We're at the bottom of the scale, with all due respect low revenue for black people everywhere. Desperate are black people everywhere that is no joke low are their advantages. You give Hispanics more. Let me inform you desperate are we against this slavery act let me tell you 98 to 50% even 80 to hundreds of thousand could have been more, including missing in action are buried somewhere legal their operation. Here is a sneak preview their exit moment development happened a no charge a sneak preview.

You could have been one of them the system. The clowns signaling that is your own story delivered the problem. No more gangs in this house. Amazing incredible that monitored negative their birth certificates, hats off to them. One more time they were eliminated to the extreme all were killed the words. So it matters light bulb their history draw attention—there are many soldiers in the graveyard to prove that alright? Incredible regret you missed it you are walking in the dark. You won't even lift a finger to help us. You look at class elevation idiot against the black man stop he deserves it; and the young black generation before immigration reform was a big subject, they deserve it recognition. They should be included in reform, he gave his all to help freedom his neighbor no less than a privilege the African American now this is it—a privilege the African American. You ought to be thankful, officially a testament why not, because they are not salmon in a can, nor a fruit in a box. They are real people indeed in the earth and their children. Now don't be confused many of them volunteered like you all did wanting to fight for liberty. I want to stress that. The military knows who they are. Bring it forward it will improve race relationships, that's a good idea that is the issue the real issue here. *Your banks are sweeping with Mexicans violating the law, dangerous big company wanting more capital income acting like *critters lately they are. That is the wanting, wanting reform knowing no boundaries in the United States illegally, they ought to be deported by immigration authorities back to Mexico, and they're not real citizen's people. Cabbage is there brand their not real American citizens, half of them wanting a new program. Cheaters of another land they are, if they want legal residence here let them do it the right way. Missing are we alienated we the people American citizens are denied equal access. In the hills find them and depot them back to Mexico. Let them make it on their own shuffling more power to them; you carry a suitcase with you everywhere. No accident they are here, they are here to deny us equal access. Denied are we now let's not go backwards in society? The big sheriff knows best, the skin color doesn't matter to Him, even the apple of His eye. The Latino's are asking for the Government to depot them who break the law. Say, I'm from New Mexico or Arizona this is the avenue—race is an issue defined, the only issue with no reasonable respect for many Blacks less the Latinos. Go after them Congress let the Black people be treated fair; more Blacks down in Jacksonville than there are Whites ten to one. AND ANNOUNCEMENT SURRENDER TO GOD ALL EVERYWHERE: To the Illegal's cure your madness. Stop it right now and immigrant gets better treatment. For that reason a host of them have been getting away with mistreatment of Americans who got here the right way, not a provision for Americans, their pass a green light. That is a reality your panel standing up difference in people, now put that down in your records you keep on us physics the right way delivered. You do the math. Call me crazy colored people this event a dream our real view reality this generation, now keep a lid on this definitely ours, but we're thinking about our grandchildren politically their rights as an American freedom that is their right. Now say, you've been touched by God. The African American struggle many died doing the right thing, during their patriotic duty the Black man hoping God would hear their cry. Give an offering politically that is the question. Hallelujah. By the way in this city I have no quorum with officials of mix heritage, just give us a break one way or another black people. We first got it started the movement, then Latinos thank they own it. They snob us we secured the advantage tell them their brother did that not the Latinos, republicans. Hundreds of them are in school; because of this they received busing rights evidence illegally, well congratulations. Then they rushed in on the fence in America where we gather, and have equal access. A pronouncement: where Black Americans don't. We are in a feud in this State. We have our strong feelings. BIG ANNOUCEMENT: all for nothing and acid reflux revenge tasteless society, and their *juveniles* here no offence are the results, they are rough on the city they don't care, don't blame it on God, and the middle class knows they make a laughing conservation out of it their whim, their treatment out of their mouth. I'M telling you everyone knows. You do the math on the table. We don't want immigrants in the city of Nashville, TN pure opportunists that are standard pollution. The government makes it a laughing matter watching big crooks every day, their argument. The infrastructure that is how they make their living the infrastructure, Spaniards seasonal, God knows their infrastructure regardless of what Metro Government says Chief of Police. Chief better head it off act now police been waiting too long. You need a back up. Things are problematic if we don't face it super rip-off—your offense. African American's and the Republicans fastest growing nation in the United States, identity theft war lords and drug lords wants to establish them cover for them. Know about them they are ripping off pretending to be Americans, wanting to be Americans. Ya'll hear that? Washington is watching them they know they are trouble politics the revelry, definitely. They don't like the U.S. Constitution its principles many of them come over here illegal, take it easy and it won't be and American Government, Hispanic's will control everything, Latino's next. America will be crushed. Things are happening and we say, welcome come on in. Drug lords are behind it all. Enough is enough we've heard that noise enough. Exactly behave, a lack of insurance people provided behave those people. Some officers are weak; exactly we want a breakthrough in our society one hundred percent. Put our enemies away, the stowaway's backwards. Their suicide rate is up, but ours is down. Their just thieves centrally make sure they don't get away with it anymore small crimes justified; things are difficult enough that is the problem. Platoon rate build up colored folks is what we're facing, believe me. They pick us up when we are minding our own business. U-Haul catch them we got them now book

## A New Article

them. Why don't you tell the Spaniards that book them anyway? We sweat it all the time chief of police proprietor in Nashville, TN the interior. We feel trapped just want give us a chance dirty the police are. Hear that white America? What is left on this occasion? Catholics who aid them (illegal immigrants) love to have you on our side, the most these republicans in our beautiful city of Nashville. For argument sake basically trash they spread trash loosely, and we the people and Metro Government, it is showing end up fixing it we are the victims their credit. You think we are brain dead our argument against yours, and the newspapers conveniently. I have it on tape this absolutely a new issue. Favor the American bomb, and in Tennessee low down is this mess a kindred spirit this season against the public in Tennessee. PART ONE: A KING WROTE A BOOK A TREAT. Good measure the White House our friend legally. Number One-JOHN BOEHNER: House of Representative. Mr. Speaker and his friends got their hands all in it, and some wayward democrats this is a reality the gulf, and fellow democrats he can use regular, including the U.S. Supreme Court. A new sequester your harem, you do the math just charming your way in diplomatically. Dirty business your stimulus under the table against fellow democrats. Finally, trust me JESUS CHRIST; people are paying you are all lowdown, and dirty fiscally John Boehner and House Republicans. You are a bleep away—your term. You're trying to end government republicans your nominee. Say, thank you JESUS. I'M the doctor the Speaker of the House, the developer of recent oblivion events. We are going to drop another bomb. It's the fastest growing segment of these United States population give or take a few flakes, believe me believe that Nashville, my word a big event what happened. Thank you, JESUS CHRIST you are a wonderful God. Chiefly *physics* the wrong way, the difference trust me lawmakers. The FBI knows ERIC HOLDER knows that our lean brand of CSI with weapons, definitely. See how they do us we the people. Dear our Heavenly

Father; help eliminate the segment. Thank you, JESUS CHRIST. Lift your voices black people everywhere, argument of the case white America nuclear a battle for conversation. I AM a witness. May I make a suggestion bring back the powerful armed services, beef up patrols crossing our borders illegally; create a zone defense that will stop illegal traffic. They commit Pentecost all kinds of crimes. They are our constant battle, most definitely. Your acid reflux smudges they have been running away with influx, your acid reflux since Bill Clinton was in office it's amazing. Now they are on the rampage citizens that live in the city of Nashville do the homework. They aren't our friends, you see it around you the influx our people. We found a new investment the details spectacular here comes some good news Mr. President. We need a pipeline of human investment. For the past ten years here in Nashville, they have been ruining this country it's just that simple. What we need is an accountant our country these United States, our native homeland supreme of our America black people as well. Worrisome are these people they can't even speak English, some barely can speak English. Many can't even read Middle America a lot of them look at what it's doing to us; people of the United States block it citizens of our homeland as a second language. Rushing to get here being bilingual isn't that big of a deal. I love GOD ALMIGHTY. Avoiding Custom's Authorities, avoiding legal entry to our society a debit (recorded debt) to Mexico's trash a retainer filling it with trash their people. We are blessed the Negro; out loud give them a big hand clap. You're going to let them consume what is legally Americans. No weapon formed against us shall prosper (*ISAIAH 54:17*), no weapon! Education we need more education educate yourselves finally, we need more power go out and vote, definitely. It's amazing your own zipper, key word settlement. Give them a new tax advantage right here now let's take a look at it right now. "Oh Rock Of Ages" desperation we've got a new ship, a big new development headed our way thanks to him, JESUS CHRIST.

# A New Article

Hooray for black people colored people everywhere. You don't lift a finger to improve race relationships; for Latino's in despair you march to a different tune you think we are ignorant. Language poor are black people ethnic black people, we pay with a cost. Do you know what I mean? Daily we have this silence for black people. Breakthrough we need a breakthrough Council at large hear me, absolutely. No honeymoon for black people. Get me, get that black people? White folks let me speak to you of your record, your sins now come on now your arrogance it isn't strange. We are nobody's fool even to this day black folks, and the results no puppet African Americans till this day. President Obama finished his race against Republicans, and the Clan. Till this day any African American all White Republicans nobody's fool, and sequence elevation we are not a prisoner. More will be uncovered. Puppet we are black folks all those years, and your white trash the Clan, they are the same. Don't tell me I seen it all. Spanish speaking people taking advantage, my opinion. On you watch your step you all my opinion, your objective robbery. Your language against us, now watch your pace out there seriously. Don't ask me I know the difference okay? Your objective your address your people you say you are Christians, but a different class. We don't deserve it the Amigo, the snubbing you give us. Your objective "the niggers" you know what I'm talking about, the white people trying to act like them backwards platform politics. Born here in America we are. Lord, I'm free against any white folks, I'm not a prisoner. Agreed, ugly they are. Stop snobbing your nose up at us—black folks, with those Republicans cross cultural republicans crossing the white line. You know what I mean. Yes we are different class Mexicans my friend; we're in the middle legally in this country Spanish speaking people. You want some advice, do me a favor take your place in history! You understand? Give us better treatment, okay? We deserve it. Listen to that give us better treatment you are prejudice. Remember our station in life the ethnic people republican candidates we want justice, and Merry Christmas to you the chunk. Viva for black people. We come here alright. No justice for the black man until Thus saith the LORD; Dr. Martin Luther King Jr., helped single handily undoubtedly racism. Racism a big thing ROLAND, the friend representative you see that. A fascination greatly holds your attention when occurring politically, no joke the hook on the eye when occurring. *JESUS said unto me; Dr. Martin Luther King Jr. was the same form of black man a Baptist *cool-edge* a messenger. Roland I love him to death—it's just and expression to me, of GOD'S great admiration for him. Excellence is his dyer report on current activities. CHRIST JESUS just said to me; CNN missed it, he's my friend unofficially focusing a friend of GOD. For security do your home work for the news my friend, friend of God? My friend, I will give you details. News let the people see I'M telling you the injustice of colored people my friend. Roland, you are my friend let me introduce you to Barbara, a witness productive. Hey look, let me break it down to you a seer this night on paper a friend of JESUS CHRIST; heaven watches her, a lot of black people do. A little bit of edgy on behalf of JESUS CHRIST; with her sacrifice with no objections, for the picking, Roland a Baptist with razor strength, I see your strength and opportunity for black people, and other people of color including your location Mexicans, and other people of color with dignity against white injustice. You've got backbone courage to filter through all kinds of poverty and racial injustices; I see it all the time, most definitely. You have middle class blockage a new episode. Canon, you have some tools like Moses, and JESUS CHRIST; the author and finisher of all things. For black people preparation for JESUS CHRIST now use them, definitely against white people a whole lot of them, for the treatment against the African Americans-black people in our society. And then black people be nice record what you have seen. Be comfortable and live with it, injustices all over this entire country. Skepticism set things right check the race relationships in a moment in time whites against our people, against black people everywhere. Raw footage can make a difference go do your thing. Get on board. Thank you, JESUS CHRIST we've had enough of it against our race overtime. Black folks we don't need any black rock stars in hopes to bring in more cash. Be better pay the price be a film crew that group urban people actors and actresses, they have raped us enough legally. Courtesy the person JESUS CHRIST; He is my pal he is so cool the one and only got his dividends. I've got the evidence. I AM a witness to that. Here is the battle ground, the battle is drawn. Hey, be creative in the industry any actress or actor on the history channel do that. Sell out your agent big man taking a lot of money let him share some of the wealth. THE ARGUMENT: fight against racism. *Hey ACLU graduate move that mountain, you know what mountain stop it. Where is your bed legally representative in Washington, D. C.? People of color you act like they are nothing. Management African Americans get creative be big against racism, we're one step away achievement get it? *How about that REV. AL SHARPTON the other man? Problems things are in our favor ego it loud please! The people will get the message we pay taxes as well. Call their bluff. Film for the people, record racism in response be a film crew your observation at the root a chilling thing recorded these things people, and then things will get better. They will be looked upon, and frowned upon negative perception everywhere. They are diabolical with their political strength! Witchcraft they use. They've got their own created energy bravery. So political their strength they gain strength each organization. I swear to God. Tennessee Towers, you hear that? You don't begrudge us our public opinion. I'M telling you people lots of loss capital everywhere. Right in the same territory flood gates are coming open a lot of traffic on the highway. Evil people a new revelation, evil people seek for shelter. Hear me no arguing battlefield you contributed this is a social thing, you are in desperate need of a new address. See you can't do nothing seek for shelter even in a small town many were injured. I felt His presence pushing through. Try understanding it's all up to you. Aftermath shock people everywhere, this generation lazy grazing your vintage. Hear me, number thirteen fast and curious, fast reaction people. We will turn it up right in the same spot with a hit, tornado an eerie feeling more than a half dozen of tornados at the same time. Bring your Stetson, have a group of them destroying farms, and all that is in their way. Sickling urban solid bricks hitting windows during the month of May blew the roof top off of houses worst one touched down rising like a blizzard. Sneak preview, no one wants to be here shocked between 6:30 A.M. and then noon, 9:00 P.M. like a gun killed a lot of people everywhere with an exception, they hit about every 30 minutes. See that tornado hit like a launch pad. Crowds were standing by just jerking people thrown everywhere, the whole thing about 70 people were killed dazzling hot weather that cause it. Eat breakfast early Nashville. People were trembling even until July. Show America your rich neighborhoods beats laughing. You see that? Impact, hit the grass people keep the key won't be nothing left yall's fancy new home, don't you know your home was lost in Nashville. I'm nervous. Twice remembering total, I will be watching use your intelligence lawmakers this time. *Now here's the point: all my children that are in Pentecost neighborhood affiliates the African American, with exception of the Apostolics of JESUS CHRIST; the backbone gathering for Nashville, trusted people that are on television I'M telling you the admission free. Here's the entire now children I AM your friend, that I AM the third degree, and injunction a missile this place. Don't trouble me; I'M tired of this mess folks. On the lookout better control your meter your pencil cap. Pentecost unbelievable your mess, Christian Church your services. You all agree you would rather see foreign faces forgive them, the black's whites today. Adopt a Black African American Church, show them the way Pastors, do you need a word before your funeral talking about and explanation Pentecost Christians, cabinet for the record for your information? Your long term your anti-aging greedy, wherever that you are want and injunction follow me, you can be toast against the future let the Holy Spirit look for you. Better yet let's have a rematch nobody can keep me, no human being stop me adopt a church in their pool. This is my world. I AM a witness Pentecost legally. I keep up with you, everyday of your life. The basement you've got us singing songs it is pitiful, you are a fool. Business telephone, business disconnect, your revenue spending in this city a mountain mole hill of despair, libertine they are—marked difference in African Americans in the public school system bleak outlet here in Nashville, particular in the African American community. Pray for the children. People are complaining bleakness liberty for the black man. A martyr you seek that is the formula ladies and gentlemen, the white man. That is where they come from or do you want some, an earthquake to hit at your house? That is what it is coming too. See the message then things will start happening then. So good luck see the dark house coming around your table, if you can't pay the black man back something. Give the black man something a diamond, a cheap necklace, your wives wear mostly plastic.

SANTA CLAUS NO OBJECTION

Thus saith the LORD JESUS CHRIST unto me; clearly no good intent politicians in Nashville, I AM no fool get that? For Nashville the penalty your group in Nashville, I remember no more *Santa Claus* your wild bunch. I hear you at the time of iniquity ice cream, I see your waist bulging. Santa Claus, the template isn't coming to your house anymore. I see rescue at work on your day motivation any kind of pain to their rescue. Now here is the answer. GOVERNOR BILL HASLUM: you get my point a mandate for your evil hope, you are listening get it now? Here comes Santa Claus, with nothing on your shopping list for you this year. Have a good evening your discomfort. Ticket been bleeding for a very long time is what's wrong with them locally. The Republican's are full of hate, the Republicans is what's wrong with them against the Black folks the election, and DONALD TRUMP is leading them against HILLARY CLINTON. JESUS! Based on you *Humphrey's calendar* it's almost like a legend of saints (ants) hit the White House grounds unnecessary, literally to that. Against all the accusations of we can't perform our duties; I've got good news to that you are the villain. God is my witness; you keep blocking us a custom care here in Music City, with emphasis looking in the back with your foot in our throat! Get the buffer pull up a chair famous, setting we've had enough we bleed enough against your tax. *Going out of the tax business an audit should come to the States' budget, and to that the best comptroller Ringgold payment given to where all our Federal School's dollars in Metro-Nashville, are being legally custom fit too fit Rutherford County, and in Williamson County, their school's budget. We want freedom. Hear that want some more? Don't throw a fit now you hear me? The emphasis what's happening based on your swelling liability. I see your pain wanting more. I see your trouble. Say God, help us remember me. Republicans, they are out to get you in this hour no freak show. Never give up you understand don't give up in Nashville, you can't give up and go home? Follow your religion and to that don't doubt you understand? We can fight them legally now stop giving up. One more time, they are just white trash including the Governor, the author of those gates. Put that on Facebook, Democrats. Listen to me concerning racism, I'M going to stop this mess this statistics. Hear me now a new break up of politics here in Nashville, and across this city of Nashville, and across the State. You have a lot to be thankful for we agree. I need you all to take advantage people, okay win in the next election you are my friend. Their women especially in Green Hills, watching behind closed doors they are dangerous with their purses. They will come after you. I

## A New Article

have the evidence. We don't carry a gun, nor a knife people anxious in circumstance big bully. Don't walk up besides them they will walk all over you, I guess they have a lot on their mind. That is why they have guns for sell, and their shooting ranges in the city of Nashville, a legal weapon. They carry a loaded gun armed and dangerous. Branches this is a reality. The white women in this town in their place expect a bully their wives, yes it appears as an athlete. Up to bat they are batting a home run in this town. Monster they have become especially near Vanderbilt initially in their home place. Monster portrayed us near Vanderbilt that is how they feel in this town; I do not like Vanderbilt that is their nature. Beware of their station their criminal intent their husbands. Don't knock ever, when you are going door to door asking for a vote. Stay in the yard people never cross the fence, or they will call the police. Do like the experts do wire them. They are hungry for deliverance, the white man from our intrusion on their grounds. I know how they feel. They are monsters in this town near Vanderbilt. Just a gesture or they will send a big dog after you, not just any dog their secret habit. They don't put that on the news. They are watching eventually just a distraction, they are strong. Messages a bang you can't come in here, just a few to keep us from legally voting in this town in the next election. Ignore those politicians don't hear them; throw them away those who don't back our issues we suffer. Okay enough is enough? Just imagine we need a miracle black folks all those racists in this town, and against politicians that are racists in this town and across North America. Stop complaining and do something about it just keep it up. It is our lives. Stop your complaining you all are the ones that suffer the most in this town. In the next election beware of them. Say God, we made it made a difference now open up those windows no substitute. Defeat those hypocrite politicians. No more rolling over and playing dead. I'M for you, so people can vote government in to keep this country running the right way. Flipping are the parents who view their kids as backwards all the time, because of TCAP final scores the emphasis here on public schools performance. Racial energy has always been the concern of many whites in this society; they are obsessed with it very legal they are and all that junk. Dr. Martin Luther King Jr., wanted to put an end to racial bias, keeping kids from getting a good public education. Amen to that. Racial prejudice even among Democrats has brought it back—reflecting conditions in public school system. Low, I hate it. Give an account of the fitness of top 20% of people grow accustom to that. Bottom line, relevant to your destiny anti-christ has hit Nashville, the Governor and his members in Nashville, peacocks! Tell the news media NBC Nightly News, and all the news media be the best. Watch it on CNN their live coverage. This is no game Republicans are out to get you in Middle Tennessee, even my friends just keep up the good work you have already done. Let them lash out at you many of them will be stepping down, in fact a new revelation beyond racism guilt on all their hands, racial bias top subject. There are people watching every day. Do nothing is the word for the Governor who's proud of his campaign, his issues, defeat them next election year. Republicans ugly they are. Jim Crow racists is alive and well on the other side of town, including their children. I know their stand believe me, they are fake. Do I need to tell you which camp they come from, Beverly Hills this country? Look at it a new development a ballot that works in this county. Your Savior is coming with a brand new election, new revenue. Governor denied knows he is tangible afflicted this time around. Remember the day. Listen to me, freezing hate. I see the authorities they are after you all the time wanting you to give up black people, the track. They are crazy. Stay in control view black people next. Look after me don't give up. I've been watching go independent. I AM your friend. Cut-throat behind it, I view the tongues all their messy business. You are aggressive and merciless in striving for supremacy, that's how I view your behavior. Flipping

## A New Article

the heat is up in Nashville, TN your offense. Help improve in Nashville, your relations I can't. Dozens in the city all kinds don't be upset with me Pastor? At the request know the bible you passed the test a true test. The snakes are up to something been up to something against the black man, or are you more comfortable with the white man extreme, far reaching the country? Say, thank you, JESUS CHRIST you told it right. Don't blame me. You are amazing for frying all those years even independent. Hallelujah. Just pointing a finger you say, it's no evil you are bigot your moral offense. Get revenue this river. All thumbs down view your compass then measure. You could get by with less. Learn it, bothers me raising your capital, while putting a burden on the people; they've had enough everywhere a true reality for all black people make a big difference your organization, you can afford it. You are under arrest. Hear me JESUS CHRIST; total reality for your collection this book a lesson in its self. Daily excuses the help word from me, backwards are your tendencies improve your relationship with the black people do better. Ms. Oprah Winfrey knows a lot of great black people, a lining. Get that just a suggestion public policy? She can make a movie with donations about the youth in this city, and how they are brought up struggling. Kingdom in Nashville, honestly view Oprah Winfrey as one of the apple of my eye, I'M depending on her not viewing racists and racism, and the children you have robbed of a good public education both. Rich my friend wanting to help, not as a Little Richard an entertainer. Love him white folks here in America; view him as an icon cabinet anywhere with joy his presence including the elderly. Rich my friend, and to black people everywhere as an icon with clout; and MUSIC INDUSTRY ENTERTAINERS: respect her authority not dangerous to our society planting your fears personally, your platform in the "Edge Hill Community". I see your schools and all across America, even Alabama, the voices hear her voice Pentecost. She serves me well. Neo-Nazi groups are the same way painting racists pictures, even against President Obama, I have the evidence. Don't take away the African American community its legal right. Now listen to me, for black people everywhere your community and history this evangelist, and across America legal her authority for freedom and racial equality for black people total a reality. The black people not a novelty commentary your regular old Joe, have not been indenture servants hate groups. Racists this Epistle Republican Party rescue across America, for the people. You want my opinion get help. Contacts improve your relationship. I know how that you are. Say, thank you JESUS. The difference for the people colored people, people everywhere Republicans, Democrats as well no more racism. We can fight. Do you understand in the kingdom, God has eyes in the back of his head? Listen, for this country push for a change the purpose. What you have been doing Republicans while you rob the fiscal year, and then you go off and say its conflict. Enough we've had of you. Enough is enough hear that? You are twofold child of the devil. And Pentecost the large group, JESUS said unto me; use this scripture reference without a doubt practiced *MATTHEW* 23:15 the KJV; you all have been doing it a long time. I'M going to teach you all a lesson. Pentecost, believe me. I'M raising up a standard real quick enough is enough. I've got Government weapons looking at you right now isn't this exciting? I'M sure that most of you are watching television right now you did everything right including Mr. Obama, but God will see us through. I'M putting my foot down, "*Oh Rock of Ages, Cleft for me*" (Hymn-Text: Augustus M. Toplady; Music: Thomas Hastings). If you need a weapon, I told you a long time ago use your weapon; the average Pentecost to clear the way, the mountain out of your way. No other way no accident give them that medicine, they went to sleep on him, and don't you know the kingdom. Please don't do that go to sleep; you're larger than life. Is nothing to hard for JESUS CHRIST, our family? You need a weapon make one, you're larger than life. Your debt you caused it against the nation your budget. Increased deficit say, forgive me both chambers not the people. Dirty you're back in the same deficit extending more wealth to the wealthy, while hurting revenue of the masses, even black people. More and more people are getting hurt. Take the elevator up and raise taxes on the wealthy, and lower taxes on the middle class tenants of America, who are funding both houses legally ill effectively. You are heading for a fiscal cliff, a black hole. They are combustible. I view everything JESUS CHRIST the official the argument simple, the answers gross negligence legislation on both sides for Americans. I view all neighborhoods. Give them a headache those Republicans, create more jobs; I've done homework you can depend on me. Things are difficult get the deficit down. First, increase spending revenue for the fiscal year. Cut defense spending budget, it's alright by me for the people pass a bill. See Obama ask for legislation. I'M passing laws on your spending, before you send over the fiscal cliff. Both leaders Republican and Democrats who stand for true conservative values they are onto you. I view both sides. View both Houses, Democrats with these tax cuts, and the fiscal budget, and stop blaming the rest on the people of the United States, reviewing the stats now those Republicans changing fiscal leg. Say, they got their tax cuts suffering the consequences since Bill Clinton was in office. Give them your vote change leg. Now I AM watching you. On the 7th day taking advantage, I watch you shaking your heads 77% vote with the Democrats. Crazy you are filibuster, don't want tax cuts for families, you will ruin the economy. Make the rich pay their fare share, they already have enough. Why don't you? We need cuts. It's a miracle, definitely this example; I speak first hand Republicans, can you handle it Republicans? Pentecost follow me your network. Understand this particular your particular Pentecost, *ISAIAH* 63:1 ... this that is glorious in his apparel, traveling in the greatness of his strength? I that speak in righteousness, mighty to save. / Now here's the truth not a monopoly event rescue us all, your city your people, we deserve it we're all under the gun Black people we're waiting for you your decision a unique possibility. CHRIST JESUS, we thank you us individuals Pentecost. PRESIDENT GEORGE W. BUSH: planned it in the first place the happening. You left the door wide open for us several years ago. It is not a monopoly get out of the way, white people no offense. Drum roll now even black people this side of the branch. You have dealt with enough—those Republicans.

THE IMPACT ON INDIVIDUAL'S ORGANIC URBAN CITY, THEIR HANDS ARE OUT A NEW ADDRESS YOUR CITY

Thus saith the LORD; some of you may recover from the oppressor, you have oppressed my people enough run them out of that house. MESSAGE-ELEVEN O'CLOCK: warfare Republicans, you want war this is our goal. Come with me JESUS CHRIST, it's all about me. Hey pal, now look all due respect for teachers and new announcement, a new package. Metro-Nashville, District Attorney time to give them some medicine, and a little to Metro-Council; all due respect your ass is broken. Now interpret that please. Plead the fifth. Throw the ball hollowing now many public officials, now brethren serving notice. Be prepared, TCAP be prepared see you when you run away, be prepared politics. When you get up in the morning meatloaf on the drum, you may need somebody to plug you up to help you to the bathroom, preachers as well. Buckle up—convenience then can't plug up the fountain, when you go to the bathroom familiar your ass. Imperative that you stop this matter move quickly supreme on your vehicle, on purpose this is a Council damage leaking mileage, I see a lot of water running in that place out of the bathroom. Yeah check this out influence; we're going to have a good time. First of all people get ready listened to my initiative. Check this out influence now buckle up, I've got the keys. *Former House Speaker U. S. Senate your Jim

## A New Article

Crow class and counting, for yourselves I hope you make it. Then in Tennessee, it's almost impossible to make it, Knoxville under bench being interpreted Chattanooga as well. Your service event in any event wasted instant-gram nine millimeter shocking your sugar pie, and things of that nature physical. Thanks, for insulting me. Black folks a miracle your reservation, Pentecost say God help me please. Please rescue me. Oh, I like that car if it was reduced for a fraction of their cost. Say well I could have purchased a motorcycle Pentecost pitiful. "Salesman help me this year value plate buying it did not go well." In the U. S. follow me this night say I surrender before I start, from above unto me Jesus said, JESUS CHRIST *whipping asses* this very minute. Council you don't know I will give you details keep watching the news, News-Channel Five it's special a documentary all you rich guys its free. And on CNN watching and it's free to all. Know the ministry your ass whipping the outer behind it's free. Say that again it's free three-dimension, clue and opening F&M Bank somebody. There you have it, yours truly JESUS CHRIST. I'M watching your job you are a threat. Now don't be ashamed. Women can't seem to get enough of you. Taking a trip think about it. Anybody can still eat breakfast. Having dinner country music, Jacob's brother head thick block head you are. Their on your case people everywhere see their false advertisement. Atlanta knows may function later view the crisis. Her attorney cost him a lot. He withdrew a lot acting a fool no respect for GOD ALMIGHTY, about a drop on your way to heaven friendly hurry read the *ATLANTA CONSTITUTION whole lot going on. Now they are going somewhere else finger pointing saying on the news and elsewhere, "Everything is going to be alright." Take out your anger on him and the Godiva. End up trading personalities their stumbling block. See their recovery. Your name is on the list. LORD, JUST AND RIGHT A MIGHTY SOLDIER, A MIGHTY WARRIOR IS YOU OH LORD! It's just and real. I AM looking context you could do better. Many challenges you say "Our religion sets us apart," outcome no guaranteed your predicament or any other predicament. You have been duped. Heaven is for those that is doing what is right. Are you operating properly Republican Conservatives working from this side, working by the young people? Nobody owns you. For the people view the basic rule from above the exodus of all things, the bonus right now. Let me counsel you this says JESUS CHRIST from above; *REVELATION* 3:18; – From above to that: you say that you are rich, any excuse you are not. Are your robes white dispensed, your shirts that you are wearing? Already providence JESUS loves you. Question: your name is higher on the list your pocket of thinking? Be emotional your drama place to all that, "You say somebody has got to lose, definitely." You feel uncomfortable? Your fist full your glee your weather, you say to that "That somebody loves me," read a piece of paper for your give way. For your crackers it's only been time people independent your nourishment, that is where you are walking everyday right on time shoebox. According to the Bible Republicans, I view you a lot defense bleak. According to scripture I've got their receipt, their number. The recipe imagine that *DANIEL* 5:27 TEKEL; you are weighing in the balance. / And to that view from above, Pentecost I will destroy, things are bleak I see your bleakness, and your weakness, and the Apostolics in Nashville, you can't escape me did you get that your cafeteria, your ministry kiosk standing your university, your power you have lost me your portion? View and then read *DANIEL* 5:27 Thou art weighed in the balances, and art found wanting. / Thank you JESUS CHRIST. Trinity your new record, I'M not playing conclusive your treasure you're hurting people going nowhere, no self-defense, amicable double portion third degree conference. Thank you, JESUS. Still remaining underhanded white people like you. You get the music? I view government amazement as well. We have to move on. Another teachable moment outcome persons there is a public investigation going on now, just starting the investigation with no exceptions. I see the crisis predicament moment things are a mess your substance, I view you extreme. Now here's the possibility the pick you up 11:30, you get the half. Republicans, I hope they change their minds. Their game prohibition cocky is their game cracker jacks solemn their rank and file, their entertainment no crème there. Gas they are. Solution to the Republicans have you heard, we've got plenty to beat you with immediately, an opportunity? Take the businessman private industry flipping, you're ruining their business weak oysters they have become. We've got news, we've got plenty to beat ya'll with your Federal spending that is what you're famous for, ya'll behave. Overseas it is out of balance in Washington D.C., and our deficit over here in America, Republican Party sin takes pleasure 180%. What's complicated about that? A new development home improvement level, the prices just went up driving some out of buying a new home, many are already broke try saving for a new home. We're all are going to be outside. The real complication there might never be enough for the next generation; hear that Washington D.C.? Many will be in the poor house the rest of their lives. You hear me people? Pentecost in Kentucky and half opportunity look at the treasury of this nation. President Bill Clinton, he's the best his administration had a policy eraser Nashville. In Nashville, across the board the Federal budget cut spending, raise higher income taxes on the wealthy Americans. Let that be business income less profits, they sure owe a lot. They take a huge chuck of savings revenue, and come clean. *And in Tennessee the Clinton initiative it paid off brought the deficit down, the economic freeze close to home. We the people we're caught right in the middle of a Federal Income Tax, meet the deadline. We got to stay focus. How about that? We've got to protect what is right. Hear me; tax idea we the weak in this country in capital income the treasury deficit reference our burden, while the great big guys don't pay restitution to the treasury, the Federal Government. The difference of tax freeze of the nation without a doubt on the wealthy of this nation. Cut federal spending domestic spending on the rise, and the rich and famous claim they are lost. Now this is not complicated their economic policy, chicken for the wealthy that do earn mega bucks. Now hear this, he is the apple of my eye his policy not Carl Roe technical, Mr. Obama is approaching two fiscal cliffs. And evolution burn out the banks. Oh thank you, JESUS. Jobs people need them and cut the tax revenue on them, the wealthy need to pay their fair share simple rate of fair tax, flipping are the people in this country. No more Carl Roe. No need of complaining over your revenue, when people are out of work put celibacy on tax allocations for this nation, before we go over the fiscal cliff. The people know about your crazy people, want be back by popular demand guarantee it that's a window of opportunity, for the people and agreement. Take responsibility Democrats as well. It's all witnessed now. I see it all over my fingers. Oh matching! About matching God Republicans, God is matching the right way. The feature you're wrong you will reap what you sow. They are wrong. Thus saith the LORD; *GALATIANS* 6:7 Be not deceived; politically God is not afraid He has an understanding, a record, and a blueprint. God is not mocked: for whatsoever a man soweth, that shall he also reap.), / be pitiful your test.  ESTEEM FOR THUS SAITH THE LORD; GO AHEAD DO SOMETHING I VIEW YOUR NEIGHBORS. GOD IS OMNIPRESENT IN MURFREESBORO TOO. I'M PIPING HOT MAD. Move over Casey learn a lesson your city Murfreesboro, your town robbery. Your trimming is coming just like a garbage dump. You would think I'M selling business. I see his images now I'M telling you children legally who you are, I know who you are. Praise the Lord, rivalry I'm blessed. You cheat abundantly—on test scores. I agree in Middle Tennessee, Christians on purpose you do your dirt now throw that away. I see the evidence white people. Poor Metro Schools they are at risk. Thank God, gifted on Nashville. You brought it on your own selves.

Better give up now an audit. Oh thank you, JESUS. Listen to this metro, review your method and stop. You're not a pill box Nashville School their diet. I know all you've been through. Call a Nashville doctor. DONALD TRUMP: a trump away I AM a witness. You will be successful. Call commercials. I witness other groups. This has got to stop. Listen to me, permanently a big boulder is in your way a double whammy on Metro. Role model Pastors, your congregation, that is deliverance your organizations the young people. Move over theft get them off the cold ground, and then things will be alright. You are God's servants. A new sentence looking unto me JESUS CHRIST, look back we need your help in this matter, think we're stupid. We need a role model. We need new role models in Southern Churches. You Baptist, you hear me? Thank you, JESUS you are a friend. Nobody even cares anymore black people, since integration. We blacks outnumber whites in the South, we can do something. What have you done to settle this, your advantage not their advantage. Waiting for a coin toss? GOD SAID; I AM ANGRY F&M Bank! Take another step for people of all races; too keep pushing for higher education justice for all in this matter your duty common denominator. Weak we have become to other nations in the world. NORMAL: Pentecostals backslide, and the single friend of JESUS CHRIST the Baptist they self inflict JESUS CHRIST, they hurt when they inflict you offend me. Let me explain, Baptist people whitewashes everything they are a mess no pact, they are the queen of everything. Under that remain true they are asleep. I AM A TRUE WITNESS PENTECOST HANDLING ME; YOU DON'T OWE ME KEEP THAT A SECRET, DON'T YOU KNOW THE DEBT IS YOURS NOW JESUS CHRIST. Thank you, JESUS. You are my friend. The latest results shocking, we have a candidate recently making millions caring nothing about why our children's schools are in a predicament, chocolate brown and their babies. Cutting a new resolution for example, big government auto spending make them better, help make them be persistent the government. Give them an opportunity, Mr. Government Official. People we can do better. I will perform my duty. I will be alright. I see the address legal escape. JESUS said; Republicans obedience weak in society in plain view of everyone, created offense cobalt attack see how they run this race it is no accident. A pinpoint hat off to them is how we act. AN EVALUATION: SET UP MINUTES THE CLOCK IS RUNNING 12:00 O'CLOCK A.M., AT THE MIDNIGHT HOUR ....THIRD WATCH. We are desperate obey the LORD; providence on Capitol Hill no one bothers anymore not even the Senate. He tracks your every move rolling down the Delaware River anti-christ. Let us gather here's the Ox, Ox this circle. I've got three words for you; evil-social illiterate. People see you everywhere. Did you get that? Does anybody care in the first place, the people? Benefit people I dare you to work on this to the door. They are literally out to win. I hear laughter believe me people of color, I AM going to walk them to the door. They are like an old refrigerator over a break down in public schools, a meltdown in community schools. Republicans that is for real so many parents have told me so; saying, what have they done to America, the results some have serious issues? Evidently I have to understand remember ready or not their predicament, I will always understand not dirty politics that is why they come to me some need counseling. I told them a long time ago the ingredients heaven.

**METRO NASHVILLE RESEARCH TWO AND HALF YEARS A PROVEN VALIDAITON, GIVE THEM CREDIT THERE IS NO TURNING BACK**

Thus saith the LORD; weighed down. Metro-Government, and the press, Metro-Council elected officials gave to them services, and the consequences we were waiting difficult to find. Problems regular blue collar schools funding all of Metro's allegations,

## A New Article

legally for regular schools funding voting for keeps Nashville's regular school funding, not to be found. You pay property tax, pay gas bill, and your electric bills, keep the pumps rolling everything you pay taxes on. We don't think of the difference cast your vote. Start voting in Middle Tennessee and in Kentucky; be easier than that change your Representatives, a ripple effect—throw away their wine bottle, throw more wine at them at the base. A ribbon effect they just keep spending our money throwing it away. It's like pouring it down the drain, I'M telling you these Republicans they are mean. They are Americans, and they are European Ku Klux Klan elevated money Nashville. We pay taxes now handle that Europeans. Students we pay taxes. Are you in agreement the rich man? We are all in agreement. No more second class. Otter racists, we got class. We are equal class. They took advantage ya'll get on the revenue these Republicans, the belt operation given away to Williamson County their advantage now, enough of that Williamson County. Think about it. You can take that to the bank Capitol Hill. March right on in there make a new Government and City Council for Metro-Nashville as well. Broadcast buffalo no more. Can we mingle?

Hooray—their new year, a new policy. *The President will override, and pinpoint their maximum decision. View more collection income not to fund Metro's Schools properly that was their decision. Now look at their revenue. JESUS CHRIST told me that I'M on my way; I've been staring at it this situation for a long time without a doubt. Eventually our children will get the right kind of school funding—matching dollars from the Federal Government, the perfect solution, and TCAP scores they will go up the conclusion. The operation the real captain, the real architect, the Federal Government trading none a new law passed comfortably, embedded they are in abundance. The ABC'S I meant action hear me the Board of Education in Nashville. Let's hear more games. Wrestling some parents stay up all night making an assessment of their child's future. *And all the Metro teachers in Metro they are not responsible for all the things that have been done to Metro Schools, for years they have been lacking behind everywhere. OTHER OPTIONS: a smoke screen it is just a smoke screen your public interest; show some action quick we have the evidence. Every day you hear them in the hall way, they are looting our educational fund sheer negligence. It's a light bulb moment we've struggle enough, praise the Lord. Your smokescreen our situation, you started to make the rules, bend the rules those Republicans your way for your benefit you're found out. You're going to jail people are tired of it. Complaints against you Federal Law on our side breakthrough significance, it is a breakthrough. Here it comes in the city no more watering troughs Metro's Schools budget established; nasty blockheads those Republicans. Somebody a revolution you won't offend me, bend the rules Martin Luther King did. Are you listening? Here it comes it is your fault. Here's the answer; legally we can win. Try something brand new now your practice Republicans. We need a breakthrough. Who said I can't fix it? Legally Metro-Government back in the day, and Metro-Council two institutions gave to them (Williamson County) services. The consequences every day, I'M telling you difficult problems regular schools funding, for keeps Nashville's regular school funding. You pay property tax. Start voting in Middle Tennessee, and in Kentucky change your representatives a ribbon effect their just spending our money throwing it away. They took advantage ya'll get on the revenue these Republicans operation given away to Williamson County, their advantage. He is looking at the paperwork now, a new Government Ordinance against the Republican corruption government home grown against the President. THE APPLICAION: we need a community leader following the Republican Party, the way they do the black man— the white man. It's time we said yes Democrats, we need a lot of intervention put it all in perspective. They are all racists my perspective, the white man going after his own agenda their program, the white man government in our society being cheerful. The Democrats know the white man has crucified us enough. We need more government to fix it. Our children poor black people against the Clan in our society, that has made it a race issue. They have ruined us financially. We have to fix it to try, and curtail their naming of their own funding budget taken from Metro Government what a trip. Hallelujah. We've got to hustle to keep up with Williamson County no more. *Jurist Doctor Student's: a stress test please help challenge the Republican anti-christ, and their substance abuse take it all the way to the Supreme Court. Hallelujah. We can't afford to waste anymore time. Fight for the rights of African American children, and poor neighborhoods in East Nashville, ABC News help please raking more, and Jefferson Street too receive a quality education assured by the law don't relax. Millions have been wasted already. I have the evidence. Get on board, before it's too late. Fatal recklessness if you don't lawlessness already. We already see a surge of crime. The Board members know. Take it outside for a better solution to the problem, the development of proper funding for Metro; 1600 Pennsylvania Avenue, the White House is a great place to start. They are your pals. Hollow the kids need therapy then we will get somewhere, no breakdown we need some help. Then Jim Crow days will be over for Metro-Nashville Public Schools screw off the top. There is no other solution to this problem in Metro. I'M warning their motive illegal solutions wiped away. There is no other solution to this problem in Metro-Government. I'M warning their motive illegal solutions wiped away. Let's beat them the gang at their own illegal game. Steps say I will take the challenge. Come on take a picture, I dare you to work on this backwards if you don't. Say, I will take the challenge. Funding for Metro Schools was it an accident no, or was it just a chimpanzee cluttering the highway toward higher education distinctly issued for Metro-Government. Show the heart make a difference in your neighborhoods, the victim. Pentecost you need it in your own neighborhoods eviction notice, likewise look the Mexican students as well. We don't need schism enough of that. There is hope Metro, if we all come together. Church what a great idea. Metro going back and forth tally a remake politicians, for the future of our kids fill up the gap lesser, learn your lesson. Amen. You can depend on me JESUS CHRIST the keeper, and then turn around and the Metro, more service adjustments can be made exactly and absolutely, definitely. Hallelujah and amen turn around. Save the house Metro's School Budget. Careful we have got to get something done right away there is evidence, look right away mistake if you don't. It is grueling have confidence, you will get the answer you've been looking for evidence a pivotal moment. We know the cubical event where the election is at, at the poles the poling ground. It's an emergency please help get funding back for our kids. What does it look like Jurist Doctor Students across America, help final notice? There is hope. It is grueling all the way we need your help. It's an emergency please help get funding back for our kids. We know the public wants to help get real funding your insurance agency. The balance is righteous for your engagement.

MY FAMILY GOD CAN FIX IT. A GREAT SCENARIO WE'RE TOP OF THE WOODS THINGS ARE ABOUT TO CHANGE. AMERICAN CITIZENS WE DON'T WANT TO BE A SANDWICH. WHAT'S THE IDEA CITIZENS, THE CLOSER WE GET WE WILL WIN MORE CHALLENGES WE'LL FIND OUR OWN LITTLE PATCH?

Thus saith the LORD; get the picture. The Tennessee value full amount the effect for us, Williamson County and their public school system spasm for Middle Tennessee, when asked treat other school systems like dogs; dirty dumb-ass even their country music, their influence, their conversation. Hail their music low down they are. Legally fully affect legally, I'M telling you. Praise the Lord; we have the evidence. We've got JESUS CHRIST on our side watching out for us, who's working for us completely. Two addresses their drop. Top group what time is it? It is time we were set free let's proclaim it to the Government in Nashville, the NRA even in the bathroom. LET'S MOVE QUICKLY: a special investigation is needed first a new audit. Their teachers got higher cost of living salaries everyone of them compared to Metro equal with benefits, while Metro had a handful a big mistake. WOE, LAMAR ALEXANDER: definitely a friend no. It's an emergency they barely get by they have little funding. Did the masses see and increase? GOD IS ANGRY! **But the masses saw decrease it's a buffer civil lawmakers in their earnings due to a lack of concern at Metro Nashville School Board. *Push for higher teacher salary increase for Metro Teachers. Thank you, JESUS CHRIST. The difference the-none like you today help change our destiny. We earn more in tax revenue Pentecost, we are laden. We need an audit on tax revenue. Show their revenue income, and then ring the bell. Have you viewed white bathrooms, or have you viewed them particular in black and white an opportunity protest? Set your market on isolation Williamson County, and their funding resources potluck is your answer in this area. Nobody wants to be left out anymore see the difference. People everywhere are going to respond to this outrage. Do you want to be horse whipped keep up the good work? I view your sentence like a big brother Williamson County, you're dangerous—whites. Let me encourage you a whole new brother, Congress, new taxes saw to it against serious allegations emerged public forum demanded. ONE HUNDRED MILLION DOLLARS DEMANDED ON THE SURFACE, MORE REGULAR FUNDING UP TO EIGHTY MILLION UPFRONT, AND ACROSS THE BOARD, SHOCKED. They've trampled on Metro-Nashville enough evaluation no debate. Ever heard of redistricting you have favor black people; black leaders were able they emerged to talk about their burden of proof, the lack of funding for their school district, definitely? If you live in Williamson County where are you going next? Stand up and vote if you are hungry for a change, we are going the wrong way. Let me talk to you they have a loophole prove this economy. Let me explain, local schools will continue to rob Metro School System, they are disabled due to integration your journey public schools. If you don't we will continue to be disconnected. We are going to have to wait a long time for proper funding; it will be like looking for a needle in a haystack. Create more funding the best kept secret in town the criminal intent; the kids are in trouble look at their test scores look at it MIKE HUCKABEE, we are not in bubble land and MITT ROMNEY as well, they could use a woman's touch imagine that? There is no comparison easily done. Create more funding bottom line, before we can get anything done in education turn things around, change southern rednecks the option, before we formalize create a quality education for our students black students, brown students, and white students, the average for all students we can afford it. There is a need for it now. Sports figures get more attention than Metro Public Schools on NBC. Publicity specific often we hear a cry this is skinny cracking. We need more transitional lens effectively all around the block. There is a gap that is the gap remove the gap. Mannerism is what we should be standing for, that is and heighten alert. Alert more people young people their advance. We are desperate here in this situation would you agree? Dyslexic we are not. I AM against you. Absorb that. You are warned. Substitute no more just a reminder; reconsider where your funding is coming from. THE MESSAGE TO WILLIAMSON COUNTY: the district school distract ran by Williamson County it's a failure. Your Franklin Special School District lowdown imagine that, eventually was separate created to keep different ethnic races from attending potentially all white individual schools? Curb your benefit. The promotional your game welfare is out. Regard the clan elementary principle stop. The persons created it for minority racism against black people. THE BENEFIT: you are taking from minority recess, and lending it out to other institutions for investment. Black children financial keys for success the ramification, a personal note a great argument come next year its ramification, and leaving them with nothing. Their equal rights afforded them under the Federal Constitution, more equal rights down the road. They qualify legally you are breaking them, taking from the black cinder man. It's a splinter trying to defend it making them give up, they bought it with extreme poverty what is legally theirs, and defending their funding, their resources, and so is the university your special interest. The District Williamson County, your Franklin Special School District was created to keep black people from getting their education. You are taking from the black man what is legally theirs, and defending their funding Nashville's resources. Black people to the community, definitely potluck is your banquets, call the "Red Cross" service advantage, definitely in this area a violation. Don't be a dope head. You say, stay out of our business. Change your mind and return to Metro Government every dollar you took. It's been a long time coming plus much more, and overpayment for robbing our school system of its resources, a really great education for all. We value a good education it is important no junk we deserve. Democrats behind the woods speak you need to; we know all about it, I know all the written word. So bad is our thirst for a good education for Metro School System. DR. MARTIN LUTHER KING Jr., would have found and opportunity to be counted. He would have been leading the way the right way. He would have been going into churches telling the foxes to let my people go, most definitely. Silence is golden; your business owed none to your lack of moral awakening. Congressman kick back the choice is yours. *Praise the Lord, apocalypse of Williamson County School System, and Franklin

Special School District look this way; definitely the sky is falling on. Your free fall taken over by the FBI, sent to take away your right of independence to rob Davidson County, Metro-Public School System, Republicans the head. THUS SAITH THE LORD; HAUGHTY ABOUT IT. THE TIME IS NOW 9:30 P.M. ….SECOND WATCH 9 P.M. TO MIDNIGHT; THE NEXT WATCH EVERYTHING IS NOT WRAPPED UP. PENTECOST, I WILL BE THERE SOON. Your haughtiness engrafted into your society will bend over backwards to repay this debt, tacky going back to the 1980's bench press no more public welfare no more your debt. We are producing the evidence your host God now eager people. The reign of the anti-christ messengers in Williamson County, and elsewhere your days of society's rule is over. Help throw them in jail, CHRIST JESUS. Leave it to Heaven to make a difference no need to think me, CHRIST JESUS already has over and over again. Somebody's present my daughter. Walk right back up the hill like everybody else. Just walk right back up the hill, courtesy the HOLY GHOST JESUS CHRIST. CHRIST JESUS said; try taking funding away from them the Williamson County School, their funding. THE MESSAGE: in Williamson County an outrage you would hear to Metro Public School System to replace their lack thereof. The cry would be so great you would hear the bellowing in outer space. Is this a cancer in maple gardens? Turn a stiff if you will, but catch them. Help us our friends all the black people. A lack of discipline cost us much. They're going to arrest somebody soon. DEAR WILLIAMSON COUNTY: neighborhood people another pep talk, the Federal Government are looking into your school funding from Metro-Public Schools, consequences your robbery; you steal from the majority-people. You have set a record majority funds needed, of destroying their record your people. Radar is up it is on you. We've got the victory poor amputation leaking it now. You can handle it you get it. I AM, your friend. Thank you, JESUS for everything great amputation out of this world, JESUS your

## A New Article

offense. We hope to see you soon in the clouds. SECOND OFFENSE - A MAJOR ISSUE: it is mounting trouble their legal offense for the accuser. Your direction I would seek counsel. Good luck. Cut their big toe off first. Thank you. No problem. I'll be with you. Who won the game JESUS CHRIST did nothing tied? Say Barbara, we are friends. Hallelujah! Incident the police are coming after you, the police are coming not for me, flipping (turning you over), they are like the Coast Guard. They are after you marking you they are for your mess you started. I read the headlines now. For the benefit the service against the people you robbed publicly carried it on, count it your mistake you made your influence it's a jungle out there. No benefit left. Are you listening? Instruments careful for me thank you, JESUS, I cleared my soul. Thank God, for using them. Donation a vacuum cleaner for the future your donation, the government digging people out of the ditches a gravel opportunity this boat legally, this ship for people headed your way that have been abandoned; black people, good people, running the race who will pick you up. The results I smell your fragrance. Your condition you're in a mess your divers are a ton away. You need protection jump on for the ride children. Get on for the ride. I will watch for you. I AM the tailor. Many of you live in poverty a double whammy there. Many of you have forces dragging you down long standing, the ecology, race issues, and poor people. Hindrances just like in the Bible. The ecology, I know how it affects you your families warp minded, blood stained opportunist they are. Many of you are decent. You are trapped social stigma's you're black can't make it out without a good education. Your families are going nowhere. Civil Rights brought you a long way, but poverty has dropped you down lower need a balance more structure, we need it. Change the situation say, I want to go to college, get up early in the morning don't throw it away. You will turn yourselves around get up. Say, I want to send my daughter to college split the tuition you must don't deny it. Get your Associate Degree, then a Bachelors Degree, and a Master's, then a third degree a Doctorate. There are colleges in your neighborhoods TSU. Make a defense build your own wealth. We need more Entrepreneurs, and Doctors. Be above the hate crimes, you can stop that get your education show performance. Go to college create your own wealth stop playing the game. Get your Masters and your Doctorate. Go to school open your own business, even if it is in restaurants-investments, annual income. Take it all in they are dirty keep you servants. Ladies and gentlemen we're not wicked as some has suggested. I know where the wealth is in society even in Michigan, the agency their backup this country. These people are snakes, crooks, they are terrible live off of you greedy public politicians, and public officials waiting in line to grab the silver, their piece of the white pie; that is the point they are loving every minute. Aren't they something?

BURNING

Thus saith the LORD; Don't wait for Islam to be your backup the next president of the United States; their answer that is what the white politicians accuse us of, get the picture? *Republicans are bringing them over to torch the flames. That's what this movement is all about. They are developing a nuclear plant, (a familiar spirit, demons) planning a nuclear attack near Ohio, and near Nashville, with nuclear devices. I have the evidence immediately help. No offense the water is so polluted from the nuclear attack, like a heat wave drowning us all. A nuclear attack they are planning a nuclear attack near Ohio, to destroy customer's homes politicians gave them the lead way just to attack the United States of America in Ohio. Our leaders are helping them doing right now bringing their brand of Islam, to the United States they are mean. Listened, interested a ribbon what ribbon for their wipe out in Afghanistan? The hunted—"I deliver the nigger to be president the black man, and the vice-president, kill the nigger the 44$^{th}$

President of the United States Barak Obama, over Afghanistan." OBAMA DELIVERED FOR THE AMERICANS! Yes he did other group Mr. Obama global chapter. Mr. Obama, be on the lookout go to the source, the power JESUS CHRIST; Hallelujah, your only source their slip up will soon be manifested in Washington look out White House.  *THUS SAITH THE LORD; the Islam community naughty they are.  You're not in soup heaven. People of earth follow me.  Republicans planned this whole thing.  I AM going to a banquet.  Do you hear me?  They are developing a plan, developing an evil plot right now to overthrow our regime people- THE WHITE HOUSE.  Be grateful for my protection already, PRESIDENT OBAMA put it in GOD'S hand.  Be thankful against them with special guest, I'M telling you Mr. President, of the United States of America.  Round them up even U.S. Citizens people like that don't belong here.  They are crazy with a microphone their own agenda.  They will attack U.S. Citizens, even Ku Klux Klan the evidence often surfacing.  They've got guts legally behind them, their always watching Mr. President keep up the good work.   NOW PRESIDENT OBAMA:  is capable of winning the next election I'M telling you.  All the Democrats have to do is go out and vote him in his own party back him up.  Say, come on Barak he is a young President.  Put more Democrats in.  Go to school open your own business ladies and gentlemen; you're not doomed as some would be quick to think.  Plug in make a nickel for yourselves.  I know where the wealth is in society.  Let me help you I AM your friend.  Let me encourage you, underground railway your own opportunity.  Nashville, can't see pass race hello thank you, JESUS.  I'll bet I'M more powerful.  Agreed people?  Operate their religion.  You're headed to Nashville; guess again we're actually in a flip off better back away enough on that I've got the evidence regardless.  Learn how to work excellence.  It's like watching a football game somebody has got to win, be class oriented with high moral, and high academic standards.  Seek jobs with fairness for African Americans, and a high ratio of opportunity of economic fairness. Never rob God. Be fair in your business dealings with another. High standards require greater accumulative. Promote family values among your children quick it's in your blood line, excellence. Help yourselves separate yourselves from drug lords you're spending way too much time with them, monkeys and gang individuals. If you have a meeting with them the issues can be corrected. Here is a pinnacle this laser against them black people, college people then move. Mexicans do it all the time find an apartment by themselves, they are like mosquitoes be more like them in their housing, even just let it go in Los Angeles, there are no excuses for gangs running drugs pushing cocaine, heroin, there use everywhere typical and say enough is enough, I don't want to live like that. They can't take it they know what they are up against every time; let the dogs take their altercation they are thinking that. Ugly to Black people nasty they are to Black people—other people even Whites and Latinos. It doesn't matter every ethnic group feel the same way, the White man does toward the Black man. Can I say something; prejudice. Now what is wrong with that Black people? Asians their race feel the same way drug abuse damaging to their society, the principle Pentecost. How they feel the bad altercation damaging to their society as a whole Saints in Pentecost, their interest the danger. I've done my home work. Drug abuse running heroin in your neighborhood, crack cocaine, and other illegal substances, anyway obliviously it is divers attempt (just pure hatred) to eliminate a major population selling drug abuse substances; everybody knows that is the problem. Through nothing away serve yourself, you must not do that. You keep throwing away the rich man he doesn't care; I AM A WITNESS JESUS CHRIST. It's like you are looking for a needle in a haystack trying to find your way out of drug abuse. Nobody is perfect run from that don't you want something? Even if it is a dump they move anyhow Mexicans and Asians, they know what they are up against, and they have suffered too. You keep ignoring it this fact. Don't be dumb about it. Move somewhere else find somewhere else to live. Where their location a hotel enough a bonus destination, you'd think it was clubhouse where they gather. The Negro, the African American stay and tolerate the drug movement in the neighborhood; backwards. Mortified, move away be like an elephant they move in herds. The African American community, say, we don't want that in our neighborhood. Do something about it you've got overwhelming odds against you already don't take it. There are so many hooked on drugs already Pentecost, flipping keeping it up. There may be a hundred of them in a hotel they merge, they get favor they move away from the system your black ghetto. They are thankful; they are not pitiful like some of you are they want more revenue; they will say we're not going to stay here. I'M trying to give you some more wealth. It's in their home blood they want take it anymore in their development, I've been observing all the young people, Spanish speaking culture how they operate. *Move away from Black Muslims people use them. You will hear more about them move away there are other places you can live. These groups they are drug trafficking as well, people don't want that in their White neighborhoods. *Move from the ghetto look at what you're up against; move away from those kinds of people, tip-move away from them be wise protect yourself and your family anyhow, my point of view or you're be screaming murder in the neighborhood all the time, and don't let your kids hang around them after school those people are dangerous. Get it? In Black ghetto neighborhoods trafficking, you've been battling them for a long time. They are drug lord's activity people everywhere, surety that is where most of the crime is in teen violence. You don't want to get caught into that illegal activity in society, alright in Black neighborhoods? Older folks know can't stomach it trust me I know. Talking you're headed in the right direction safety. You have to run away from drug activity, and gun violence, throw that gun away be independent. For example, they are equivalent to practice random acts of violence. Don't do that get a job dummy. Ugly they are promoting their own kind of wealth. Many will be locked up for good, when this nation turns around. All they want is your money. No excuses anymore the difference: Crimson is coming to carry them away. Biblical principles truths will be taught everywhere including the White House, ignored long enough. Discipline yourselves to become structured in society. Always put God first never leave me out. Thank you, JESUS. An infection never look down your nose at the frost follow me, early rises accomplish more during the day. They protect themselves from poverty. Cultural deceit will fade away it is irrelevant. Never look down at someone who is uncultured it could have been you. Be brave about it. Decide what is good with the word of God. Banish from your thoughts it has got to be this way. Know your case, and transfer yourself put it into action. Don't be a diversion. Never leave me; I will always be there to help. God's grace, His favor, own it a quality a good recipe for success it's a blessing on you. Put away all foolishness the African American community. Sad, can't get your education. Team up on that. I can see through that can't pick you out; back up stop you young boys forces they are. Some say just do your best. They are stabbing you in the back these people. I know you are hurting isolated dangerous. Low down they are, I see the criminals' criminal minds great attitude (For the battle is not yours, but God's - *II CHRONICLES* 20:15). / For Nashville, I will fight your battle. I'll help you. We're talking about a moving train fast approaching your class indignation. For the conclusion, your influence you are a liar. You can do better. This edge for the children, for citizen's influence, for people wherever you are. For this record caring pertinent for the future, the issues without a doubt celebrate me. Your influence has died. You are under arrest now by GOD ALMIGHTY. I am just a servant legally accomplished. TEMPLE: My friends Jewry don't laugh; are you watching we need help now and more in Arizona? CHRIST JESUS said; I see your arrogance with regret I furnish you with a lot. No man is an island. Some of you may have a heart attack, the rest jumping out of buildings many Jews as well, when they've lost everything. Go ahead live on patio furniture Jews everywhere. LORD, your influence give them a bath by me. I see your authority looking wherever you want your eyes to see, you are OMNIPRESENT everywhere. I'm so glad. Always for ever present you are peeping nowhere. You know all things knowing all at all times and places, definitely. Protect me LORD legally, I see a group of them watching, questioning. View your hands upon this situation. By the Bible I do live, I read it. I am unloading on to you my sleep passes, but I will remain calm. Middle age belly have I now so give me an edge for everything, before time is left. Your influence always will I see quick on everything. I dearly love thee Oh LORD JESUS CHRIST, my strength for everything. Yes, we are friends. Remain calm. Just listen and work. Remember me and your duty be comfortable. I AM your Master, and His Excellency the person JESUS CHRIST. My strength my supervisor agreed, I AM a witness. God bless you. Remain calm now let me do the rest. The police they're not after you. I will not complain this time. Let me explain, a mountain glitch no icicle threat let the Post do the rest. Your duty keep it up. Universal every day I will appear humanity. We have a good understanding this time. Support me vigorously. Acknowledge me always. Let me encourage you, I will be there to help. Support me JESUS CHRIST, there is no getting around it follow me everybody that is simple.

BREAKTHROUGH A WHOLE NEW BEGINNING, A NEW MORTGAGE LOVE THY NEIGHBOR. THUS SAITH THE LORD; A NEW BEGINNING NASHVILLE, FOCUS ON ME. MANY DON'T WANT TO SEE THAT IT'S AN EMERGENCY ROLLBACK ARGUMENT, AGREE? A BRAND NEW BEGINNING

*The Original Barbara Payne*

FOLKS, ANNOUNCEMENT: WE ALL HAVE UN-DESIREABLES A NEW UNDERSTANDING. TRY UNDERSTANDING TIME TO IMPLEMENT. IMPLEMENT NOW OR THEY WILL BE SAUSAGES. MAKE OUR SCHOOLS BETTER ITS RACISM. RACISM CAN DIVIDE THE WHOLE FUNDING—THE TEA PARTY. MOVE REAL QUICK BEFOE MORE VIOLENCE OCCURS. PEOPLE HAVE NO JOBS. LOW ESTEEM EVERYWHERE PEOPLE HAVE LOST THEIR JOBS, OUR OPINION IT'S JUST RIDICULOUS.

Thus saith the LORD; a new beginning, a new series, don't fall asleep single individuals, absolutely. Say, help that is what I measure you by. This is a reference your average flipping middle class people individual, Catholic people as well, been looking after you for years with all due respect. Say LORD, I think you. Blood is on your hands. I'M ready to cut you off after a week. I've been viewing you for thousands of a year's it's an outrage the way you carry on. Can your group imagine? Say, hallelujah, JESUS CHRIST is my friend. The group you ought to be glad about it your movement have torched people since way back when, good people put in chains for worshiping GOD. Read *MATTHEW* the gospel: the apostle he was an apostle of mine and what about me? All those years you never give up. I take my hand off of you and your devotion your wrestling now a typical. Glutton you are. A whole new program, I'M going to let a snake eat you alive, penalty. Prepare for it specifically meatpacking now brace yourselves. Pentecostal's you want to stand all by yourself, your collection plate is ready. Listen, Pentecostals I know their game. I rolled the paper your department you are individual backwards. Wait a minute backwards confession guess what, and your parents too your game. Don't tell me catastrophe novelty recipe, and then you danced the crowd your barn wandering hanging friends; throw the curve ball backwards unidentified objects blowing up a novelty way back then, lucrative growing up curve ball to each individuals task his own,

## A New Article

Pentecost your personality your grandchildren as well big loser Pentecost. Individuals with a passion your operation you eat from the same cupboard, the same meal. Did I open somebody's eyes? Say we are friends, people that discriminate against monitoring central the black man; let me explain it to you each individuals hollow is that wisdom, signed now JESUS CHRIST. I hope I AM opening somebody's eyes to various other reason, let me explain my point of view. Chocolate a new possibility say, open your eyes your character we the people are asking you. Obey GOD. Know that GOD rules. This is the way it happened, the curb you blame us, your shot extent your *neuro* abnormality, antecedent complicity, your Monroe Doctrine can't move one way or the other that weakens alive in the basement. Open your mouths State Senators doctrine a thermometer. Let me explain, officially I'M in the middle your profession of this argument. Don't be stupid grow up individuals put in a little practice people. Say, I oblige you're very negative, you'll be out there all by himself. The Keeper beacon a whole new campaign legally all by myself I've got connections face it. Go ahead face it put the brakes on it love thy neighbor as thyself then apologize, have compassion. Say, forgive me for afflicting. We've been struggling with this for a long time. Can't block anymore you don't have the right. We must seek compassion. NAACP where are you pointing a finger? Say, you will look after me NAACP. Say, I accept. Racism nobody can see it will no longer be tolerated in the House Of GOD, you are offensive. Do you copy? I told you that a long time ago. You are growing and there will be more in the population your mothers and daughters taught you better Jewry as well, or you will feel the backlash, because we come from the same equipment. See our present President I did it. No wonder you want baby setting for your collection of racial indo-crescendo's. You people are ignorant very insulting. Racial people the undertone of racial lies you are all king. Give God a hand clap of praise acknowledge Him. He is King absolutely.

Because you are splitting the churches every one of you make a difference. Highway robbery if you don't I have the legal edge. I have legal people ready to fight? Listen, these people are people too, you have no right to discriminate against them. Look at Arabs how they hate you. Do you want me to catch one of them to legally for the next President dark horse? This is a grant I give you. NAACP knows it well, Black people talk to GOD. I will burst your bubble of iniquity. ANOUNCEMENT: your Temple is long overdue in the Temple for a second phase of Jewish purifying. These are different people black people a group of different people they have children too. They can walk ahead of you whenever I give them favor. Distinguish them make a difference white and black in the slums, they need help. Author and finisher of all supersede each and every one of you. Think it not strange that I ladies and gentlemen can give them resources far out seeding your own. Make a difference Jewish Christians give a message put aside your animosity, and humble yourselves making a difference in some Christian's life. Ends-Worth your destiny you are amazing your right, your version, your value, your own without thinking of others. Evil incident you have become. THUS SAITH THE LORD; ENSWORTH SCHOOL is privately funded amazing, by the Federal Government used Metro Funds as well. Government funds built THE ENSWORTH SCHOOL: Metro funds yes, federal funds this is important. Hallelujah. BELMONT: cut the racism out or are you still arguing GRANNY WHITE PIKE as well? IT'S ABOUT ME JESUS CHRIST? DAVIDSON ACADEMY their district, I pulled you out of the dirt you are my friend say, thank you, JESUS and have never regretted that I did. Sources have come to you seeking a new avenue seeking your help, but you barred them from the entrance. Black Brothers pour their heart out to GOD, the difference do you? Seek yee first the kingdom of God, imagine that JEHOVAH-JIREH: (*GENESIS* 22:14) your provider it is official. I AM JEHOVAH-NISSI: (*EXODUS* 17:15). The LORD is my banner. But watch me secure others to answer the call to your brotherhood. "You have got to be kidding me you say, or we will hear the backlash." John Lennon, died before he could cry for mercy from heaven. JEWS have come a long ways you blame all for crime. Your destiny threatening to put more white men crooks in the Oval Office I regret that. There are purchasing blacks many African Americans, veterans, great role models in the black community that would meet your approval, the government's approval. Tunnel them into your home environment be a friend wish them well. I know some now that desire to see Jews, and the African Americans get along to a greater degree. They are striving now don't snob your nose up at them. Get along they are your kinsmen as well. Sisters are always reaching out to help the situation, when are you going to change and do better? Bleak moment in history, when you *yellow-tithes* bought you nothing remember civil rights again, you suffer the same discrimination working against you. Your kinsmen manage to soften the blow of hardship against white supremacy groups.

WE NEED A BREAKTHROUGH A GOOD EDUCATION. THEIR ANGLE SO POLITICAL EVERYBODY THE KU KLUX KLAN AND OTHER DANGEROURS HATE GROUPS, WE ARE AFFORDED U.S. CITIZENSHIP THE DIFFERENCE TO PERFORM. THEY ARE GUILTY YES; WE ARE WEARY WITH THEIR HATE GROUPS PENTECOST, NAUGHTY THE HATE GROUPS WITH THEIR MESS EXTREME THAT IS WHAT WE ARE FACING. YES, WE ARE WEARY THE USUAL OUR GOVERNMENT THE ESTABLISHMENT WE GO UP WE GO DOWN, PENTECOST THE GOOD NEWS IS GIVE US A BREAKTHROUGH POLITICAL EXTREME, THEY GIVE US A HEADACHE. WE HAVE EXTREMES EVERYWHERE. BAD NEWS THEIR EVENT DON'T BE AFRAID THE OPPOSITION, THEIR GATHERING SAY LORD DELIEVER US THEIR

OPPOSITION, AND THEIR RETURN EFFORT RECUIRTED. THEY KEEP STIRRING UP THINGS GENTLY. THEY HATE US; RENEW US AND PRESIDENT OBAMA, THE RETURN TAX MONEY OWED OUR NEIGHBORS AND THIS TOWN NASHVILLE AND THE SURROUNDING CITIES THE PEOPLE.

Thus saith the LORD; we are over-comer's people did you know that what a privilege. But we have the coats groups we wear during the civil rights era, and the march on Washington during that difficult time; *John Kennedy died, and so did Dr. Martin Luther King, Jr., on their back. People of mine lay something down, oh absolutely. We are kin did you know that? The alternative you want to know what is happening, thank you, JESUS. Open up right now. This time groups lay a shout out to them, even Democrats. Groups during (throughout the entire time) don't be offended like the clan, and their money, we've wrestle with that enough. During the civil rights era we wrestle with many issues addressed putting them all together for this country adverting issues saying, "I'm getting burned" never stopped the endeavor then like it didn't President Abraham Lincoln, who was my friend. Had it not been for them where would America's resources and destiny be around the world, just a rumor granted and argument in the street needing new construction shingles, a window blocks knocking out windows no Home Land Security to protect anyone, not even in Dallas a true epic. We've got evidence, gangs no other way to describe it no Halloween saying Norwegian, let's make a wish to JESUS CHRIST, your ballistic vintage revealed against us in this Country. We have the big-proof colored people been watching it a long time, even talking on the phone the messages. A different attack this is the foot saying, big time African Americans make a wish-brittle, or follow the incumbent their record. The average black man saying, "The white man to that level of glass slipper we are peeved, the beast racist's they have deprived us enough." Maturity saying from above to that, we can't hold up the racist's battle continuing nor a Republican, their list enabler the weak of society think the impossible on the record on his honor. In the meantime an apology your part, Blacks they would like it for the African Americans—the settlement, enjoy it while you can. Desperate are people of the south at this moment to have an improvement in race relationship superficial, absolutely in race relationship the White people. Yes, this is true completely Pentecost, if you ask me. Don't forget Catholics take a look at yourselves. Facing it the upper class all Catholics, your encounter with your neighbors the residents, we are merging. Unfortunately Catholics, then you can see how others feel. Thank you, JESUS CHRIST. Roosevelt and the Governors they are friends. Disgusted they are average black man dear JESUS CHRIST, they are in relationships with devil- man the average black man. Initially lay something down, please remember the other side. Before you of yourselves be careful your camp individuals. I'll be frank okay, about yourself better watch yourselves enjoy Judaism your camp your services? Pentecost don't be afraid. Soon they will be hunting Pentecost, I'll be frank that is what they are after your voice zero; white supremacy are behind it they are after the black man, Indo-Euro politics against the black man. Listen, President Obama, I'M telling you Pentecost don't throw them away Pentecost in this country, ugly it will be. Finally times are different now don't be afraid, your preachers in Pentecost cover you and advantage. The Cadillac preacher's globe hoping, preachers preaching public to the world they have no choice. Pentecost there is a difference, Black people have been done low no matter what the cameras are saying. Guess what is amazing it is an amazing sight seeing how they help the people; they all run after me. Crazy some of our white brothers will say, even country music. They go around the entire world working for JESUS CHRIST, pitiful how some of them live. I have the evidence just on the move liberating many to justice being frank, the hasten for

God black preachers, and white Pentecostal preachers, lifting the veil from off of the eyes of the white driven section say, amen Pentecost exactly, definitely. They are liberating around the world handling their fish everywhere just their regular message the pulpit, the chosen, of this world thou afflicted, and often misused could be absolutely prevented pastors if you get my understanding Elders? Take me serious help more dozens need your help, you are comfortable Pentecost. They are afflicted help those people those people elder people, so help the poor people Catholics as well. You act like crazy people. This is the difference welcome, ya'll are welcome. They are saying will you come to dinner without houses, preaching the gospel of JESUS CHRIST to millions, preaching justice making a difference. There isn't but one justice, imagine that Mr. Speaker. GOD'S justice for all hear the LAMB'S. These Republicans and Democrats, blacks they don't care about them in other countries just millions, believe me JESUS CHRIST. Pentecost their relationship to God, serving people in advance going through serving other countries. That in perspective go to Africa, some horrible situations not enough funding God saying, I'M depending on you, watching them from heaven giving honor to whom that honor is due, not enough money on their side finally by themselves, trust me. I AM watching, Pentecost that is your answer. Amen. FALL CREEK: watching them through difficult situations like a regular prison what I like about them, exactly not wondering sneakily running around with no clothes on, buck naked in public. My LORD! Hallelujah. Look up proclaim many. They are thankful to have been born human beings legally Republicans in this hemisphere the USA. Dominate the USA when they hit the U.S. soil again. Nashville, when they come home many need counseling, definitely when they come back to the United States just thankful to be worthy. Candid they are about their challenges the battles they go through around the world. Challenges they are amazing they look out for me every angle, I know their value true pioneer. More are strengthening they are liberating believers, on hand with their relationship with me GOD. I put my trust in them totally, I give them faith. This is America Pentecost Euro-people, and other people they are a blessing Pentecost preachers. They are moving forward in their advancement creating more justice streaming down politics rapidly are Pentecost. For GOD'S sake, they are not a wild goose just laying their egg; anything can go down in Judah, they have the love of CHRIST, marching forward with messages of JESUS CHRIST, given an opportunity to help get jobs to those people everywhere. How lovely they are fortunate you are to have them Mr. White House, (*ROMANS* 10: 14, 15-trust me); go after them in trust next election will prove their character no joke believe me. I don't care what the black film of the Republican Party says, trying to defeat their purpose to them it's just politics searching, now imagine what would happened without them. Oh incidentally, for the curious Pentecost talking about Pentecost making a difference that's the kind of people they are Pentecost, not crowd pleasers, not drug people, they are not coconut experience. Pineapples is that what you want not experience wheat? They love you Mr. President, wish you the best. Ten o'clock, the message for Pentecost from the Keeper of the universe: even the Republicans read the book that I rose again in the book. Their book their bible, Keeper of all with no afflictions has no function. THIRD HOUR FLAVOR: JESUS CHRIST HIS DOCTRINE; [THIRD HOUR . . . . . 9 A.M. TO NOON]. Nashville, Tennessee the Government of your watch. HARRY BELAFONTE: knows that he's part of me you know? Black people your friend they are your friend be concerned. The people perfect their watch not bothered with politics and all that mess. I'M done with politics all those lies get me? Get the cleaners out. The Bishops, regular done away with politics quite frankly they are my friend no more sleekness. It's time to say, like Pentecost not crowd pleasers young man. Your course for me do not act oblivion, I'M giving an opportunity even way down south, you hear President Obama, believe me that I rose again operating on a different channel than the devil? GOD help you if you don't, the second time around. Pentecost they have never been afraid of worship for the country, an opinion of JESUS CHRIST.

THUS SAITH THE LORD; TO THE PEOPLE CATCHING OUR HOUSE ON FIRE THINGS WILL EMERGE IN NASHVILLE, DECORATED IN HEBREW SET YOUR HOUSE IN ORDER. I VIEW YOU EVERDAY POLITICANS. DON'T FORGET ABOUT ME YOUR ANSWER. I REMEMBER WAY BACK IN THE DAY SEND A FRESH ANOINTING. YOUR MISSION, RAISE SOME FLAGS FOR THE COMMUNITY. I AM GOING TO TAKE THE COVERING OFF OF SOME PEOPLE. SAY, HALLELUJAH NASHVILLE, WE ARE GOING TO SEE A WHIPPING HELLPING PEOPLE GET AHEAD, ALL KINDS OF PEOPLE BLACK PEOPLE IN NASHVILLE. SO LET THEM RUN THE RACE ALL PEOPLE.

Tonight after the midnight hour JESUS CHRIST our Lord spoke to me and he said; he had a major difference the turning point. *I have a secret to tell you privileged are you. Look at what I'M going to tell you, a couple of things. Privilege for me golden a turning point. Get your pencil and write all of it down. It won't be on me people Pentecost. I'M going to tell you now. You are my servant, legally you are forever. I know you personally. I've got things to tell you. I've been viewing you a long time. I dearly love you LORD. Say, it once again. I dearly love you, oh Lord. MESSSAGE: battling a long time still suffering you are a prophet unto me; the rest of my life, Middle East as well span the globe. You're a Wonderful Counselor you are. You are a great man Son of God. I never want to go back, the intended a complement. Never let me down your answer. I see things on the highway essential to the betterment of mankind, the results your betterment your kind the enlargement.

Got those pencils follow me, write these down please write? I am a Christian saved by God's good grace. You own that for a life time. Are you ready, outline? You've said enough leave it that is enough. I don't mind. You change your mind. I will show you get your pencil. Be ready. Next I recorded. Don't drop that book again. It's amazing. Get your pencils. Ready? I view from the fire engagement, when He comes to talk to me a new fresh revelation, a pinnacle. It's not about you a new measurement draw closer to God. Pinnacle, it's about God His services, and His redemption for all a life line. Oh absolutely, His grace. Regular finger pointing instructions, I don't want to go there. Now Hear!

THE INFLUENCE THE PROMISE LAND

Thus saith the LORD; regardless so many things we agree upon, there is hope for tomorrow at last, the negative your fruit box. Trust me principle in everything you do. Take me friend principle I have a better offer. You got the stamp all you did was nailed them my friend Pentecost. Waiting for the pillow look private school now look where it got you, your power ridiculous. Quality action needed quickly no more roughen around. Get the point already? Help my kid's downtown it's a mess. Send a telegram okay? Oh thank you, JESUS CHRIST. THEM (those) idiots-executives Civil Rights needed to the public get the point? The funding provided for Metro-Nashville Public Schools are pretty bleak, things here in Nashville are looking bleak, Government here in Nashville, typically hateful. Yes they are. Open that door immediately! *The evidence, I have the evidence due to the past puppet; it's a male Pentecost okay no doubt about it, white male culprit not a black person. He's a genius. Yes daughter. **The guy who affected it his name *desperate stupid navigator impromptu, didn't have the guts to come forward thru the system he committed a crime. For that moment was working at Metro-Nashville Council Seat, courtesy a politician. *MR. PRESIDENT: elected come and break this up, come and whip them this time they are performing. Politicians we are affected, those devils no doubt about it. Oh my gosh, big finger pointing including F&M BANK, only the announcement Williamson County. *The Antioch that is a problem the offer, I'M sending the ammunition. I've been watching you the agency. *Hay DR. REGISTRAR, you're leaving. Don't you know? Carry on your legal right publicly elsewhere, complements of JESUS CHRIST. Say that one more time, the emphasis add closure no more nastiness. Change the situation many are destitute. You have nearly destroyed them. *Now legally the group business as usual, politicians their dream world municipality achievement call it robbery. Job incentive the bones of it. Public construction on behalf it happens all the time for free it enables us. See CNN for free we are threatened our municipality, they think we're all on drugs those politicians we're just disgusted. Their pocket encouragement invent just for spite legally, true. Please come and help us here in Metro. We need a miracle, a restitution needed to help our program. It happens all the time trapped. A new budget program created—through racism backing it. Now guess what we all know that. See their appointment agreed disaster. Motionlessness now let me tell you in the meantime we are threatened; we are making different arrangements. You watch it the ball will flip okay? We will get them back people, our adversary already done the unusual evil at that. *Their municipality created from Federal tax dollars. Call it racism! For the people black and white, our Metro School's budget principle Federal dollars was given black people our local—a University and now we're naked Metro's school budget, but not theirs in Williamson County. I'M naming no name to Williamson County get it? March then we will get results! *THUS SAITH THE LORD; MONEY FROM OUR METRO'S SCHOOLS BUDGET GIVEN TO OUR NEIGHBOR IN WILLIAMSON COUNTY, THEY ARE SO ZEALOUS, FOLLOW ME NOW? *^WE NEED A MIRACLE.

## A New Article

What an incentive continued it has trap people backward for years a memorial their memorial, and then things went haywire here in Metro in the mist. Greedy they are they did that to Metro shocked. *Our families Black and White we set up crying pitiful, and scratching our heads and un-imbalance going nowhere the budget lost believe me our budget, downtown weren't aware okay? Get me? COMMENT: dispersion back – please note Pentecost and Brentwood. I found a needle under your bed. School Board in Nashville, action finally here in Metro-Nashville Public School System it was no accident. Can you replace it? *Simple fenced: they fenced much Pentecost elected officials: that is why so much came up missing from their budget the Metros school's budget in Nashville, they committed a fraud accounting knew that all alone technically this year as well; they're doing it all across the Country this is very important, view it Democrats people ought to know that about stolen money. That is the bones of it here in Metro, unbelievable. Guilty they are! THUS SAITH THE LORD; THE BOARD THEY KNEW WHAT HAPPENED TO REGULAR REVENUE! THAT'S A NEWS FLASH! By the way hear more testimony, I'll tell you all about it. You ready Pentecost? Breakthrough Pentecost, they got witnesses here in Metro at this point in time in Metro-Davidson County. Let me make it very clear yes, a substitution alright here in Metro? Negative our schools budget here in Metro down the drain, a double freeze hurt poor Nashville. *Technically, let's beat the ordinary man will give them a freeze. Pity me a common man, white man these people give you the yellow freeze zero while we are still struggling with a nightmare. Straight-shoot the word; the big establishment don't care and then zero balance in principle nothing. I've got news I'M telling you robbed Metro's Schools. I'M telling you their appropriations (Metro's) Pentecost not lost. The big ones money yes! Designed you need to do the math. Enough unfreeze the revenue money here in Nashville. The capital budget money plus interest

School Board, before you get a whipping. The direct hit meaning basically saving your neighbor's budget in Williamson County, by authority their education application backup. Locally here Pentecost it was backroom ambush the happening. Dummies part of the plan local politicians and the Mayor together. In Williamson County the city, we are heavily armed against the city officials in Williamson County. Local politics the lead a small town problem, a blanket for their budget stole from Metro-Nashville urban by authority. We pay taxes government. We are paying for it this season. They are having a field day, their advantage. They are comfortable, while we fall by the wayside. We thought it was an addiction Nashville. They are the alligator to Metro's School budget, it's just that simple. We're going to their funeral next, is my hope's desire. The old ones "I can deal with the emotion." We here in Metro can see under that bridge their budget, do the simple math Federal dollars. CALL EMMANUEL: we need and explosion yes, we need and explosion. Thank you, JESUS CHRIST. We need a cleansing. We need an Upper Room explosion. *Corruption in the State Government. Corruption covered their fence Mr. President; a slip up they have made President Obama, and Pentecost. They don't have it fenced so high. Welcome to their dream world. Where is it now Metro's State Budget appropriation lost to integration? The number of people didn't want it that way. You have to think their social status changed, they didn't want integration in the city. What's wrong with these people their adjustments. Anything is possible; listen to me I'M telling you anything can happen its part of the American dream. Our dream people blended. By the way the African American may blow them away this side back to "Disneyland" the person JESUS CHRIST. Their dream keep them down its part of the haves and have not's. They know where they all come from, their descendants as well growing up in the fifties the subject. We African Americans are finally getting an epiphany with no dismissal, showing our value to the rest of the world each public accomplishment to the rest of the world. Yes, we are marketable our accomplishments with measure. We have value unnatural feats accomplishments saying, we deserve it getting a good education pointing you in the right direction so say the experts. Get ready with a stick of lemon, definitely your agency allocations peeping, and the open definitely. Ungraded United States Republicans engineered, and Federal Government, break it down people a study the intent a social welfare class engineered servants. Our branch monkeys they think we are, but things everything are looking up for black people everywhere. THURGOOD MARSHALL knew he was the king of integration. Hallelujah. I can hardly wait. Follow me now? Many are complaining from Metro-Nashville on their budget. I'M going to speak to the governor, what a difference a wild card the question. How about the general public "we are desperate no red carpet deals for Metro." This is an emergency granted. The whole purpose understated a pinnacle, a memorial, absolutely surely their big intention advantage from big Davidson County, you do the math okay? Terrible appropriated should have brought Civil Rights issues legally against them in Franklin, a lawsuit. NUMBER ONE: THE PRINCIPLE TO START WILLIAMSON COUNTY, FRANKLIN SPECIAL SCHOOL DISTRICT, SOMEBODY SHOULD HAVE RAISED A QUESTION IN THE DISTRICT. THE SCHOOL'S CHANGES A MESS, I WONDER WHY REPUBLICANS, DEMOCRATS AS WELL? We're ya'll asleep filtered? Our classrooms are overcrowded way overcrowded. We're taking it one day at a time. What are you going to do about it Williamson County, we need a breakthrough for convenience sake it's a hazard chronically way overcrowded. Metro's budget needs rescue now. For GOD'S sake help fix this mess now. Dozens knew about it understand Pentecost? Open up the door place wide now. DO YOU HEAR ME GOD ALMIGHTY: just speak out Metro Council can do the rest follow me? Put your emotions aside in this matter the group.    THUS SAITH THE LORD JESUS CHRIST; family and friends the *Otter* people, the worst with your webbed feet your irrigation naturally LAKE PROVIDENCE BAPTIST CHURCH: let me tell you something negative. Now listen to me, Matthew gentlemen, this is ridiculous you know better we are the majority. The argument it is amazing, epic the final conclusion. Another epic you are the *Otter okay? So be prepared to the people exit means a new episode for blacks. That's all I've got to say. We are going to have it out can't keep malt liquor out of your church; your big shots your reputation at home close your mouth. You've been caught once; undergraduates know what I'M talking about. Read the book the big shots, before you get a whipping. Haven't you notice fraud your special interest? The facility the exit of public school funds in Davidson County, read my counsel the dent incredible people. LAKE PROVIDENCE CHURCH: home disaster for the future, for us here in Davidson County from the politicians their neighbors. A miracle; check this out open house Williamson County. Say Dr. Registrar, their local they need surgery their school district. We didn't rob them and their district Mr. President Obama. For no good reason now we are paying higher taxes for their debt tax that was their purpose. Their loop-hole money allocated, and what do they have looking at a palace Williamson their leverage, their brand common here in America the agency? They now dunk a big foolish resolution can you imagine that clear politics by design here's the details early on in Middle Tennessee in Nashville, TN. We need NAACP help organizations voices ultimately, definitely both houses politics their appropriations, and the University project their hiding behind like a museum for convenience this is a huge project government appropriations government tax dollars their toy leaving a lasting impression millions of public dollars, our dollars. THE STATE REPRESENTATIVES: EVERYDAY PEOPLE OF THE GOVERNMENT, LIVE LIKE OTHER PEOPLE THOSE ARE THE BASES AFRICAN

## A New Article

AMERICANS IN NASHVILLE, PEOPLE WERE TAKING A LOT OF PUBLIC MONEY ALLOCATED FOR METRO'S SCHOOLS, A BIG BUNDLE FEDERAL DOLLARS FROM THE COUNTRY. MORE THAN A DOZEN OF ELECTED OFFICIALS WERE INVOLVED IN IT. Politically no bumblebee we come out smiling others can't. You can tell all your friends, most definitely regardless the people get the point no embarrassing our school's funding here in Metro? Does that answer your question? Roll call on their budget, you guy's we all pay taxes legally this is an outrage we pay taxes the foundation.   Help me JESUS CHRIST, to draw the line so that more people can help against these Republicans. It was founded their school budget design a group of people being pretentious, obviously Metro. I'm not picking on you our tax dollars expense. Now look at Metro now.  *Ten million dollars of our budget people of church, went to our neighbor's camp—Williamson County from Metro Davidson County people, burning Williamson County business annually. They robbed the schools thanks to Republicans, *upper crust. What a burden we are in.   Look in hard places President Obama. It will not be tolerated. Their blueprint a fact; take a look at it and their makeup, and budget, and its design Charter Schools as well especially: a big *kick back.* Send our condolences. The recipe keep a role over an executed resolution by elected government officials. They have no argument. Don't be upset with me. The district schools Public School Education money, and the University their emblem on this network Metro-Nashville, Davidson County the Republicans framing it. Now we are not covered amazing we lost our revenue. The alligators got it all. Soon it will be hurricane season in Metro-Nashville Public School System, their funding, their system its director. I live for the hurricane immediately. Apparently private funding detected came from somewhere. Government officials locked the doors on Metro from getting their money, upper crust did it like magic guess what they are the *culprit? The issues no defense they have robbed

Metro, and the Country, the people these elected officials politicians. No more stumbling blocks for Metro-Schools, Charter Schools as well the people degraded relieve our tax burden. Move quickly our kids need the help. Framework Metro Council busy bees, I see a lawsuit in Nashville no beating around the bush. Stop them from getting it. Congratulations on your networking people guess what lawyers will take it, amen. Enough excellence a new resolution go eat out of the same trough. We're crossing you. You don't have to kill each other they will. Won't they GOD, your Excellency? THEIR EMBLEM: you meet the people everyday no pretentious. You can make a difference go ahead and write. I've got your back. You are covered by me a single weapon. Some may have a heart attack. You my daughter on the other hand are covered by me that is your answer. It cannot be repeal by me. You are not a criminal. You are covered by me personally. Multiple cities are covered by me, their philanthropist, JESUS CHRIST. See the rest of the story by me. Amen. We aren't going to accept it anymore. Poor Nashville City Schools Davidson County a day branch delayed family. What happened to the money given to the district?

## WILLIAMSON COUNTY PERPETRATORS MANIPULATIVE DONE, A GREAT SECRET ONE IN A MILLION

Thus saith the LORD; on F&M BANK. Pentecost, *perpetrators F&M BANK legally took the money investors not their money coming out of Federal Tax Revenue our Schools District, the budget too Williamson County, the funding to Williamson County this bank, and then bossed it and now we have debt. They stole our money for convenience, for a ransom elected officials. No more borrow back. Did they pay it back? I don't think so in Middle Tennessee. People did they keep the money from the Government? You *betcha'* people! Cabinet we need a fundraising. *STATEMENT OF

*A New Article*

IGNORANCE AND UNDERSTATEMENT PEOPLE: A large chunk of Metro's Middle Tennessee school budget disappeared doing what is best for them, F&M STATE BANK a federally funded F&M BANK large corporation swallowed a lot of the money. Hooray for F&M Bank. They took the money okay, for their own investors the rich folks in Middle Tennessee? Let me inform you; yes believe me a big chunk. They owned the mortgage investment bank member of FDIC, the power bank speak to the Governor, the FDIC Board. Thank GOD, I have it because of JESUS CHRIST. STATEMENT: They committed a crime. NAACP knows. Here is the message to you a reality check double check give that money back. Their school district is successful in Middle Tennessee why isn't Metro's? Fair enough it will be uncovered. Good afternoon, your trade is equal exactly that is the fact! Their teachers are not qualified. GOD will fix it up front. JESUS CHRIST will uncover it. He sees the crisis. Perpetrators took our money from Metro it's an emergency, the evidence we have the evidence they camouflaged it to the other side, in little bitty pieces incredible! *THE BONES OF IT AGAINST THE SCHOOLS: They move by square foot a tremendous amount of school money, that's a legal fact, bones here from Nashville area schools, Republican lawmakers did it. The white man did it. *Want me to tell you why? Come again, let me reiterate it people the news people. They move by square foot, so things will appear the same in Nashville. Country, definitely spanking they will get, when the Federal Government ceases the records take them from their desk—the shrewd! METRO THE MESSAGE: Metro-Nashville Public School money Franklin, they are stealers. Williamson County, they are having a ball its base medium their standard and we keep funding them. JESUS our bunker for this house against those Republicans prejudice is smart politicians Metro. Give me the base line. I've got a defender Federal Government a heavy weight now. I hope it comes back to bite you typical racist.

## CONCERN

Thus saith the LORD JESUS CHRIST; I declare it my word my honor in Nashville, against Republicans, Republican Governor as well, and the Mayor of Nashville, that was in bed with them their brand of politics, I'M breaking them the whole house down, and that group Vanderbilt investment tearing legally their revenue highway damage, their stinking racists investment it's a blessing for us to keep industry it's an outrage, their infrastructure (the bank involved in it) padded from the inside down 100% young people that are in the valley. Ladies and gentlemen changes the government loud and clear, the Obama Administration they will fix it. You can't keep people down away from a development just for convenience. In terms of these issues publicly calling 911-their rescue okay, and it is written I don't hate? I don't break a word my word, Xerox that. Now bite that a development. Persons have leaked on the other side wanting to stop you this is not their leak breaking; this is not the FBI, Pentecostal. I would never accept that verdict, I'M telling you that I AM authorities operating, I AM looking for a public change to the bone this end industrial holding all men accountable, that is what I paid for. For what or it was all for nothing? Respect me, I do respect you. Floating comfortable they are grazing now. Forced segregation was its cause those Republicans. I see dooms day now. Congratulations, your defense make room for more your Christmas present on line now, the normal that solves the mystery. Say, bankrupt now. No more segregation we're talking Mexicans. Integrate! No more forced segregation in America those whites involved in this matter these are the issues. Hatred way blown this time around we need a backup, I can't believe it behind us those times were dangerous like the devil. Hallelujah to JESUS CHRIST that was a problem for way back then, and elsewhere in the Country. If you didn't notice backwards were we and they knew it. We were a train wreck? Amen. Funeral was our last pinnacle in this country, because of segregation, it was like a tornado coming after you. We lived through the nightmare segregation oh thank you, JESUS, and slave labor. Now look at us we're right back in the news everybody. Can you imagine? The immigrants fared better coaching; the original recipe going to America us way back then you don't celebrate us earlier way back when rough on us individuals, definitely we were threatened people, below rank the message we view real quick JESUS CHRIST, hatred for us the whole community. *We were persons of equal status twice a moron, they thought we were dirty in the basement. During the holidays in the department stores specials kept us going physically, the adrenalin would roar keeping us thinking we were the same-Black folks, as Whites thinking they were superior. Welcome to our world. Going that extra mile we had a lot to overcome. I'M a witness, JESUS CHRIST. Setting the china out, and putting food on our big dinner table, the Negro meal fabulous! All in our textured living room where family and friends would gather to bring gifts, and setting at the table to eat a very thankful dinner with family and friends. We had every reason to be so thankful! Uh-HUH to that. *No pot-luck, and not hunkered down. No hungered down better, that is aloof to this day our manner Republicans, a mistake your cattle britches a written art form. Don't fall in love with that ridiculous, for heaven's sake why don't you think can imagine backwards if you do? We are more than that don't brag on aloof. Do you hear that from me? Things are changing now all of us need military nesting. Teaching is our asset brilliant is what we strive for do your best. Don't draw on myths. Love those dinners, we went all out with father at the head of the table asking God's blessing for Christmas, guest as well everybody was thankful. Oh be grateful for homes today no extensive spoon feed living just like us. Candles lit everywhere the same with Easter like at Christmas; we're making it out of poverty keeping it together our house, and no second class. Amen. JEHOVAH GOD, thank you for unity, for blessing me with hope. I remember way back, we had patience and hope every year.

Now we are thankful for that hope, and a little bit every year. *Christmas one of my favorite times of the year, GOD'S gospel preached at Church, and basically freedom from racial backlash of racial hatred every day, the turning point you have no idea Pentecost. The epic we endured every day, we've been treated bad more negative than positive. We were gambling every year at Christmas, *the Christmas tree and the Christmas spirit* the other avenue would not be a fluke anymore like every day. The *Christmas spirit* that time of the year, the other avenue in a sense would not be a fluke a "Burger King" your address anymore. Praise GOD. Things would get better; I wanted it inside so badly. No one badgering us we were happy, definitely. But just for simple normalcy with family, Pentecost that is your answer Keeper knows, no more badgering us (tormenting) that was us we had our backs against the wall, for the season of CHRIST had come; (normalcy) even in a bucket the avenue for the Black man and his family, and all the symbols Christmas gifts, and the playing of "*Silent Night*" with a Christmas tree in our houses. I love Silent Night festiveness; it's a festive season that time of the year no darkness being held against you, and all is well. He's our CHRIST as well. JESUS, I would definitely agree. We're caught right in between two mirrors. I would agree. Thank you, JESUS CHRIST for delivering us, the underlining of it all. Dogs we were thought to be looked at like an animal on regular holidays. But the current did turn for the better or so we say, definitely safely no stereotyping anymore a commercial at us. No joke, businesses wanted your business even the Jews my friend. We only wanted that type of normalcy with no regrets a lot of us; we were hungry and thirsty for that. We were U.S. citizens through a peep-hole standing Black society. The government did recognize us moral support was what they were lacking our privilege our heritage, but the rest of society did not. Then it came it was official I cannot complain a real breakthrough however, soon came in Washington D.C., for us all Black people Pentecost even most recent you missed it, when the

Federal Government took action the Olympics for the Black man no doubt. The other mess people going ahead and they Republicans against the Black man, the other man the White Republicans, arguing the issues those were the key issues for the Black man. Republicans they are rough heads terrible with a backlash our offense, they couldn't spoil our Christmas anyway. Democrats crossed they are even at Thanksgiving and New Year's. One of our policy issues used to be in restaurants eating with our White counter parts. *Forget about racial slurs it's Christmas go ahead, and make the down payment bargain if you had to. <u>Their regret:</u> my parents Melvin and Ethel; that we would see the toys-big toys before Christmas had come. I love them to death and they hooked me, and now I love that time of the year *for safety produced.* We only wanted that type of normalcy with no regrets. It would start with flower arrangements throughout the house, I remember that. Thank you, JESUS CHRIST for Christmas the wonderful Lamb of God. We would hang up Christmas town, and stomaching our Christmas gifts scattered throughout the old house that we lived in, and walking the floor minding business desperate to find what we were getting for Christmas. Keep the pal waiting was their motto—a secret gift. Bare feet on the living room floor not just me, *and pine cones not a negative scattered throughout the house in fruit bowls going nuts with pine cones seeking normal obviously, we would run Saturday's to dress the house, and to have *a very Merry Christmas* just like Republicans our White counter parts. Talk about it the event most people you know it gets in your blood, and you can't wash it away it's a good feeling! No other way to describe it people of GOD. *And about us we loved presents our homes vision upfront the African American, mentioning it backwards the African American-the Negro at that time. We have come a long way. We thought they were our friend no joking our family, I'm being serious a lot of people thought that. *Grace brought our redemption. Praise the LORD for that. Eternity base camp our play to me, in the neighborhood we were the trunk barreling to pay taxes our human right we were anxious. From GOD, we're on top of their world peace and tranquility—play Nashville, not walking on a two way street not flipping trouble not in our way.  That was the event there is no other way to describe it. *Talk about a battle, we practiced conducted ourselves the right way. ABOUT MY DADDY: Mr. Payne my daddy Melvin, GOD JESUS CHRIST holds my daddy. He wanted the benefit on the ground to cover us. I joined him in that if it's okay? When there was trouble in our neighborhood generally people sought his advice, they were reaching out for his help. They did not want to be separate—the victim. *My Daddy argued for mercy: pitiful was those Black men.  Pullman in their camp a pickup thought; still we were all together many good people helped, they were not full of hate. Been done Whites overcast people the African American full house manufactured, they were just to be their cheap labor everyday on a daily basis. And daughter that was the way it was says God JESUS CHRIST, they found favor.  Except they had their faith against Jim Crow rule, and prayers at night to protect them; and you know what I'm talking about for Blacks, while they were asleep. At midnight a double mint country we were just mixed. THERE WAS A CRISIS: Way back when no sleeping audience during those times in the community.  We knew their meanness it was no accident, but all slept well in the country. *Dreams we shared a lot with our friends good White friends to the Black American family, and our neighbors and our White neighbors as well they wanted people to beat the stereotyping a unique opportunity.  There were a lot who shared this dream against racism; ultimately the African American our point of view Nashville, not worried about culture, the American dream was what they wanted it was their point of view. *Their purpose: they wanted to beat hatred with a *double edge sword* so that we could all be free like in other schools of instruction management, *What heaven must be like at that level.  Can you imagine, they did not think we were lazy the African American?

*A New Article*

Thank GOD, for good White friends a balance home edition. I can't complain we all wept, but all slept sound Nashville. They didn't entertain britches those people who entertained racism dirty they are, and in their book White people who sought for change was enviable. MT. ZION hear that? There is nothing wrong with that people a unique possibility however, and not being racists every day a projection of things to come. Many did not think it would ever come. Zero tolerance I have Black people for Jim Crow activists, who strut around looking for an attempt to attack you fellow Democrats and White Republicans, stop running up to them they are environmentalist former racists activists carrying an event on sale. Can you believe it Springfield entrepreneurs; Christians we're fighting them here in Nashville southern Whites people? Their walking in the mud without a doubt the incident we're not evolving Nashville. Listen carrying their legacy who thinks they are cool? Generally they are racists. Do I need to say it one more time? I wouldn't think so. *PARTIALLY BILLY GRAHAM-A TRUTH: Dr. Graham, hooray Dr. Graham. He sought for decency. He would have fought for decency for the average man, even in Europe and their capitals. That was his policy. Racism today it's a battle these people white people everywhere they are nasty, these people are racists. *My father was doing fine keeping us up, we were fortunate. He mattered to our family. He was forced to work demeaning jobs all kinds— performance their best a pillar of the Black community, and just was Thurgood Marshall, and others who fought in the city for Blacks, the African American people of the Negro race. It's a wonder they made it. Sometimes people he was quit mad (my father) eating dinner they had to cope with that, but he made the sacrifice. *For that we love him till today. If you are from the south buying your own home Republicans, obviously we could not afford debt we were empty. He paid for our home there was no debt owed. When he would get off from work turning the corner in his jumper pickup truck we waited, our watch for him it was good news all around. That is how it was way back when. "He's a tackle some would say. Good job a big success." Still the average man liquid to them dumped on the ground. Their leadership qualified. *Here is a pinnacle tip for the younger generation, because of low skills cooks and whatever their cross for labor making sure their families was looked after. Didn't pay that much. Don't frown on them we weren't any equal. *I know those Black men they wept sometime in Cheatham County, Tennessee a long time; and then the police officer, the Sherriff came and arrested one the lingo— bad hatred against my Papa royalale like a cancer. Hit a home run my papa royalale. He had a great attitude. *Melvin Payne-Papa Royalale in the kingdom of GOD, a citizen an attribute so beautiful, a beautiful thing! The avenue for that hiccup racist's judgment followed later the residents their house the trial had ended. Yes, indeed the revel incident fowl play mirrored, Whites trying to teach Blacks a lesson rebel trash officer, the government in that town. I always suspected the tailor (the makeup of the incident and other incidents) their biggest source racists energy, their hatred against colored people those Whites against Blacks, the Black community. Our preachers prayed to clear the atmosphere for all of them in that incident, they were praying things would get better, the home of the brave in that town us, Whites against us the condition even the middle class. We wanted a revolt things had to change. THE INCIDENT: there was a trial, incident I remember my brother then he got picked up by the Sheriff, they said he had stolen did eleven twenty nine their incident, the Whites the keepers. We were striving integration of schools. Haslum do you understand or are you blind? Please pray for me now! AND ABOUT MR. PAYNE: it bears repeating Mr. Payne should have been a State Representative. And our giant moved quickly, he kept us my family from going under in Cheatham County Nashville, Tennessee he moved with diligence. He kept working hard despite the hardships imposed. Family you think you are a Christian; you should have lived through that, the

## A New Article

years of segregation during that time, but we were not afraid JESUS CHRIST watched over us unlimited, there was no breakdown in our household. Friends know that GOD is eternally able always every tribute he won it the KEEPER. HALLELUJAH Nashville. I never will be ashamed of the gospel of JESUS CHRIST! He held us together in that town. *Alright, Ms. Rosa Parks! Absolutely, things were horrible at that moment, they were trying to do us in can you imagine things were smoking for Black people in the South we cried mercy unto GOD everywhere, before integration then they put the hose on it changing somewhat. "Absolutely put the hatred down let us rest in peace." A really good Christian man, try a neighbor GOD gave it to him being a watch out making a good neighbor caring a warrant backlog for his side skin cancer that community making the difference total advance watching like an eagle ready to run if he had to a pillar for that community. Exactly" Pentecost, "Melvin we need your help against Whites" greatly honored every day a wonderful man, he was a wonderful human being, Pentecost and America esteemed that he was. When we were young caring a dinner plate to pickup emergencies wrecks on the highway, believe me a job that he had for years even to Nashville from Cheatham County, and then be at work in the basement in the early hours before anyone else was at work. He worked at a Chevrolet Car Dealership second hand caring their bull shit till his death their mannerism frame of mind, the whites throw down at him the lonely Black man. YES! YES! YES! Peace anyway even falling down a couple of times particular-Papa Royale, but in the end striving to get back up again. Saying, "Papa Royale everything is goanna be alright." *SOLVED THE INCIDENT: was Mr. Howard Dawson, and Mr. Philip Hunter. MR. DAWSON he wasn't racists know that for sure, he made a check list, I love Mr. Howard Dawson. A lot of White people they were blind operating a ring all around the work crew, he just saw survival for a man and his family the Payne family nothing to all those racists out there. No other event checked pointed to opposition his specialists cut them off from being a ringleader of that event; cut them off run them off the camp showing people who he was a leader of that group. Mississippi do you hear that? What kind of leader he was not out of bounds would run them out of the camp; evidently that was no mistake about it. People are equal get the job done. I can see my daddy now, being proof being a caddy for him, traveling around everywhere people not speaking to him at all times, a real success not looking backwards as some would contend all those years, and Mr. Dawson I love him to death no onion that one. Melvin my daddy admired him greatly for being on the front line, with institution not caring for racism on the job everywhere he'd go. Not causing a riot just being natural he and his family, being a good old boy stretching the limits handed him on the work calendar forcing others to do the right thing, and it wasn't that long time ago; it was a big deal a long, long time ago there watching as I was growing up in Ashland City, Tennessee in those neighborhoods. Now look where we are now at going right back to the way we use to be. This development a new summary: times were hard my daddy knew that. Lexington, Kentucky for me front and center, I'm not being rude, just trying to remember I haven't forgotten you throwing pride away the exchange. I hope you read the tribute about a long time ago it was for free the calling you had on your life. Hey let's have a reunion sometime at yall's house. Can I stop by and we can have a tender discussion? I drink coffee. Persons relevant to the point, and put our cups together over a meal in the early mornings, and remember the man called Melvin Payne and his wife Ms. Ethel, and their whole life together. There are a lot of memories stored inside of me. Or we can all do dinner sometime. Specifics I will bring an olive branch with love enjoying great peace, and gratitude shown to my great dad. Daddy would like my gratitude. He definitely would like that, and our friendship. And JESUS CHRIST, will be watching from the sky. Signed this woman of God JESUS CHRIST; bearing tender emotions for the kindness shown to my dad. LORD, I think you for him and the sacrifices that this man made befriending my dad Mr. Melvin. This industry these two men you are not an embarrassment either of you, courtesy arrangement to you and your family. Thank you, JESUS. Skyline take a look at that it's for free check your inventory, positively. Ms. Barbara Jean simple fact, he kept it equal what a blessing showing respect for an older black man, not synthetic not armed with racial prejudices, and Mr. Dawson and Mr. Philip neither not wanting to draw a wedge because of the color of a man's ethnic skin. Think it strange they both worked with him equally, now why I don't know that I do not know catching a rabbit they did not, thought him equal in the wing working with them. Not a big mistake those individuals. Let him make money a little be more than the average uplifted him. *Salt and pepper just a little bit. They had a family as well. *At a distance many thought they were buddies letting a black man work in their camp, and not being prejudice just going by the book, makes me put a smile on my face. A young man, a fair white man not the average Pentecost, he didn't tolerate that kind of stuff making a difference politically made a turn around. Giving him a chance a poor black man my father in their camp, he graduated from a diesel school as a mechanic. No bunker under the hill was Mr. Dawson not like the average; so I'll tell you about a long time ago, he broke the barrier made ramification facing it. I view a revival for us and them. They both broke the color barrier legal defense, and let a poor Black man work and earn a decent wage the establishment. *My daddy was one of them everywhere he went with them. *Mr. Charlie Shoemake, was the same great individual was that man, during his time of opportunity defense. There are a lot like him and them pure icing on the cake. *President Bill Clinton was the same follow his example, "when out and about." To quote him a long time ago (Mr. Dawson) "Saying to the crew no time for that mess a little bit nervous, you treat him right you better honor him; we can always depend on him." THE GROUP: Others saying "we ain't got time for him the racists other White man." Away with that I'll tell you all about it ascertain doing what you are suppose to do. I declare benefit GOD'S mercy no doubt. Be grateful this generation you've got a life not always controlled, even in the military like the Black man was way back when. That was the way it use to be. Never did wreck my family my father always kept food on our table, my mother did the same. Generally in any event JESUS CHRIST watched over me and my kids, for that I am thankful. I don't live there anymore. He kept us together my father, when I was a ten year old girl not anchored in JESUS CHRIST; it's a wonder that I made it not crying to this day true hard knots. I don't look back anymore. *So have *a very Merry Christmas* whenever, and wherever all around. Pass it on our refugee. I'm just looking at the race our race for the Black man and his, their struggles during the era's of segregation in the South, it was a terrible time their bigotry and hatred against the Black man, except for a few White men and their wives who view segregation from another point of view. Congratulations to all of them, the Keeper of the kingdom saw their lives and how they knew too do better. Their big accomplishments will be rewarded one day up above. I was having a flashback episode. Thinking I had went crazy during the writing of this book. Thanks, to JESUS CHRIST; my Lord and our Savior, I have written this book. My father he was there when I graduated from high school; we thought he had to work. My father a naturalized U.S. citizen; he kept us together not a broken home, not living on the tracks, no charity like most people. Couple of advances thanks to JESUS CHRIST; we were on the ball advantages could walk with our head held high, wherever we wanted to go no deceit. We are thankful. He loved me my father did. He tried hard to cover it his debt and his house both parents did, even though there were racists in that town of Ashland City, they made it. Yes they did my father and my mother, the whole family we made it. We spent years in that town. Christians, we were all taught about GOD, to be a believer and yes moral ethics believe it or not, not grease as some would think the race your kin there's good in all races. Nobody knows this better than I, hallelujah. I am still the same chocolate citizen I've always been no hiding that check my birth record, understand? I am proud to be an American know, live in this great country of ours settle down raise my family, and be honored to be educated with good CHRIST like values not a fluke. Know that we are equal. *The race over the years this race he mimicked your grandmother did, Colonel Parker mimicked, signed JESUS CHRIST, it's time we cleaned this stall out its time we quit if I were you. My parents took a lot we come from a small town, I joined them. Thanks to them my parents we were not the victim, we band together, and not in a closet room. Oh thank you, JESUS CHRIST. Challenged we were. They were just people like everybody else. No matter how perfect stuff was African Americans was still considered backwards, and unusual we wanted normalcy in our house it affected Blacks, we were the Negro stereotypical grown up a typical. We needed protection in the kingdom of GOD from those racists, *the vestibule we wept, we wept a lot there on Sunday mornings growing up. But just keep on coming to the House of GOD that was the concern even lately a new program; there we could weep there out of sight from the racists outside, the darkness. *Now the average Jew, pitiful like the Black man is today Pentecost, the White man felt the same stereotypical; the Jews they are significant people no kidding about that. We needed normalcy in our lives. The usual was what we wanted not treated different, you couldn't tell that to people trying to separate us. Let's face it; we were desperate to be normal like everybody else. My parents were affected they suffered a lot, and so did all our people. Be thankful to the Democrats who kept us free from getting hurt my friend. Mostly work at "Dairy Queen" restaurants the Negro, my mother and other Black and White women of lower class in that town a film-crest. Colored people our advancement our jobs scrubbing on the grounds, if you ask me that was how we felt our whole life. Bomb premium us, like a bomb your true destination a lot of bombs, we were already afflicted. Thanks to JESUS CHRIST, hallelujah, our own investment, and the Keeper of the universe things got better people. I have quit shopping don't buy no more Christmas gifts anymore. I don't do it anymore my family isn't complete, a breakdown in communications because of him. He doesn't want to spend the money. He's a mess. It's okay though I quit shopping he's a stickler. JESUS looked at me and He said; daughter you've had enough much difficult that I know never give up. Too bad it has to happen. Now I will perform a miracle, it's all going to come together. It's the third time this has happened to you it will happen again. I know his accent. I'll finish discussing it, I ought to hang him now been a dog for a very long time full of hot air with his old girl friend, can't take his eyes off of her. Pentecost Ms. Barbara, you're obedient and that is enough. She's got a gravy train Pentecost. Her race yellow laughs when he's not around, he's making a big mistake. He sleeps with her their ornament, just like today Pentecost, they are yellow ^don't have pity on her you're under attack by them both. *I will get you out of this house. Did I tell you you're on your way to eternity-heaven not laughing nor crying Lord help me, here's a clear signal oh thank you, JESUS. Now here's a record on that independent a clear signal, know that legally, I will protect you no matter what. Know that he is a fruitcake walking offense all the time. *^He insults me. *^Let me tell you, hateful he breathes it all the time Pentecost do you understand? And about you Ms. Barbara, evil intent that is the way he feels about you and the children their blessing and grandchildren, and art form he has become an embarrassment without a question. Don't tear up at this point; I've got my hedge all around you. / Raggedy he is doesn't have a brain wore out need maintenance; understand management level from on high? Hear that all that are lying to your wives now do right. Keep going with it bottom line, I want you to take my advice, JESUS CHRIST and cry mercy Nashville, after denim we're going to Nashville, you'll never get in living the way you do? Christians don't mess with drugs. Gentlemen you are dirty supreme, it's the fastest growing sin around the world. Maintenance no weapon formed against you shall prosper. Evidence legally nothing is going to happen to you. We're alright you shall not perish, catching we are distinguished. He is on his way to the grave no open gates, and facing judgment the wrath of GOD being called a Benedict Arnold down there. The aftermath you will be safer against him just hold out, I promise you. In this town I give you a miracle better than you think, I have already hold your breath it will take your breath away. Thank you. You're in the middle. I know that he is ugly against you negative things. Like a pizza pie rolled out the storms keep coming at you, *Nathaniel your husband, you're the real winner awful is he? Why negative, ethnic group he is not grateful for the things he has this year. We're talk more buy groceries and dine well alright? Don't act like stickler like confusion. I give you credit- back door. What people want it doesn't matter the physical evidence. Negative in the kingdom is he always makes him happy to see you with nothing walking by faith. You've got more faith than most people have. I see him not a friend of JESUS CHRIST not my friend. Oh so thankful you are, just look up my friend, the occasion I capture it with you, your sunshine gray. I can pick it up a notch a two this season. Anyhow take it out of your hand you go pray you'll feel better. Put a song in your heart relax with me catch the spirit anyhow. JESUS said unto me; be a friend my friend ROSA PARKS was a friend, she raised up a generation to fight for their equal rights be prevalent Pentecost, don't be backed up take your account prevalent give grace a chance your number one game. I'll be right with you don't forget the Olympics, you've won a lot of metals for the people the anointed. Now keep up the good work. We had better quit talking. GOD bless you, I'll revive you. Go get revived for the gain take a miracle.

## The Original Barbara Payne

I'll see you at home plate take a miracle get comfortable, JESUS CHRIST. Thank you, CHRIST JESUS. Enough of that I know the species walk with me place your burdens over the mantle of GOD. He's crazy; I Quit buying those gifts trouble in my way GOD; people don't care can remember the KING another way. Yes remember me, it's still Christmas. Remember JESUS CHRIST our Savior always. I love thee oh LORD GOD, very-very much. Glory Hallelujah! I honor him anyway. Be thankful, and be grateful for that time of the year. Oh be grateful! Ungrateful, my family not beautiful anymore it's okay that husband. Cash he's unbelievable, just keep it throw it away deposit it where he likes. That husband went industrial he drove it away Christmas, the blessing from on high, the anointing, embellishes his sweet heart the thing JESUS. Don't approach him, I will give you a breakthrough the difference surely an offense your husband own his record above. Don't blame me GOD so confuse the event, anyhow a mess the record keeper upstairs records his many offenses night and day, spoken against you created always. I hate it. You are so beautiful read *1ˢᵗ THESSALONIANS*. Nashville no confusion with my confidence all hope justice the right way, the mediator JESUS CHRIST with no offense. Now be grateful I will establish this written book Antioch, can you imagine, I heard JOHN ADAMS, MEL GIBSON? This book, this writer legally, not just another writer typical. I know his background legally in the kingdom next to you he's a monster in the kingdom. You on the other hand are a fairy princess, no offense you are a Christian recorded. *He's a werewolf dangerous; I'M talking about your husband dangerous are his attacks incredible against you. On attack after you all the time believe me. Believe a lot of people are watching him; he's a person of interest there are a lot of people watching him waiting for him to do the wrong thing. He doesn't think. Picking up a bible number one you considered the lateral advancement move; you've never failed me you want to go upstairs the big event judgment day. Wouldn't do it the natural way, and you know what they're talking about. Terrible some people do those things no recourse, all the time they keep thumping like a rabbit undercover, I know the address their big hang out. You've written this book, they will go after him after a while. Keeper JESUS CHRIST with a gun in his hand will take your breath away. They are after him already, the worshipers he better do better church politics no more. He's catching mononucleosis; be grateful kissing him no more physically. Stop him get that? I'll change the atmosphere enough is enough. Your father I know his address, I adopted him and your two younger sisters your whole family Josie included and your brother me JESUS CHRIST, and the one that is ailing fill with jet fuel. You are jet fuel filled with power from JESUS CHRIST. Quickly view the equipment. I come to support you an agent of GOD JESUS CHRIST. There are witnesses in the earth trusting in your discipleship. Now don't go back your performance keep being a believer. Trust me. Oh thank you, GOD JESUS CHRIST. Believe me now be nice, I know the kind of weather you are under your attacks. He want be a gentlemen. Your gifted pleasure knowing me all night long still loving GOD, you have written this book for me. Keeper, move me out of here LORD, remember me! I will keep you safe done. Finally, now we're in jeopardy our relationship for sure no more brown sugar. Oh be successful is my goal. Thank you, JESUS CHRIST for success anyway. OH THANK YOU, JESUS CHRIST MY GOD! THE END OF MY DREAM LET IT BE POSTED ON MY RECORD PREMIUM, FOR JESUS CHRIST NASHVILLE.

THE SIGNIFICANCE TO PERFORM GETTING MERITS BY YOUR RESOURCES P.R., BECAUSE OF A LEAK EXECUTIVE I'M TALKING ABOUT JESUS CHRIST. WOULD YOU LIKE FOR ME CITIZEN TO REPEAT THAT AGAIN? CONFIDENCE FROM GOD PROTECT THE LEAK THAT PERSON SPEAKING FOR JESUS CHRIST, ON THE OUTSIDE, WE WARNED YOU CONSERVATIVES, WE SEND CONDOLENCES TO YOU, JESUS

CHRIST. JOIN US IN A NEW RESOLUTION. CHANGE YOUR MIND A LOT OF THINGS DOZENS OF THINGS IS GOING TO START HAPPENING IN NASHVILLE, THIS YEAR AND NEXT YEAR FOR JESUS CHRIST ALL POWERFUL, AMAZING HE GAVE HIS LIFE TO RESCUE US FATHER OF THE EARTH. CHANGE YOUR MIND. DO YOU HEAR ME? DO THE RIGHT THING, OH ABSOLUTELY.

Thus saith the LORD; pleading urgent the force field can you imagine Nashville, they are Republicans big-time? Say, turn around your system where in the world are you, your maintenance fees the evidence? THE OPPOSITION-NUMBER TWO: ABOUT-BART DURHAAM: can you imagine that the convicted opposition, they want to kill Bart Durham, for prosecuting them lucky he prayed, can you imagine? They are a private group; they are members of the Tea Party Political Organization. Why he is trying to take their money away by authorities? Next time he won't be so lucky, they follow him all the time since he was a prosecuting DA attorney. The west is wild. Be careful Mr. Attorney things are rough representing clients, the Government knows. About this writer-BARBARA PAYNE: the lone Negro about her, want to murder her they want to kill her too this organization, and her children, but we're patented. It's not just your children. She went it alone. Go after the Tea Party. Look at the Tea Party they are a mess. Barbara Payne, criminal my husband, and my children I live with no respect. You hurt your mother. I don't know why. My oldest and my youngest the two they have attack me enough. I am not their property. A newspaper clipping they have become, they accuse me malicious in the past because of their friends, their neighbors they are a gun. Your blessing GOD said, stop talking to them I know their number your defense against their attacks. Anyway CHRIST JESUS said unto me, my defense this article I am writing be it known to all. A drapery my defense set this record straight. You need to be dealt with by GOD by me I AM superman detergent JESUS CHRIST; I see what you are doing to your mother you the boy spreading all those rumors about her, the guy you are responsible for a wreck in her life falsely a tattletale before GOD. About you I am writing a book okay no cliché about her? You're carrying baggage around you and your associate in crime against her. I love her to death, and I won't change my mind this is a reality. You get on my nerves spreading all those rumors about her. You do your best to knock her down. I AM the contact JESUS CHRIST; better go your own way. Innocent am I your mother. Contradicting company your ticket you think to a better life yellow is your father by me. He sees me as his property that is why he is so abusive to me, old school he hasn't learned a lesson, the abuse trouble in my way, he's in the driver's seat. I see a technical a plan of event this house wife beating observed this house he threw me down, and then attacked the nerve. JESUS said to me; don't take hold of that, I will bless you. He's a fool worship me instead no doubt about, I know you are hurt. I baptized him with the same HOLY GHOST and now he stinks JESUS CHRIST. Lean on me. Setting the record straight in this event of massive difference, that is all I have to say. Don't rush in to tear down what you didn't understand. We've wrestled with this long enough understand? I am your family your mother. Stop talking about me, control your emotions GOD is watching understand? Stop passing judgment on me. They are against me Barbara. CHRIST JESUS said; leave no doubt, your children they are ugly, they need to be born again. I see your struggles okay? Current event you are not by yourself, they need a whipping talking about you like that. Desperate to succeed thinking that you are rich you attack her character. It's not necessary doesn't show intelligence have it your way, and what I stand for. Stop trying to fit in your segment like a Christmas tree, wrong launching an attack against me your mother. You will be saying LORD, take me back one day grateful that he didn't launch attack against you. THE OPPOSITION: my children, when talking to them it was like talking to blank everyday strangers the opposition, regret. I was considered by them an everyday low price. My finger of love pulled them through a lot. We went through a lot. My only regret opposition from trying to raise them being both parents a tendency. Loving them hoping they would be regular and normal, and now they back slide its trouble in my way. GOD will turn it around. I pray for the forgiveness, they have been ugly least they fall into a greater pit. I hit my son wanting to make him mind me. JESUS CHRIST said to me; mother never give up be nice let it roll off of your shoulders. Mother you are unbelievable your attraction ungripable you will win respect, I AM a witness you are my friend no doubt, the King JESUS CHRIST. They hurt me their abuse against me. I AM a witness you hurt me children, their abuse against their mother stop bothering me. Grow up and read *MATTHEW* the gospel be more like me understand?

CAN YOU FIGURE A CLOUDY DAY ON LOCATION

Thus saith the LORD GOD; we're going to get them the rule, the law is on our side both our sides. The damage has already been done. That is where they got the money to start Franklin Special School District. It is done. Some allegations are false believe me. THUS SAITH THE LORD; CHECK YOUR NEIGHBORS BUDGET METRO-GOVERNMENT FROM THE BACK, AND SEE WHERE THEY ARE GETTING THEIR SCHOOL DISTRICT MONEY FROM. LORD! Please watch over me this season. Don't worry you are anointed against their attacks. Thank you, JESUS. Robbery it was under the table, their self-defense mismanagement. Inadequate your address both of them, the answers are wrong they view the Mexicans the same, actors. JESUS will fix it your bath, when it is discovered your bath. SEE THE HOLY GHOST GOD's TIMING IS ALWAYS PERFECT. Improved method the center evidence will surface before next Christmas. Something is emerging now quick advance. I want no more separation. *They cannot deny it see Franklin basement. Don't throw them a lifeline their schools not even a hook. Trouble they're in trouble. Don't throw them a lifeline. Hallelujah. Their organizations hid under a rock, when they found out. They treated both White and Black the same no respect, if you did not meet the *their *class criteria,* they were originally that was no accident remember that typically. See the link it's your duty selection is their process. Congress inflict them now, the way they have done our children just like a snake. We have a right to complain. As you see CHRIST JESUS said; I mean it you don't have to wrestle with it anymore just write. Tell me. Go back to regular public school system; trust me that is where you were at first. That is why you are leaving. Don't trust them anymore watering fence against Metro. *Beware Nashville better get ready no more funding for Williamson County, and their School District. Imagine that are we their slaves entertainment the Negro? THUS SAITH THE LORD JESUS CHRIST; NO OFFENSE YOUR NEW COURT HOUSE FOR THAT CITY YOU WILL BE LACKING NEXT YEAR, AND EVERY YEAR AFTER THAT SIGNED, I JESUS CHRIST. Thank you, JESUS. *Kill the valley it's a valley killer perpetrator richer, definitely done for Metro Nashville Public Schools former Davidson County Metro Councilman, an unnatural thing done on the school system ended. Say that again, the killer perpetrator for Metro Nashville School District Republican Senate, former Davidson County former Metro Council member public elected official, and his wife a big litigation big Republican people, Congressman now in any event. GOVERNOR PHIL BREDESON, and Jim Crow White trash they knew even in Kentucky, Republican politics implemented zero tolerance. Low down he was too, the big chief now the Metro cat is out of the bag Metro Government ordinance. Let him make the decision answer the rules this year you and your wife are going to city jail at the Metro Court House. We solely understand it's a miracle read the paper don't get comfortable. The U.S. Supreme Court will decide against elected officials Republicans. Memphis there is a hundred out there like you. You mean a threat? PEDRO GARCIA: should have been arrested he ruined high school for Davidson County people. I will tell you Nashville everything. He saw how he could make a little extra money. Then he withdrew his support for Metro Public Schools he was dangerous trying to get an advancement a nickel, and now he is up north. Hallelujah. We the salt and brown pepper of the earth, the public school system are left with nothing. Good news you can't rob God my Father, and his people anymore. *Bad news you are at risk *Williamson County seriously your operation. Thank you, for misleading the people of Nashville, the country your fellow Americans the people, the whole nation the young people, and *Sumner County. Knoxville do you hear me, we have forgone hardships, we will get to the bottom of this? We get no respect they dug us to the ground I'm telling you. Say, I'm going home. We need a follow up more experts. WITH CONFIDENCE THANK YOU, JESUS CHRIST FRIEND BREAD OF LIFE. You say we've got a problem then fix it. There is an easier way out if we reduce. Cut funding, cut your mark up, cut Federal funding from Metro Public School System your welfare. I AM shocked your group. I heard you decades ago over a quarter of a century. Bridgestone helped you some you know Bridgestone—pointing a finger? Thank you, MAYOR CARL DEAN: for letting it happened. I see the affidavit now. We see your attorneys. Clean up your mess for the present administration. Metro is full of tax revenue. You can't mislead people anymore like in the past in previous administrations, the documents courts in Nashville legal edge courtesy FBI. Gotcha right away salted hands known as the rock. More accomplished come on freedom just as then righteous we deserve more. Independent jealous you owned it.

## A New Article

You are doomed any objections? Your followers afflict that is the principle. Jealous you claimed it locked up now group percentage. Now the cat is out of the bag. Basic threat takes the joy away, if you stand up close first impression that is the way it is current administration. In the south now days in Nashville no authority, I AM a witness saith the Lord; in neighborhoods have no defense. A great opportunity just ruined everything everybody to this day; I'M a witness. Yes Vanderbilt view their risk factor. You thought I was blind Vanderbilt Executive Branch. Get your education be an adult. Get rid of it ignorance, you are smarter than that your development correctness. Throw trash talking away. Manners make an improvement pretend like nothing hasn't happened, and sing "*How Great Thou Art*" your religion, your shelter agree? You need some shelter, definitely? Get your families, your family members away from this affliction, white trash nothing but trash trio public. Get your families Pentecost; away from this do you follow me? Get an associate degree do you agree, and then get your bachelors? Get those degrees, dragging you through the mud they are their traffic. Yes, get your degrees Pentecost, even if you have to move away to help clean up this mess. They are backwards. Get more than one degree not just two. Then turn around and go right back to your cities where the hoodlums are these are animals, and help clean up this mess. Dogs they are living for free off of everybody else. They don't want to clean up the house. Get a river, get a map, get smart, and even higher make a difference. *Masking like Lady Gaga-impulse connection, your branch demonstrating on the side of the road in Nashville, and we're like turkey sausage just ground meat. Can anybody help us get the correct funding for public schools, the task more super-natural funding Pentecost? Cover a bride, CHRIST JESUS. Thank God, for your children my fellow Americans. Thank God, for His grace, for His goodness, His mercy legal integration. We love him very much CHRIST JESUS.

## NOW YOU HERE IN NASHVILLE, MAKE ROOM YOUR PACKAGE STORE

Thus saith the LORD; Pentecost I've got a ton of stuff to tell. Can you imagine that? In the basement your physical activities, your perimeter go on leave us like meatloaf, definitely just low like ground meat rural tendency. I just can't wait to finish you off like you have done the people. Protect me say the people they treat us like animals. We're like sweet potatoes not meat substance just gravy we're finished. Republicans the stress, the confusion, you block us from preparing for the future bow excessively. Get the bonus out of the way. YOUR CHARTER SCHOOL PLAN FOR METRO IS WORKING: MORE BLACKS LESS WHITES. Even the university sublet your activity, your adventure, your policy, with earnest activity your policy, you have a point. This is an eye opener your physical activity. Give them a ribbon play ball with Rutherford County School System, they think they are great. Release the funding near 80% deficit for Metro-Nashville Public Schools. That's where the battle grounds are the wealth accumulated like a club. Huckleberry Finn you are wait until your season comes your garbage sweet potato your virtue. Things could be better. Give God praise for stopping this! You wrestle with this. Give out of your pocket. You swindle $20,000., $50,000. We can turn the schools around produce more wealth. We can make a difference produce more wealth. It's my responsibility. You've got a union making a million. Give them protection faculty. They are run ragged this is reality this is an exception. ALEXANDER: meatballs you knew, I see your face on the cover. I see you in prison eating breakfast. Seriously you general Republicans White shrugged your responsibility. No more "Super Bowl." I view you 99% two hundred percent. I see your inhabitants loading docks; they are actually wearing robes occupying space government. Rough you are I see you in prison eating breakfast, Newt Gingrich to the underprivileged. Wipe them out now sever their needs. You control billions. The whole Country bankers 42% thought nobody the Americans, would see the bullet those Republicans some of the highest paid political Americans your political needs. Your character to the people, you have been running over them long enough. We won't have any more budget crunches next year this is a big deal. The down side the job end Charter Schools, end private lessons. I told you two decades ago. TO THE AFRICAN AMERICANS: Brothers and Sisters say, they aren't going to drag us down no more. To the clan: rewrite Charter Schools. We are independent you don't scare me. TO THE JEWS: that we can depend on use your influence finally great complement your anniversary. Say GOD has kept me your Kosher my friend. They did that to you, you Jews I have the evidence be a friend, the adversary cool watching we're all Americans. You want my advice people are watching, exactly. People are looking at you every day, and you didn't know it wonder why backwards if you think otherwise. You are crippled before you walk out the door in New York, all eyes are watching you. Be a citizen do that for me, you are needed, a community tearing down some walls pass the rebound that is the whole coverage? Don't walk away a pat on their back, be a blessing that is a real anointing. Say, we no longer will walk away on purpose, heaven help us all from our calling to help the Black man a mere image of GOD, in this country. Offer blessings your event. We are all kin remember that. A ripple effect—remember the holocaust in Germany, no one took the time to defend? Don't walk away. Hear that? Remember your past make a decision. You are responsible to GOD. Make a decision while you still can, while I'M talking to you this time. Remember GOD he made a way for you. Know that GOD remembers your past, and that He helped you out. Make a decision help. Know that GOD can make a way dozens of you want to help. Better not walk away war has a way of tearing us all down like a cancer. Well Black people are the same, I have the evidence sprawling the African American downhill, and nobody cares with no repair here in Nashville, due to the White man. They benefited in tax revenue. See the White man news coverage all coverage White their leverage I declare. TO THE BLACK MAN: unfortunate you are walking a free canister. Get yourself educated you are the victim, the way out of poverty. NAACP The Group: they are a great opportunity; I have better things to do with my time you know-*The Original.* They are so disadvantaged the Black man. For all the wrong reasons Nashville, did you hear that Mitt Romney? His season of rejoicing is coming accompanying counter police, the event Nashville. The KKK try pulling us down with its mass transit of disease liberal organized rebel integrity against human beings. Veterans they are against human beings, their influence the low life Pentecost, scoundrels Pentecost I know all about them okay? Pentecost I see their reference against the Black man, peaceable are the Black man in trouble against the Whites of society. Your advantage know that GOD is able. Some are inherited influence criminal injustice having a break down influence. Take a stand. Others are billionaires walking the streets peddling their influence. Mitt Romney have you used your influence the right way—bottom up? Are you listening Mitt Romney don't get mad? Use your influence I hope you are listening quickly. Use your influence you've got more time before the election be a friend. Some are generic that is the problem suffered inherited damaged brain waves. Often the person in a state of confusion disease function their memory that is the problem. Industry most request the racism, the hatred tap into it big companies they are all alike. It's a stench that won't go away. Are you listening? You can go shopping for it any day the film of racism. Say God help me looking over your shoulder. Believe me I know Pentecost, I've been here long enough. You never think about that it is not healthy. It's not like looking for a needle in a haystack organized racism funded. TO THE BLACK COMMUNITY: your story the untold story be a role model. Don't cause a riot. Just walk away your wreck. Don't trespass. Work with me just a little bit. Documented everything even the way the women wear their hair. They have knowledge of you White Middle Class politicians, they think you are dangerous. They think you will cause mayhem, okay? Politician's healthy activity raising false sense of hope, raising rebel flags against a democracy is always making sure looking for ways to reinforce their stigma package, in the neighborhood that is so dangerous. Just look at Nolensville Road in Nashville, your local government does it well. Good advice we're not a national close out. See the general elections cross your ballet the right place. Say it's on me a great idea. Say I'm hungry for GOD. Briefly they are being transferred right now. We are full of it say nobody is laughing now pigskin labor done wrong. I AM the middle man. What they see injury what choice do they have. Be free what a mighty GOD, we serve! Okay fasten your belt. Long mess do you think you are better than them? White America change the situation big government. To the public throw a brick what is the difference to the citizen? Argument, they are laughing at you. The result come on have an avocado give them a glass of wine. You can taste wine. Dry up you are evil you know the rest. Keep impressing upper White middle class, the result no chocolate no more. Have you ever squeezed a lemon, an apricot? Never push GOD into a corner. Go back where you belong. Stop the suffering. You think superman had attacked you cross your finger; I've got radar even in apartments, Solvent. You know who I AM? Triple attack Newt Gingrich, I fault you I have a bone to pick with you. *Superintendent of Metro Schools you obey first, exactly. You align first; it is a privilege your compass get it? You get paid thousands nobody is doing business publicly, advantage improve your operations to the Negro persons. About the average, you think we are asleep your voice of operations at this time. When your contract expires get out. *Go to greener pastures understand? Help we need help this is an emergency in this Country, regardless what race you are in. That is what we'll all about. We're not giving matches at the door Christians to Whites or independents, and non-White men, the Black man, even Latino substitute, and if you're Democrats Latinos, Black or Brown, and definitely White Latinos eating a cake the host from the White man's hand Latino politician you think we're crazy? You understand? You think every Black man or daughter is crazy, pitiful our race the African American Latinos? Black people they are racists, the White man racists in Nashville. Do you understand? My dad worked for Whites, that didn't allow it racism on the job against our people, Black people. In the south there are racists. Let me explain to you how racism works. Look Latinos the next export could be yours. You're living in this Country on *social welfare.* You can't come into this Country, and live for free off of the Federal Government, creating *a social class stigma* many would agree. They have bending over backwards even the NAACP to give ya'll a pass the measure, the Obama Administration have created equal access that is the standing right now people coming into this Country illegally for free Hispanics. The next exit could be yours. They deport every day ethnic group's people walking into this Country illegally. Believe me Jim Crow law still exist under the table a group pass not a settlement. Agree; don't break the law hazard for your health running drugs for drug lords? You are a thief committing a crime. Stop breaking the law under the tracks. Do your best live right; their equipment moment giving crutches away your racket playing to their music. I know you need shoes a lot of hobo's scattered throughout the Vanderbilt area waiting for a meal, waiting to be used by people Black people. Learn to walk right. Shoes or no shoes gangs are keeping you in hot water mistreating other Blacks, and then you're locked up in the basement. Live right, act right don't be a beggar to someone else acting like a buffoon, a kindergartner in the basement. Un-doubtingly the system approves of your activity; they keep making the same mistakes. Let me give it to you Corporate America is your friend; they decide who gets their vote Corporate America. Go to greener pastures whipping up on some other race any objections? Hallelujah. Do you hear me? The rest you are racists. Hear me! Oh thank you, JESUS CHRIST. Just open your mouth. The mess politicians industry Charter Schools, just open your mouth wide you are flipping. The result I'M going after you first nothing can stop me. Initial understanding to residents there are two questions compass: the health question, the deficit on each end pointing it out. Know the process the big questions. Thinking better know that I AM bigger than you are Franklin, Williamson County. Committed technical adjustments before GOD equipment this edition, I thought I was going to have to shut you guys down new construction your technical many have suffered losses, you keep breaking the law. Read the book you stand at accusing Black people at every avenue ridiculous. Say that I'm burning up your mess, your location. This is critical in Nashville all is well you have a monopoly driven on everything, your institutions big campus dividends your institute fixed. THUS SAITH THE LORD GOD JESUS CHRIST A BLACK MAN; individual Pentecost pointing a finger war zone your moral character, your funds, your moral support leaders-Pentecost, and you Baptist especially Black Baptist, strange I see you with your hands under the table all the time one hundred percent stop complaining, all Baptist this season no matter what your race, you hear me counting your blessing. Typically the fixed image the issue, saying you'd better hold back your equipment. I'M not just beating up on individuals anymore. This is an emergency in Nashville a new development. The case, I'M finger pointing to individuals your new development word; after all I AM the referee. Case-in-point you can do better. You have had a leaky faucet. The real case individuals and Churches, Church leaders, all ministers, Pastors, Black Pastors viewing segregation big time do not be afraid, Pentecost Brothers say, behind the cross *"Nearer My God to Thee."* Pentecost say it now the case even to individuals Pentecost, the African individuals.  Say it now even in council be free.  Say, JESUS CHRIST is a man who hung on the cross be free.  Say it now even to council guilty to individuals who try and bring up the race issue, He hung on the cross your blessing. Pentecost the race issue to individuals let's face it even to those carrying the green card and paying no taxes.  And you all know you aren't paying taxes individuals.  You don't have to pay taxes like anybody else. Guilty to individuals do not be afraid the poor African American have been wronged enough.  Pentecost say it now rubber neck even to the American council guilty to individuals Apostolic Preachers your establishment.  Your tribunal tour individuals being quick with the words why don't you run out of words, there's no cause for that the spot light.  Let me say it one more time to the rubber necks; the other necks that gave a lot go pick up yall's individuals snack basket, your race track where you live guilty to individuals.  Apostolic Preachers agree?  Are you all listening?  I hope you agree, if you don't I will be shocked? I know their budget. THE PEOPLE AND THEIR RETLATIONSHIP: TECHNICALLY I'M JUST *ASS WHIPPING* THEM THOSE PEOPLE, GOING IN BOTH DIRECTIONS SAYS ME JESUS CHRIST, BE IT THAT AFFIRMED DEFINITELY THOSE INDIVIDUALS RIGHT NOW, AND MANY OF THEM ARE BLACKS AND PARTIALLY JEWS AS WELL. SAYS ME JESUS CHRIST, IN ANY DIRECTION BE IT AFFIRMED. Culturally I'M breaking through a sound barrier that is technically equal.  You're at the bottom of the pit now; my children are under tremendous pressure.  Naturally a new set up, a new course for them, a great idea what another option for them? No malice in the heart fighting for them.  Number one individuals your leak is out in your system over here and in Europe.  Your makeup in this city you've been making fun legally.  What about you Catholics typically you as well your literature.  Your filth don't bother me no more your institutions with it JESUS CHRIST; start improving. You got the ninth hour do your duty. You got the message gentlemen? Believe individuals you take advantage do you understand? Get the message? Ninety five percent understanding now see royal. Now just because I AM the best Pentecost you get on my nerves, I AM ALPHA AND OMEGA individual preachers no retro. I give no latitude. Everybody else bud out this recipe war zone understand? I AM not transit Pentecost. You get on my nerves come next election the race is on. Let me explain, you're filled with theology keeping your income profile, it's like a cancer your religion establishment each individual. I've got good news local churches are going to attack your watch; seminary's a dumping ground adjacent political razor. White seminary's you're already dying you're a big monster look with confidence. Remain with optimism that is what Islam do. Come on let's celebrate. Now did you understand? You got sense purge trust me. You asked. Good news I wrote that. Hear that Baptist religion, hear the HOLY GHOST. Don't be pointing a finger? I view you a whole lot. Let me tell you, pointing a finger huge mistake Baptist. Discourse before it happens, and your balance I make a decision you are getting on my nerves, JESUS CHRIST. Read the instructions defense what you've been peddling. You're all going the wrong the way turn around first on you now turnaround a big turnaround, then I will help you turnaround. I'll let the whole world know how you really are. You're far from your Savior's home His saving grace. You're leaving children behind in this country, the African Americans, a good investment. Put on the "*breastplate of righteousness*" Ephesians 6:14; / Baptist like Pentecost humble yourselves; The KEEPER. Look out for me now be careful in what you do. I see your struggles you big ones here in Nashville, TN turn around no other recourse come to me you got that. We will win positive. Say yes Lord. GOD'S business you can't ignore White people first. AN ANNOUNCEMENT: I smell the roast. Are you ready for some more? Amen. Pentecostal preachers do you hear me? How about those Baptist elected officials? How smooth can I get? Do you understand? Knock out with the HOLY GHOST. Say go to the Upper Room. I created you favor Baptist, Southern Baptist as well. Now say pass me the freebie Republicans. Say open your mouth giving thanksgiving. Your appearance will soon be found out Republicans. Prepare Newt Gingrich. Paper get me the paper the result will show where the money was spent, and who took it. Obey God now! The results get the result. Hand me the results to Black people fight no more. Drum roll to the preachers who have some backbone. Stand before the lights fall out. SAY, WILLIAMSON COUNTY: a threat it was founded on deceit wealth, a lemon introduced on Metro-Government. A whole new wealth created Charter Schools for America, thank you, JESUS for Metro Schools as well, anyway Nashville Charter Schools the difference ignorant they were in this city improving self. We Republicans brag, we can keep up the good work okay; enlist more empire shoes we can brag more. A SILO WAS CREATED PENTECOST, TO HOLD YOUR NETWORK STORAGE THEN HOMES WERE BUILT. GIVE US PEACE OF MIND REPUBLICANS. CAN YOU JUSTIFY IT THE INVESTMENT UNDER THE TABLE HAND CRAFTED? There is plausible emptiness in your attempt to cover up your mess, your big daddy food for waste. Do whatever it takes to pay them back. Somebody will pay them back. A giant is about to take its place. We don't need any more of those pig-pins. Are you listening Metro-Government—delete Charter Schools, non-authorized? Brainstorm you will stop at nothing internal crime. I've got your number. Give me liberty. A NEW ORDINANCE: we're talking about a new language casting (throw away) public schools shutting them down in Nashville, redirecting them to private schools, Charter Schools their bonuses. All of us have to take their abuse. You ought to pull up everyone of them from ground level. Direct the funds to Nashville Public Schools. The second opinion: the house no accident those poor children. Here's a comment; are you ready heaven help us can you take it Pentecost, in Nashville? Accident it is not okay understand it in Nashville? ARGUMENT NUMBER ONE: can you hear me, I read your address? It is a dark mobile sailing around apparently in Nashville; across the city everywhere in the south even in Atlanta, GA Gallatin, TN apparently make no mistake about it you are looking over your shoulders. The demographics you are looking over your shoulder. I know your struggles you as well are the results of a true attack in the system. Great big Atlanta you're snob as well it's time you took a bath got that? In the city on the interstate in Nashville, Rutherford County, Williamson County so are ya'll. The contrast true investment the focus its moving around in America you hear it every day, in Black neighborhoods moving around reflex covered mischievous, let's change that with a salary issue politicians construction. THE MAYOR: Mayor Carl Dean, a nightmare raisin chocolate covered syrup annoying locally, that should have been gone over the last few years that will be a big mistake. How can they survive the worst recession ever without a good education? What is to become of them? The enterprises have collected a lot of their tax revenue, and bank it free money over data to start what is their own worth individually. Looking to borrow more a dramatic assertion? Know that we are winners Nashville Public Schools. Can you see now using Federal tax dollars free money to fund their families business? Charges will soon await them. Season of enterprise is over for many of them. Federal agents will come, and arrest them one of the last strong holds in Williamson County, Wilson County as well. The suspense will be over soon it will all be over I'M grateful, because at the end of the day deep wells run deep no more it is the law. I hear most of you the city argues wait especially a little while longer your premium secret. That's right they are being converted right now, it is relevant now a new reference covering their mess hiring more teachers literally to take their place. It's irrational their game. Whistle blowers ought to shut them down now. Say, we're not going to take it be the motorists (in the driver's seat). Look at what they have already done, fellowship away. Praise the Lord God looked out for us, He did that for us it's for real. What a wild mess entirely. Turn them over. Are you listening Board give it up? Are you listening Metro-Nashville Government? Are you listening May Carl Dean? Due process of the ignorant no more. Move quickly! Move quickly! CHRIST JESUS said; I hear the Hispanic population inside Metro ^and Arabic as well. Check all their leaders out. Don't take more leaders. Essentially cut out delete all principle public Charter Public Schools from our district, delete principle Charter Schools right away that's your agency and everything will be fine. I view Antioch it needs maintenance they need help. Help right away now, act now no more Charter Public Schools. Charter School programs robbed them.

NEWS JIM CROW PEOPLE EVERYWHERE, IMAGINE THAT TREATMENT WHAT KIND MARGINAL? THE EMPHASIS PRACTICE HIDDEN DONE ON PURPOSE BELIEVE ME EVER LACKING WE ARE DOCUMENTED THE DANGER BLACK PEOPLE; MOVE SOMETHING THE MATTER OUT OF THE WAY. WE HAVE TROUBLE STANDING OUR HOUSE. IMPORTANT READ SPECIFICS IT IS A MESS.

Thus saith the LORD; building another house, their defense to half of our Country, politicians their government waste on the inside know that we are not mud not all fun and games. We are all powerful this event, we had nowhere else to go for help, we won't tolerate it anymore our experience. The emphasis Federal Government our breakthrough this case, our people things have gotten bad. Things should not be this complicated. Listen, stop barking at us on FACEBOOK, and MEET THE PRESS negative the White man against the Black people it's not healthy for us.

Time has taken a toll on us. The wild man Mr. Republican, we would like you to know the White man your operation in this Country. The Black people want you to know to the White people shake somebody else their hand with your hatred, the next time you want our vote; makeover a complete makeover is what ya'll need against the poor. I'M not by myself think about the journey you are on right now. Listen to me, say amen. Don't take me wrong I don't want to hear anymore those racial slurs anymore. I AM fifty inches away. AM I getting it across to you? I'M not some delivery corn person illegally here—hello; oh absolutely, that ya'll pick up in town. You can dig them up everywhere. Do you copy me? Bilingual I AM. I know the difference. Across the country they are your enemy these White people, they have a different outlook on life. You have got to come to a reality these poor individuals that you hire; sinful are those White people, "*Afternoon Ms. Daisy*" their expression; the illegal's our expression "Ya'll ought to quit." God is taken us through the exception. You know that is wrong. GOD is taken back. Shocking isn't it the avenue. Stop barking at us you White people. You know what they mean—your theme. Don't belittle them. White people *Ephesus*; pitiful just like the *Ephesians* at *Ephesus* gangs that you are. Here's a good euphemism everyday "let by gone be by gone" keep racial slurs to yourself in the kingdom, the problem—knock-knock you stink. For crying out loud it's going to be the death of you, you think you're slick its ugly you ought to put it down. Let it go it will kill you. Here's an album no more Country the way you see it anymore. Follow me; know a cooler your assembly racists. Read that book racist's not there, I the keeper am tearing those things down. Let me tell you something White politicians lay it down your practices; or do you want more trouble than you can handle the very end. Thus saith the LORD; A new coupon I'M raising the bar. God's building a house Williamson County your own created production. God's building a house Franklin, Williamson County in your case all your effort this commercial, I've got secret agents behind it watching you, the policy you have created, definitely. I see Sickling be careful, you ought to be careful. GOD sent a miracle no gimmicks, a law suit against your gimmicks hidden cameras are everywhere. Glory hallelujah! Tremendous amount taping your corporation, your people, see for that reason God's making a way even in Black houses, the Negro. Your diadem even in your neighborhoods, masses secret journalist including me, they are everywhere no doubt ^no accident recording criminal activity. Be real quick White people the result ya'll gradually will straighten it out. They are suffering with violence many people. Be real quick—the case to prevent violence in your town, and everywhere even in department stores even here in Nashville, better move quick. Tell it all get up close no gimmicks anywhere it's already done, for that reason blue collar workers they are the ones that are suffering, business people—White people they are racists. The *peninsula* on the north side of town trusted you most, okay? Many have suffered. That part of town is hurt the most. What are they supposed to do for JESUS CHRIST sake, White people many are out of work? The victim they want work hard to find jobs. The mechanics are doing, okay they have jobs. Employers don't want to hire Black people, the Negro super business so they can pay less money no excuse. For some Blacks there are different avenues many of them weren't affected their wages are the same, they just need more money-the cost of living is high. The victim got no jobs, they deserve more they are innocence. GIVE BACK GIVE DAVIDSON COUNTY DR. PEPPER THEIR REVENUE OWED TO THEM, BRENTWOOD AS WELL NOW THAT IS A DETECTIVE STORY YOU SWALLOWED A LARGE PIECE OF THEIR CAKE, THE RESIDENTS DID A GIFT FROM METRO-NASHVILLE. You're in our space even in Brentwood, people don't know, for that reason some are barely making it can't buy medicine, can't pay their light bills many don't have lights. What can we do legally? What do you say about that? They are on the outside looking in surely they are sobbing, thinking, wallowing, about the U. S. Constitution of America it isn't fair not fair Mr. President; they do most of this Country's work, piece of cake for some. Know why we were created? They are paying with a price Mr. Officials, better a man a break this Country ridiculous; they are U. S. citizens the Negro. Thus saith the LORD; we Democrats, African American Black people of America, we have tremendous amount of strong force, and other force behind us available tell the President. Mr. President Obama, thank GOD, we know you. You are our President. Mr. President automatically President Obama—then Mr. President again, we see a giant snake in the middle class, we have the evidence White Republican leaders, we invite you. Middle class you had no business doing that in the first place. Need an FBI report. The FBI will move them out of the way Charter Schools out of the system, their dream. That was part of the deal making Charter Schools' part of the deal. Thank you, JESUS CHRIST. Move them out couple them down, that was part of the plan. You would not have to work long a lot of people know. A lot of you are on lockdown in Metro Schools professionals nationally. I have the evidence swinging on a bank. Isn't that a beautiful thing? This is the end of it. You feel that comfortable. I see you on Facebook talking about your activities. Can you imagine that? GOD will weed them out. I'll tell you everything. *Search the records glass schools.* Who created the funds that will give them the evidence? SCHOOL PRINCIPALS THEY KNOW. HOW DO THEY KNOW PUBLIC RECORDS IN THEIR KINGDOM WILL SHOW THEIR DIADEM (THEIR CROWN) MY CHILDREN, AND ENORMOUS LOST BECAUSE THEY DIDN'T CARE AND PENTECOST THEY LOOKED THE OTHER WAY, OFFERING A ONE NIGHT STAND PETS THEIR PROJECT? THEY GET ON MY NERVES. LORD THANK YOU, LORD. Many people know. I see the emergency. I have the evidence. Give me the evidence.

Other units will follow make no mark. You're like a tumor that needs to be cut out. Search records been curious a great opportunity heave them an offering. Who created the funds for public wealth this misery, greed off balance legally? Can you imagine? Public records will show the diadem. Hit the ceiling I have the evidence. Knead back Mayor Dean pull the magic; I need a Negro/Adult $40,000 a job with a blessing to focus on him to take its place a lot of them deliverance sure foundation. HIGHWAY ROBBERY THEY HAVE TAKEN FUNDS $50 MILLION THAT DID NOT BELONG TO THEM; THE FIRST PLACE TO GROUND (OR GRIND) THEIR ASSEMBLY WILLIAMSON COUNTY TURN IT OVER $50 MILLION. CHRIST JESUS said; mark that no defense you under arrest and your government. Put into Metro-Government good people in key positions to restrict their public funding from Metro-Public Schools. Have an open house you'll see some action then. You are counter productivity you are under arrest by the administration, the LORD a citizen's arrest. Your game is up. ABIDE BY ME SAITH THE LORD GOD ALMIGHTY JESUS CHRIST HIMSELF. The *autobahn* race is over Williamson County. A miracle needed now your defense. Dreams do come true a better life for the kids in Metro-Nashville Public School. I honor him where ever I go wish you did the same. Your bullying days are over temperament now. You are fabulous LORD, our dream come true, we honor you fabulous you are. We are listening to your every word. Case closed. No mistake about it.

LORD! Strengthen me on the battlefield. Strengthen us on the battlefield. Open up those doors, we are good soldiers. Knock the doors down so we can walk through them. We're left out on a grill like barbecue conversation. That is the way it is in the south now a days in Nashville in Black people's neighborhoods. Please help my daughter! I see what she is up against. I applaud her effort no discipline in the schools. She's the only teacher without an aide, and all the teachers mass through the school system; she's and open book no accessory standards, and invitation and all the teachers' invitation speaking English. Don't be such a fool stop complaining about Nashville people corporations as well, politicians the wrath of GOD will soon come upon you. Give me a break. Thank God. She is a pillar of her community, I have the evidence. Can you help? I know her enemy and all the teachers. GOD help keep her to stay conscious, and aware of other teachers around her that are drowning in waste useless paperwork scheduling mess, a bummer alright. They are the hunted. Can you behave Supreme County Board, Supreme guard your blessing, learn a lesson County in Metro benefit staff you work with. These people are working their butts off teaching in Metro. She created her own standards so the kids could complete their lesson assignments. She is a good teacher, and there are plenty more like her just as equal. They argue a little bit grown ones suffer while lazy ones won't work, won't do their share take advantage; and then there is the discipline to contend with disturbing up the class like Vanderbilt keep the standards high soldiers are these people, but it's not just in Nashville. Save them! Their bonuses ran out (fair wages). Sometimes I feel defeat for them myself. I want to give them and offering. Help me! She is like a coupon. Defeat has brought their spirits way down in Nashville, and surrounding areas as well.

EXPLAIN ABOUT METRO-NASHVILLE PUBLIC SCHOOLS, THE EVIDENCE NEW DECISIONS THE SCHOOLS DISTRICT.

Thus saith the LORD; the government and the children in Middle Tennessee their school district are successful. Meatloaf why isn't Metro's doing the same? Metro Nashville it will be uncovered the evidence legal weapon. They hire teachers Williamson County—finger pointing, for elementary schools from Vanderbilt all the time. That is stiff internal damage that is not qualified Metro Nashville. GOD fix it we're tired of it better Nashville. Nauseous okay relevant is their crime ultimately so turn it around. Great property value here, we pay property taxes here so why aren't things turned around. Ask us? Crossed-up evil is their general intent. Get ready everybody I see big revenue coming our way. Evil is their crime. Metro-Nashville is still paying for it—Metro-Nashville the government. JESUS will uncover it. Somebody is getting ready to walk in now to do a take on Middle Tennessee, to see what has happened to the funds intended for our public school district. Let the sparks fly. It's time we took authority. October Feast devastation he sees the crisis in our government. Reluctant are people to fix the problem quickly, but they better while there is still time. Viewing the data Republicans, say Republicans your event JESUS CHRIST. There will be standing room only in the courtroom, when the fallout actually occurs in Nashville. *I see a hundred Republicans facing a lot of Democrats-Black people demanding immediate action including the Mayor Carl Dean, walking on thin ice and Metro Council. We will recover. AN ANNOUNCEMENT: Remember one thing your event negligence confusion, your stink bomb blame you Mr. Mayor, and the Republicans this administration who bleed everybody to death. It's an Olympics you're having an Olympics. My GOD, JESUS CHRIST anointed against you, JESUS CHRIST the anointed a force field legally separating your liberty. Talking about going to work on the issues trying to get it corrected, before it goes to Washington, and the Senate declares it a big mess, for heaven sakes a disaster for Tennessee, we are just a move away. College scholarship money won't go away and example, it needs to be loosened, so that we can fix public schools, oh thank you, JESUS thank God you're on our side. Pedro Garcia he wasn't I'M telling you building a reputation that's the result. PERPETRATORS: The rich perpetrators started it here in Nashville, as it turned out no accident. The rich United Pentecostals just a lean on your desk, your favor Republicans took the money here in Nashville area schools with no regret, they have politicians. God can deliverer use wisdom everybody. Let God bishop me and be the judge that has kept me, and delivered me preachers this great house the honorable Bishops. The end of this operation this program by me, you may say over stepping my bounds church over stepping my bounds I did not. I just left the bounds directory; we all have rights most definitely. Prisoners we are not. Amen. Never over step your bounds Council. You hear me; just do what is right as a Christian. Don't fall by the wayside—ridiculous.

INSERT-SUBSCRIPTION: A TURN ABOUT SEEKING THIS ALTERNATIVE. In addition, this is another letter. Complete input that is the theme of this letter complete input. Actually, that represents be it affirmed our future CHRIST our redeemer, the original himself. Specifics, go ahead you don't know what you are doing span a new assessment Nashville, Tennessee and abroad. An Insert-Subscription: For A NEW ARTICLE (Legally and complete of JESUS CHRIST, Pentecost I follow God, your true God. He is human. The actual written by Barbara Payne recorded on Friday, November 2, 2012 9:00 P.M.

SUBSCRIPTION FOR THE
*A NEW ARTICLE*
THE ACCOUNT

A CLASSIC THERE ARE NEW RULES, BECAUSE OF CHRIST JESUS REMEMBER THAT, REMEMBER THE GROUND RULES. NON-FICTION THIS BOOK, TRADITIONAL REMEMBER THAT.

BY AUTHORITY THUS SAITH JESUS CHRIST; INCREASE YOUR STANDARDS PEOPLE OF GOD. LET THAT BE A LESSON

## A New Article

TO YOU, LET THAT BE A LESSON LEGALLY. THE TRUTH, HAIL THE GOOD NEWS INITIATIVE NEW TELLING THEM ALL ABOUT IT LEAVING IT TO GOD FOR MAKING A WAY OUT OF KNOW WAY. GIVE IT TO HIM HONOR. GOD SAID; THROUGHOUT THE WRITING OF THIS BOOK HOLD YOUR BREATH, MEET WITH ME. I COULD NOT HAVE WRITTEN THIS BOOK WITHOUT HIM. GOD YOU ARE AMAZING. SPAN *"A NEW ARTICLE"* WRITTEN BY ME BARBARA PAYNE, DEGLATED DEFINITELY LEGALLY YOUR STANDARDS.

© A NEW ARTICLE
FOR JESUS CHRIST, THAT IS CORRECT
A NEW WAY OUT FOR METRO NASHVILLE PUBLIC SCHOOLS

Copyright © 2012 By Sister, The Original Barbara Payne ™ in the name of JESUS CHRIST delivered. All rights are exclusively reserved in USA. Signed in pseudonym By Barbara Pay ne---------------------------------

CHARGES WITH NO REGRETS EVEN IN THE DARKEST NIGHTS AND INDEPENDENT RESEARCH COLLECTIVELY BY ME, AND THE GENRE PENTECOST BY ME AND THE BIBLE; EVEN TO THE FOURTH GENERATION WISE WHAT THEY HAVE GIVEN TO US THEIR MOTIVE, A FORMAL DECLEARATION WITH OVER TURN By Barbara Payne, IN THE USA THE HAPPENING BE IT KNOW FOREVER.

No one is in the middle By Sister Barbara Payne, the entire context written by me and JESUS CHRIST The CHRIST; ladies and gentlemen no avenue sub JESUS CHRIST, he's the person we can depend on, I'm telling you. For without him there is no avenue of hope, but death without hope. He is independent so grab his hand; you've been wrestling with this for a very long time. Where there is salvation we are hopeful. All rights are under reserved independent in the USA by me alone. For this reason context in this work is mine in the name of JESUS CHRIST, and only me gathered by me complete to be sold as an independent writer. Irregardless, it is written by me for on the record cherished for this purpose. Honest you have any objection for this reason Country, and your reaction blogger in any event, my address any exchange annually accountability at any place store it by JESUS CHRIST. The results don't blame it on me your racketeering, we need desperate help. We're not alone. I mean think the impossible what can He do but a miracle—but cry unto GOD CHRIST JESUS, for help cry unto GOD, and who gives unto us everlasting life our champion preachers to this Country and around the world. Handle yourself your emotions. He gives us strength use your intelligence. Any objections contact the anchor, our GOD JESUS CHRIST. I AGREE. BE IT PREFERRED IT BY ME. GENERALLY THE TEMPLATE YOURS, THE EVENT YOUR ACCOMPLISHMENTS-PREFIX TOPIC: ANY QUESTIONS YOU ARE MY OWN. THINGS DO MATTER MY HONOR CHRIST JESUS, UNDERSTAND?

FROM ABOVE: The big announcement go all the way schedule success and article written by me praise GOD, and article template in booklet form tiffany in design. Even in paperback form by me, throughout all the ages eternity concrete by me people of JESUS CHRIST and how to. They made it a success even when others doubted it. In this age give you a booklet TLC blocking any information what we have, the Obama generation it's a physical. And eye opener give you a booklet by myself blocking it literally all around their evil speaking events, the results you're looking at a picture fascinating ultimate. This Article was superintended, was written all by me and the LORD JESUS CHRIST; tablet form the original everyday serving GOD the reason. I am grateful virtual to JESUS the HOLY GHOST for keeping me, for not losing my sanity drawn by decent. Complete this emphasis no offense with deep emphasis my duty included underwritten on this, by passion to the KING glory to him JESUS CHRIST the emphasis. Drawn in ink and on paper purpose the facts received evidence not by no agent or public records, updated for you I'm grateful. Oh incidentally, this first writing given by the hand of GOD JESUS CHRIST, literally speedily whose got daily power for His people legally. I know the culprit beating me down literally. I thank God, JESUS CHRIST. Listen can't nobody turn me around no offense drum roll this behind me! Oh incidentally your inspection translated this of the real evidence pros and cons written proof by me, carrying no smoking gun all the time collectively. God cares about his people gathers everywhere, wherever they are doubters too. I know I've got food on the table. When they think pay your dues in Nashville, don't be snobbish even in Murfreesboro. Another thing, honorable is our God. The LORD JESUS said unto me; I would agree. This booklet it's a question, I have ups and downs mental state when it is posted, but I must keep it all together I know God will cover me. Have reserved talking about my marriage trouble it is for me, this person my helper in Nashville, in this epistle praise God. Dual play merit-topic throughout the entire book, I am truly grateful. Middle the case throughout the book, the given account I'm writing this book. I honor FATHER; given your permission please don't look at the innocent unbelievable. CHRIST JESUS said unto me, I'll think about it. LORD, you shake me! Closure for me, people didn't think I would write a book calling me names even my children trash talking as well. You have a testimony said God to me at that moment. Let me explain something to you, dignity I defend JESUS CHRIST. I don't know what I would have done if JESUS CHRIST, did not protect me from those assaults. *Observing out there what are you going to say next about me? I have finished a book read it now no joke. THE CASE: authored a book no remake a big accomplishment. The Jim Crow resident, we are onto your habits now. The journey oh why wait take your ticket, the gas will never run out for you proven. Look at me I'm cruising now no real negotiations no mess. Anyway now take your stethoscope, I'm not hemorrhaging. In the end JESUS CHRIST has your back. In the true end things matter to our Savior, the person name JESUS CHRIST. I'm breathing on living waters with a whistle no suspense. I'm on my way to heaven true testament tell everyone we have equal access. Think you, JESUS. We can cruise now He is taking a snapshot of all our lives. Grab your portion now, before you lay down and rest. Let no one take your place, definitely! Say He's always there, oh great JEHOVAH GOD everybody! Claim our GOD merciful He is forever.

## LIKE KINGDOM MINDED IN THE EARTH FROM ABOVE YOU ARE A JEW

This article each statement is for FATHER GOD JESUS CHRIST. We are covered by His blood there is no other alternative. JESUS CHRIST, I dearly love him extreme. Some have hated of me that's the atmosphere. Exhausted now; I have written this book now take it JESUS CHRIST, examine it with your favor my accomplishment with a little wiggle room on my behalf with wisdom JESUS CHRIST my friend, pillow of strength my superstar in His place. They mocked me JESUS CHRIST in April of this year. Relax you are my friend, I view your accomplishment. Because of Him CHRIST JESUS my friend struck down their offenses I won. THUS SAITH THE LORD; I know what I AM doing. I'M not laying down Pentecost, say I refuse giving up get it your anointing they refused you even your pastor, and across that street, and your husband the narrative? Stay close to me different class they are. A very simple epic are you listening big-team, their team, hallelujah, you with drew? AN ANNOUNCEMENT: you took a dive from Asia their traffic winter time, pushed you right out the door your services didn't matter just a freak. When it comes to you I'M not kidding *Abednego* that you are, you grew up and they stayed the same. I will protect you. If you ask me Pentecost flavor the underground word,

## A New Article

they thought that you were a freak, you cried wolf to them a lot that was what you were up against. Then again, your effort with them and your services let me tell you, kindergarten the whole unit, I AM looking at that church right now all lack wisdom view hot off the press, please you better believe me. You wouldn't believe a team effort Pentecost, don't you know you're not on their team. You're not going to his church anymore, and his youngest son never joined their brave team effort clearly he graduated, when you grow up different grounded you more become thanks, to CHRIST JESUS. I put more value in him can't knock forever. He sees the very thing done to them, when outside the United States of America this side of the U. S. border. *A breakthrough for him will soon follow according to the word. I view him an Elder a long time ago. And his youngest son he sees the difference; he says no return to their machine politics. He says that off the ground with those people. He advanced at the right place believe me; he believes it's just the right thing to do. The Whites they want behave single out you were the institute before GOD, accusing unadvertly prophecy protested. That is your answer to them blame, they are to blame Pentecost. Practice syndrome that kind of behavior in play on you. Jealousy Pentecost it brings out the worst in many anything can happen that's for sure, you're on fire for me still seeking GOD, a bonus congratulations Pentecost, knowing kingdom primarily their rude behavior demeanor that is for sure. He rules all the time (my husband how he stabs me in the back), specifics he always has competitive in the air feels threatened, wonder where he gets it from? From his father he has his nature, and the country rolled in debt from afar his accomplices against me, he has a new phrase— institute ignorant. He likes whites the big criminal Pentecost. He models their racist's attitude relationship, their character against me. Darn their package attitude. He makes me nervous even in my feet *a Judas*. A NEW UPDATE: I have rheumatoid arthritis in my joints because of him. *Praying, can't shake arthritis need to move from here literally even in my back he shakes me at my stomach, he stinks my husband just crazy okay? *I'm tired of the abuse. Pentecost this is an unfortunate situation, I must get you out of here so be wise. Get me out of here; says scripture no offense. They are dangerous be not afraid. The average he bothers me recording me with an instrument staying on that phone. AN ANNOUNCEMENT FOR YOU: be careful the newspaper knowing blowing smoke out their ears against you Pentecost. Just acting like a clown flapping physics on you. *People are praying now in their congregation, they have limitations even in your family against you saying, *low-down* the undertaker in your relationship living on welfare, that's me big mess done. They have observed. *They know he pocketed the money. I have the evidence not just your opinion. I AM sending you some help to help solve this problem Pentecost; you will view it real quickly. Reasonably be real smart just keep looking up to me anytime. Pentecost, I have your back. I view you every day. He is wrong the offense treachery manufactured. Family and friends got nothing for their active part. *And that company that he used to work for, Human Resource will crack it her name solo. Be on guard leave them alone "Hello Aunt Barbara" they are a mess, they use you. A finalization I will help you. Say LORD, forgive me for creating all this mess. Physically reduce my knowing off limits bring closure. I need a miracle. There are great battle lines property is their technique. I draw the battle line. You are no problem Pentecost your opinion think first I view your house stop cursing. GOD is a good God forgive me for that action he angered me. Hear that Elder Burns, the Comforter sent me to you to know oneness, the pastor who baptized me into oneness in the wonderful name of JESUS CHRIST our Savior? I can do better. This *epic* wrong I was for the language. Unimaginable, believe that challenges. Let me encourage you; forgive him and other people as well. My husband he attacks me, blues I keep I keep the blues. People are onto him now. Phenomenal, shocking, dangerous atmosphere, you are an incredible human being. Fulfill your destiny. Don't you see you are incredible, see Ms. Barbara you are chosen my friend. LORD, deliver me from this place. The agent, I AM your friend, and to your family. You are incredible. I will protect you from him now be brave. Shocking stand on guard his indifference he bothers me. For continuance be on guard he stands accusing. I view him in abundance. He is a murderer get my point so be safe? I've got news; I'M pulling an affidavit to you now your favor. He's nonsense get help. We're going to go ahead we're going to set a higher standard. Really initially a real mean devil unnerve you completely knows no boundaries. Legally below your class Pentecost, I see him in strip-joints okay? Very empty you will be very empty low-life traveling with him. His flavor way off the wall not cosmopolitan like you, a lack of can't send him places to be a representative, him and all his friend are lunar in atmosphere looking at other peoples, rates other peoples package the whole group like a nightmare. Pentecost be not afraid. I know the kind burning lust in the face with finger. Read *SAINT MATTHEW* the gospel; thought I had fell asleep Nashville, they all think that their instinct a deceiving man. Let me shake your hand you are amazing. He's tarring you down don't give up. He's breaking you down. His motives are uplifting you with a safety net; yellow interference to death so look out his numbers are crossed up off the field thinking blank. Dozens are like him move real quickly around mid-June or July, and even mid-August he is nuts the onion. Thank you, JESUS CHRIST. We're going to roast him now completely. Oh thank you, JESUS CHRIST. He's trying to kill you in that house. Men get ready he has a warrant an arrest warrant for his arrest. No banquet for him. *"Don't ruin my puppy was your screams your joy," your youngest daughter her little dog that you loved so much, and she loved you as well. I couldn't bear it a whole new bundle of joy. He frightened you every time. He is a criminal no other way to describe it even though

## The Original Barbara Payne

he speaks in tongues. He will pay for it. Watch out Nashville, his record is in Nashville, out there. Nashville, he's under arrest. And your young ones are talented young people like you. I will deliver them as well, when they open their mouth for common defense just an expression avenue. Successful you have become it was good working with you Pentecost, JESUS CHRIST. Every year Ms. Barbara, the advisory against you completely the advisory your husband, you're going to win that case completely inconjunction Ms. Barbara, people do doubt, and they are watching him. You have written a book Dr. King would have been proud of you this one. In any event understand that's your life immoveable indifference that is your life, I can help you in any event he watches you all the time. Anyhow you are the victim don't you see? Hey my assistant, personally noted by JESUS CHRIST. I fall out with him a long time ago LORD JESUS. Don't attack him no more murderer he is. Learn a lesson this phrase he's going to hell your accuser. For the crime he committed based on the evidence found 0800 Hours. Trash talking he runs it in the ground always cooking with words. *He committed a criminal act: a perpetrator with a hand gun in his hand bothers me says, JESUS CHRIST unto me. And using that hand gun a great move for him. Using a hand gun he shot a man for no apparent reason, and bragging on himself. I've wrestle with this one on his defense the package literally. "At ease sergeant your wife doesn't know." In disguise him he opened fire a man without a gun, he shot a man watch him breath, and then watched him die for no apparent reason a murderer him, he's *a lunatic* he doesn't like you. Hear me, I'll say it a thousand times, I know his resources. Easy play then he walked to the meeting, they were in a mess a beast knowing right from wrong, "I didn't know what I was doing thought we were playing" to the Government. He told authorities he claimed he was aiming to high. He was a murderer real quick. "I can't believe you did that, you knew what you were doing" The Company Guard. "Can you imagine that don't

## A New Article

trust him." "You knew better than to start shooting it was no pranking, you were not pranking." "You pulled that gun on him on purpose aim wasn't too high," deliberate the intent was his intention. "Now people hate you fastened your seat belt." Barbara, esteem for me JESUS CHRIST. "She falls short" so ugly for all the wrong reasons talking about you like that. I'm done getting back at him lying he is strange. I'M available Pentecost, I understand. Watch that language Pentecost people are watching you. I AM covering you. I dote on you literally JESUS CHRIST; other people will toast him it's a done deal. Be careful talking on the phone. He needs some adjustments. Alright okay. *Pentecost you and Camille's conversation, watching at the other end of the line creepy the mess. Mental he is Nashville, call him low-medium his brain crazy. Diamond in the ruff stay on guard your route; be on guard with a capital G he tells the church everything. Unbelievable Jewry Jerusalem with a capital J you that's you, I see him discussing you almost every day. So be like me. Don't be afraid of him. You understand I'll help you. I will bring you a new castle soon. I watch you every day. Your benefit hear me your bonus, I will break up this mess. Follow the schedule like long time ago typically anytime before 5:00 o'clock a.m. weekdays. I know you are having a hard time this journey. Now don't forget that. *I declare on guard at her best, I'M talking about you. Hear me, creepy your husband he hears yall's conversation daily. You've been through the wringer enough. Don't be afraid of him. Understand just read between the lines bugging you very mental, he has disease at the mouth? That I would agree Lord, for myself he's lost his mind. Your assessment daughter from JESUS CHRIST, hear me I hear him all the time at that house; I don't know how you cope with him. You can hear him almost every night all night long those screams, nightmare dreams ( his night terrors) those devils are after him. I know it is painful. Stop that name calling. Sometimes he gets on your nerve just let it slide impulsive is he. He could hit you under the table. Be thankful I watch over you. I view him multiple times not humble. AM I accusing him of any wrong doing? An active theft he is still active, lowdown he is actively about you. I'M going to take him to the dry cleaners. He just needs a bath one-on-one with me; then he'll bother you no more. The angles are watching him; he's having trouble breathing at night. Deceit automatically it's a fact no landscape idea easy to understand. Preachers instead of calling those devils out of him they don't. A Pastor an officer of the church, the Pentecostal leader person in Nashville, Tennessee, the Tennessee leader Bishop a minister of GOD, I AM your friend let's sit right down and talk. Don't fight him that third-party, he will attack you it's only a matter of time tell the people. JESUS CHRIST, come to the rescue! Saying let's chop his head off wrestling with you. To The Bishop, I'M warning your wife and your family, and the people of GOD, you need a meeting Pentecost. Family now thus saith our Lord JESUS CHRIST; the Holy Ghost your friend. Don't mess with him he's in your organization. Bishop, and Nathaniel a big tug on the ground this is not your battle. In plain view an opportunity presented he has you on the ground. He has you cornered in reserved. Acknowledge he'll approach you; he'll be at your station of identity keep observing him. Don't tell me you don't know any better. Tell him to lay those tools down. By the way a missed an opportunity, I AM more than able. Tell your wife don't fool with junk, he complains to her a picture opportunity his cloak fake. From a religious standpoint the obvious don't fool with *junk*. You've been told now listen. Now don't care, when you rise it will be all over you, you will be saying help me LORD against him. Painful when they are laughing at you, put that bus away—your benefit. And the women amusing jaws they are amusing stop him, he's on the hunt and they are an easy mark they are narrative with him, stop them from talking they go after him, he is one of their moving favorite it's unbelievable they come to him Pentecost. Preachers that are wise *catalyst* (hastening his behavior over you) they are content, they will be at fault; they just watch and observe him eventually he'll have that fit in their campground. That is significant people will wonder what is ugly doing here, exactly. They will be saying get out of here, get out of our house turning him out the author of deceit. A new development people are nuts about him, all subtle active lately, I hear him boasting Ms. Barbara. You don't mind if I call you by your first name? Let me explain, he's real desperate got no real friends got those devils in him. People that are keen spiritually (*discern*) they have empathy for you. They already know my husband, and who they are that are working in him, and they are prepaid for him they have discernment in their lives. They all watch him and they know. You can't win many have been bitten before. Send GOD after them and they will go away. How did this happen, he has become criminally insane virtually? Now Ms. Barbara he is your husband, you are responsible for him, exactly. The after math for you, facing immediate hate by your husband creepy they are (those devils inside of him). Let me tell you something, be careful he will pull a gun on you. Don't be afraid. I will look out for you in that region down in Egypt land (in bondage my family) just like the nation. For example, hard nose he is a battle brewing all the time with you, he doesn't care. He has no friends (your husband coming after you). He carries a gun anytime he feels threatened. They are threatening him legally. People have picked up his spirit and they know he's got devils in him. You're getting a divorce. A unique opportunity, I will change the atmosphere keep praying, thanks to JESUS CHRIST our maker, David is onto him right now. And that David the youngest and not the elder is the apostle, he has shown he is an apostle. And I will tell you the rest some other time about him. Huh David? What happens in Nashville stays in Nashville, now don't fool yourself. He will soon find out. I'M on your side. He definitely will attack take that gun away, viewing safety first legal issue. *He sees snakes your husband just (*schizophrenia*) in your house. Between you and your husband whole bunch of shouting everybody knows it even the neighbors, out in the yard everybody knows about it from a legal sense shouting at the buggers all the time, can imagine keeps you all upset it's like yelling at a snake that you are wrestling with? There is no wonder you sleep in that back bedroom because of his behavior, no wonder you are tired all the time my sister, you are tired of meditating to God dealing with his behavior and those issues. JESUS that is me, I am your friend and I watch out for you all the time. Murderer he is, I wouldn't want to sleep beside him. Those bad snakes fighting demons all the time, something has got to be done about him. Anyway before the fall of Saigon (April 30, 1975) he should have addressed it then, he's ignorant thought tablets would kill it and dope. I don't know why a big mistake. His mission accomplished being in the military all those years ruined his life. For example, brain damage a lot of soldiers act like him thousands, they are veterans. Pass suspended—in real company mere animals. They need a miracle. Daughter they are real messed up, absolutely. Believe me in their head just stupid knocking, these old soldier's demons let out. The President, Mr. President know better in this Country, we're at an all time low this nation, we're facing another war. The Country can't give up. I'M telling you watch them when they come back home, The White House our Government denied for many a year's how they get along-different wars. He has been denied some medical coverage; naturally it's a doggone shame. And it's not just an isolated event your issue with him is his regret. Got the Purple Heart pilgrim courage reported by the Congress, that's a fact anyone would be proud of him. A Purple Heart conspiracy a little weird thing, ask medical personnel "hey better sound an alarm about him," it was their public mistake and it was a mistake. And at his funeral don't accept any reward; you would be in agreement with his dirty deed committed on another. "Oh we've seen the best of times." Just for free his mission. He is a U. S. citizen unattended for the

## A New Article

movement. They shouldn't tolerate that kind of treatment duty in advance. On the battlefield needless to say, never give up their team members would say. The principle in time funeral arrangements in units, and for arrangements he had honorable discharge. Let me explain, weird number give them leverage and they will tear you up throwing a fit make you have a heart attack. Hundreds are like that wild men. You're the greatest President elected past and present. I admire you. They shouldn't be denied coverage. Be on guard angles are watching for you against Mr. Arrogant. *And you know what, yes indeed their brains suffer, the average independent suffer objection. Let me tell you something, they are racists independent in the military E-F5's and Staff the Sergeants some don't even make sense. That is sad news the veterans of this nation from above then on the other hand they need help, the good news all people the American people we are praying for them. They need a miracle right away. They've been on the front line far too long these American Vets. Then President Obama please help out we are desperate, they are your people understand this situation. Thank you, JESUS CHRIST. Listen to me, President Obama, and senior advisors we need someone to help the men when they return home, Civil Rights leaders a retro of our nation every day expedition. The final analysis, it's a strong hold on them chained them up. Don't try and ignore them, because they will wrestle you down onto the ground. FROM ABOVE: To me says JESUS CHRIST; now the cause was Viet Nam: Pain can't kill it away they need a miracle. Turning on you, he turns on you his repay pitiful unbelievable he hurts you. Deep down you are nasty you want to wash your hands; his words my friend talking ridiculous everyday at you it aggravates you. Local brand in the service just mixed up all over he can't think he wants you to then agree with whatever he is saying, in addition matter of circumstance talk like a group a calculator loosely under the table. Spiritually he is loose in the camp—real backwards, real dangerous. A jerk, always gives the appearance of mild mannered supposedly right here in Nashville, a real covert operator would beat her Nashville, I warned him a long time ago yes me, the person JESUS CHRIST. Group therapy; a lie he's never gone just sitting on the side lines like the others, regular conversation everybody passersby hanging on a cliff regularly. Hit me like a ton of bricks saying stop. Let me tell you, being the CHRIST JESUS CHRIST I will protect her real quick. I would jump on him real quick. *I whip my kids, if they don't act right under age as well. He used to pick a fight with you, but I put a stop to that. I told him the next time I will carry him out that window, and I would I meant it. His elevator doesn't go all the way up, the battery seems warm limited edition will knock you down. He picks a fight just to aggravate you, but I'm sealed conference force repeated action straight up. Gentlemanly he is not. He pees all the time his doctor says his physical condition—he's losing a kidney, the right kidney is dying his death is upon him right now cancer in his blood stream. Don't tell your children let them see for themselves, they will have a hard time with it can't be ignored just trust me, included in that the VA didn't report it. Right now tight word extreme a rare form of cancer a typo various kinds of cancer hadn't been reported yet, they will soon discover it yet those doctors of the VA system it's a very unusual circumstance. Cancer extreme will show on his bed and in his urine, and when he goes to the bathroom. In your house better keep an eye on him many soldiers have died with the same disease had the same complications, and Alzheimer's disease. Literally they are really dying hadn't identified it yet. *At Camp Shelby, in Mississippi "Well, I'll be-darn. Seriously let me tell you right now, they are looking at it now and the list goes on at many military bases. "Unusual lock it up, don't tell anyone about it just want my advice keep it a secret; then lock it up okay let's just keep it a secret gentlemen?" "We don't have leverage for it." "Exactly be it known the military don't have any leverage." "Exactly" that is said Republicans at all those military bases everywhere. And they are still counting the Veterans "Things just happened." Those people at those bases do not know what they are doing. Exactly it has ruined many men's lives. Be honest with you people that serve me, conservative they are running out of time soon it will be discovered hastily they are tracing it. This is an emergency. OPTIONAL: no treatment, there is no treatment for it. Many will die brain dead. For many it is tough to find work, they labor hard in this event, they feel no one no longer cares, the White man did this to them" the African American male off to war. Negative is their effort putting forth an effort to find an answer. Something had better be done before it's too late. My heavenly Father knows, we love everyone of you especially these Black men against the Whites, their number is thicker with the White man the number is narrow. Race Black or White we need you to protect this nation of ours. They are getting nowhere. Black men want to know. They want you all to know. They owe a debt, Viet Nam War for their effort. Soon the veterans will have to know. I will talk to you about it soon, okay? I will tell you everything coming up. Turns out at any time he is a threat be real careful. Say, thank you Everlasting. He so hurt me, pitiful I was forgive me. The accuser dare him anytime use scripture anytime, he will pay for it. I see massive grave they are dangerous. He is a pain. No open door for your husband, GOD I am trembling. I heard you. GOD you take my breath away JESUS CHRIST! I AM JESUS CHRIST. You don't want to offend him in anything people. Talking about him everything Pentecost slipping, he is Nathaniel won't go the distance lately marked as a Christian complete that was him. He is dangerous Pentecost. A regular cheater of everything in yall's house Pentecost. To top it like regular having sex with everybody he chooses, look at them in the field painful as it seems the crook many know, the White people know about your husband. They ran upon him lately won't tell on him, your husband group sex-next entertainment. *About the sex no freefall no more it's not a bad habit, he has another problem visible his character, he has an old familiar spirit (demon possessed, evil) he practices witchcraft as well tries to control her with it, even in her sleep. He uses other sources daughter to knife you in the back pure evil then he practices witchcraft a habit that he learned while traveling in the military; From Above to that and at his residents his mother used it thought it was advantage, the resident where he grew up basically his wreck. For you battle ground upon your honor causing you wreckage, a privilege learned it in Viet Nam creating insults dishonorable wanting to take you away causing you injury. Things matter I will deliver you from this house Pentecost, you're not going to sleep here anymore, okay? In Pentecost and at home an exchange at you, he is jointly lowdown follows his natural behavior lowdown all natural everybody knows, he is pretending he likes to pretend. *A friend of yours Sister Barbara, wondering what is going on, him ruining your life devastating. An impression for me physically you've written three books why you're so long away. I don't know Nashville, when I will return to church, I'm not that important. "I'm telling you, you can't trust her" his muscle, his words behind it. Believe me so fast control yourself extreme control your emotions! Let me tell you something, you need a miracle. "That will keep her away" at the church where you all attend saying "Can't trust her" Nathaniel, saying that to other people even to Brother Brown and his wife politically his defense. I admire you, I AM prejudice of you on the job indeed independent. I will beat the defense daughter on your behalf. Don't worry Ms. Barbara, about it viewing the competition trashy he is in your house; about her he created a scene—your operation. "Until death we're just going to lock her up in a mental institution, and then visit her occasionally," agreed to that your son about you for the rest of your life, "Lock her up." Pentecost believe me, their actual exchange checking her out that day, a warrant against you. It's embarrassing him around a lot of people, you can't be happy. Don't worry I AM on your side. They are watching you your personality pointed out, "Typically they all have a tendency to break out" (being emotional) your husband speaking to your son big fallout against you. Your murderer, the killer in the military that is your husband that is what he told your son. Their council together horrible against you their actions, when they had council together that summer a leak proof secret among themselves, your accuser can you imagine Ms. Barbara? *But thanks to me JESUS CHRIST, your prison better dream on so far in that house locked up it hasn't happened. They're going to get a wakeup call rely on me. Ms. Barbara what they created a mess it is no accident, their opportunity just pitiful directly wishing that on you, and your son futile trying to get back at you, he has apparent reason desperate he is. *I must tell you, he thought for real Nathaniel, you would never escape that house your makeup believe me. Just think what would have happened, if I had not been looking out for you in the camp. *I will move you away from this home. JESUS CHRIST! That is what they are trying to do too you. Here is another note: your son as well and his girlfriend. *I just want to get him and your youngest daughter as well they are confused Ms. Barbara, a revolution spreading propaganda about you they each separate, they have a front row seat. *Revelry, they are after your baby girl she is in a prison, she sucks on her wine drawing a breath even the bottle "Come on have a little bit," she didn't learn that at home. I'm a good person. I live straight thanks to you JESUS the CHRIST; follow the straight and narrow, the Holy Ghost abiding by your word. For your information your baby daughter to they are confused. I view them every year. I just wanted you to know Ms. Barbara. *LORD; my children just save them. They don't deserve it. I know you pray for them all the time that is on your record. On this side you have a clean record. I can depend on you always. Your son, loved him believe me he used to be like you pleasing everywhere his route, but satan got in his ear views dirt now won't change dirt directed at you completely. His head hard a little bit needs to get help, before I clean house both of them a real hard spanking. Their game is up. Your satan both of them a specialists, it's a wonder you haven't had a heart attack the way they have come after you Ms. Barbara, this hour the way they have acted directed at you him and your youngest daughter. Be grateful your oldest daughter cares stays more grounded; be grateful for that on her over here tough tries to be her own person with understanding toward you. *Says, I CHRIST; a beautiful person more understanding, she has a real handle on life. BIG ANNOUNCEMENT: I see an increase with flowers your increase, okay? I will finish it a reality his reality upgrade. I owe it to you. JESUS CHRIST the person; you are so good to me. You are so right. They have been bad mouthing me all this time at different events. You've been hanging on by a thread. I've got you covered. Your son he is a bully at you, and in life a generation gap he needs counseling you know that, because of your husband no respect for you? My son thinks he is the only one complete. I will finish it a reality his reality. Say, "*Amazing Grace How Sweet It Sounds.*" Understand what I AM saying nothing less will satisfy GOD, me people? I'M trying to put a smile on your face. Believe me go all the way. Pray for him. I AM a witness that he understands. Doesn't honor me I view a round up, they will recognize him. I view him gifted. Views me as a joke the bubblehead laughing at you, thinks it's embarrassing been whitewashed the joke is on him. Your son he is in the middle big cut that boss just be prepared. You understand your children they are adults, I can help you it can go either way before they repent. They should be saying I want to be more like him, CHRIST JESUS not a peppermint bar. Going to heaven a racists there are more that are racists that won't get in, including a friend your friend. *Let me tell you, your children they are blinded, it is no accident Nathaniel their father Pentecost and others like him. I will give you credit just look up. They just look at you, an epic center a pillar of strength for life an adult so be prepared whenever they come to you like in September. I give you a lesson now, I've been meaning to talk to you just say, you don't have nothing to talk to me about people. They've been watching you along the way no doubt them evil, and they are brutal they are not your friend, they have ruined your relationship crippled it stalking you as well. You have written a book you've got talent, and anointing you remember GOD, when they come and try to persuade you, mess with you giving details can't cripple you going to make it an event. You say JESUS CHRIST remember me, stand your ground your rope forever. Because of them you lost a chapter waiting for things to turn around. Look, now please stop wrestling with it all that evil all the time. Take comfort. Naturally they are my children, and with regret I pray they will turn around. Say greater is He his Excellence bountifully. I view generations coming after you daughter be thankful, I AM your friend always. You give me hope for their redemption. Now be extra quite, and stay calm you have a long life with me don't be afraid. I view an Amber alert, they will come back to me just like you. JESUS CHRIST! The premises can you imagine? All things are possible if you believe. I view an open house for you. Things will work out let me work them out those issues. I bought their frame; I will remember each of them. Each of them I will always serve them, they will be more like me Pentecost. For them Pentecost, your final destination give them a house like you your final record. Pamela hanging around with the wrong crowd, she has moral issues against you engagement all the time using her temper as a the *tenet*, her hanging around that group having no class her friends, reason against you on behalf of them causing you pain. Both of them your son as well you are cutting them off. Talking about your children the break up daughter you have experienced with them, you haven't sin not your idea it was brought on by them. What happened? Their human nature, both of them trying to make you look like a fool instigating stereotypical stirring up trouble, shame on them pitiful people of GOD, can't be a white lining shame on them bruised your heart? And your youngest breaking a window at the other house way back when, and then storming around stabbing you in the back. NOT CHASING A GOOD DESIRE FOR HERSELF: the ultimate sacrifice going the wrong way modeling herself into being wanting to be a blue collar industrialist everyday modeling herself into that, and her desiring to be a non-pedigree person to this present moment, and not finishing college the way she should have and stabbing you in the back with her actions just full of it dirt, and acting perverted and comical acting second class at that the whole way, and she can definitely perform making herself silly in front of them, intelligent enough to succeed we all know that, and a peace breaker in yall's home certainly not like Camille. We need union in that praying against those insults. Agreed! I've got proof of her stabbing you in the back. *I will spoil her plan on you. Oh thank you, JESUS! Weak minded entertain herself being morally offensive going nowhere, foreshadowing—wrecking the house you now live in disturbing you. They instigate against you, they are trying to get over without paying their just dues. They should be turned away from your face. GOD gives you credit for turning her away, them away, keep trying he sees their ways. Do your best to be a good citizen. I will soon bring peace. I see the darts in your back in this time of piercing killer fiery darts coming at you, a double wheel a bunch of lies. Your children romantics in the house they are fantasizing about their youth and their upbringing, lost they would have been without guidance and teaching of Godly CHRIST like instruction. They need to read *MATTHEW* from front to cover; and *GALATIANS*; and then *PHILIPPIANS*; it will tell them all about disturbing trouble, people won't read the books and chapters thoroughly. Read *MATTHEW*; read the book all the chapters let them speak to you counsel you will find there. They get on my nerves just the opposite of you, just evil against you worrying you to death the both of them. No norm in their face.

*A New Article*

Attention all the wise they all are doing all that dirt to you behind your back like they are holding you hostage. You are amazing. Passive they are wrecking your home killing your joy, and ruining the house. Even running away she should have been arrested all those years back, a child with one parent guiding. *And your baby Pamela, I've got proof if it had not been for Mrs. Ethel Payne her sweet grandmother watching out for her, she would have been in big trouble not walking around anymore. She would have been kidnapped and held for hostage, and ruined for life by those crooks operating in that city beyond the river. *What's your father's name, you'll figure it out later? Worrying you till this day always picking a fight with you during arguments wanting romance (her hormones gone wild), blaming you wanting sin of the world a big reflection on you singling you out, and your boy likewise stabbing you in the back Pentecost my servant for free his actions. Brown I don't blame you. There is not going to be a replay against you. Something has to be done right now. I view your life every day Pentecost. You try and stay out of trouble, learn that lesson drive real slow don't act a monkey, JESUS CHRIST your redeemer will get you out of that house. You will be alright. Don't you cause a scene no offense in that house they will take you away; they want to put you away. The deputy naturally someone is looking at you governing you his staff. I know who that you are. *One more thing, forgive them that is the spirit of God forever. You all make me nervous with a throw down of lip debate growing back and forth. You're not being constructive. Don't ever do that create an offense. JESUS! I repent I will keep my mouth shut. You have any problems bring them to me. Dozens of operators are working with him whispering about your battles, they're not on your side. They like him hoping he will look their way militant gangs and your two children. They are running a show talking about you Pentecost, "Exactly." And another thing they are not on your side you need to know. Pentecost now give it up offense. So be nice. *They shoved you in the door and kept you locked up. The group they are laughing. *Apparently he leads them Nathaniel their father your two children making your life miserable observing them and his mum, his mum mistress. I've been viewing them for decades and their *lewd* offense soap opera romance. It is a mess so mind boggling their offense romance enactment. You're the reason they are all blessed. Wicked against you, they are so mind blowing. Super star building in them they think. They are a mess. *Review Pentecost they gather together as a crew to pick a fight on you. The fight a mess created by her and him your son and daughter and he is responsible. *Throwing a curve at you both of them, like a little league battle they scramble in the afternoon by moms (your home) in the neighborhood just to worry you. Have you no shame? *She attacks you Pentecost. *Distinctly her language she is awful close to you never, hateful been like that forever. *And they are both real low down, they are a threat. Terrible temper evil single against you so be careful, paranoia her paranoia disease you be careful. You're the writer, for JESUS. A scribe for JESUS CHRIST, you follow me. The reality your department trying to succeed to write all these books, while you are tipping the scales being overweight, you keep bumping into that work on it your weight it is abducted. A little talking we're just so proud of you, while you're writing this book bumping into everything getting you upset a unique opportunity shame on them. Alright does that make sense? Every one of them is written up a little bit. Remember I AM your friend, your heavenly Father watches out for you. Scrambling whoever it is we're all putting it together keep count on base. Put that on their record angelic creatures, the angles of GOD ALMIGHTY. Organized crime against you saying you've lost it, "My momma has lost it her facilities her mental facilities" tearing you down mentally. "Then get her JESUS CHRIST for me, disturbing me I'm telling you." Your daughter Pamela raising cane, I rebuke her be it now and I'M not changing my mind. They're all too old for that be it known this day, and I'M not changing my mind JESUS CHRIST.   I view her all the time and Nate your husband.  Nate Williams can't keep his big mouth shut about you written by hand to Whites, embarrassing disaster carrying news real hateful in North Nashville.  Other friends White people they are your friends real veteran saints of GOD, believe me they have frozen him out, "Don't know where all that mess comes from." "Now that is creepy such goings on stabbing her in the dark."  Distinctly the next time do not answer the phone, if it is not for you.   I'll tell you what to do.  He calls against you stabbing you in the back.  *Dozens of rings out of bounds (downloadable hoax prank calls daily), what is more it's to the extreme.  You have got to get away from him.  Soon it will be over with he will be arrested by GOD ALMIGHTGY.  If you are asking my advice I can help you come to your defense.  Prank calls they don't call back, JESUS they don't leave a number it is to the extreme.   I can remedy that, change phones switch phone lines when you move.  In regard getting into your head messing with you catching you off guard those events lately for you.  I've got a new development I will pay her back his friend.  Knock at the door don't answer, one more time knock at the door a stranger no don't answer it, no electrician, apparently they want to put you away.  Don't be afraid, absolutely.  In the meantime stop answering the phone, they're doing it on purpose.   Even if it is an electrician wanting to use the phone don't answer, very annoying no salesmen either let them drive away.   The accuser Jeremiah my daughter that is you, there is no excuse for his behavior.  Know that I AM available, I am going to turn it around in your favor it is very annoying.   You will be a success—your book.  His excuse; they can't hardly look at you.  Break away real quick.  Let me tell you something Pentecost, difference for you open that door right now on his secrets.  A lot of people didn't know says JESUS CHRIST; the boss of the military his army. You know what, we all know him thinks he is so strong.  Now among the young thinks he is strong. Final blow, they are onto him right now talking cornered forever. Amazement killing your passion for God Almighty, I know the kind in the body they are a nervous man. Charges for him won't be thrown away. Charges for him pending my friend, don't doubt trembling your accuser and them that work with him. Help me GOD! What a mighty God we serve in this country they are hiding now. Nathaniel no passion for God, not like you. The doctor your defense I will help you Pentecost on the phone no competition. I AM like a regular guy, I will help you. I AM strong among the weak in society with a gripper. Know that I AM ready to help you believe me he can't escape, believe me I swear by it. The weather will change soon I control the weather legally. Know that I AM watching, you can't be a quitter go ahead denounce it that's my department okay? A wife competition for others to hear racing every time; "Exactly" imitator he is. That's no way to treat your wife. I see him addressing others with your issues; believing he is GOD, manifested in the flesh in his own self that level his own time. Barbara, he can't look at you straight in the face. Know that I AM right on time view the horses. Oh-my-gosh! There drawing closer than you think, they are right now in your backyard. You don't want to look at the deceiver again. Very shocking while I'm talking on the phone he picks up the phone, crazy. Good-GOD a-mighty; now let me tell you dangerous is his basis all vanity. I am trembling! You can depend on me. Know that I will deliver thee stay on the phone, let me handle it never give up you can't do that. I see his performance and her performance her and her friend. Like a pullet bird (a very young chicken) a crazy jingle no oasis just empty the whole group without a measure. Recompense my house; try and get along leave it to me JESUS CHRIST I will avenge. *One more time refusal on me; he refutes me all the time calling me crazy just pitiful says this to the community; this has become an epidemic to other people, *The Upper Room people of GOD, somebody they should step into my shoes living with the blockhead. The Bishop believes him, now believe it or not he sides with him and his organization. Pentecost you are an expert been dealing with it a long time. Facing it that is scary people don't discern anymore. That is why he likes going to his church—they don't have any insurance. Just around the corner Pentecost there is a new guy on the block waiting for him. They are already sending protests Pentecost, their brotherhood his brothers in the LORD against him now, a real mess all that evil equity coming into the church, the house of the LORD. Already equipped the man of the Almighty, he will blow him away. These Bishops ought to be more like him steeple top or they can really wreck the place, the house of the LORD. For that reason then after that get that foul odor out of here. His organization this Bishop, they don't have enough power to deliver. Equivalent he can't deliver satan out, it's in reach. Don't they pray? Your article will help them out. *I'M not like other people. For their record Jeremiah, I have taken my hands off their church and their Church organization he is in. I view you every day don't be bothered you are perfected. The Church of CHRIST, (Apostolics') now look at me now complete. Complete I can relax now a rainbow now happy am I, for this reason with the help of JESUS CHRIST, my defender. On record my defender JESUS CHRIST, for the benefit of all that are listening and heaven is my home. I am going to follow Him. It is though and enlightenment descriptive, a distinct narrative English prose composition in booklet form not irrational starting from the top. *The jest is needless in its form to say not a book though my debt is a book to publish, total access an agreement to JESUS CHRIST to be paid. I love Him very much. This time I am writing this publication a model to inform in details to leaders that is authorities, another historic moment enlightened in dept, agreement through its own complete book a historic moment but not complete my own idea. TO ALL MY FAMILY: I write on behalf of our LORD and SAVIOR a book to be sold this book around the world, and in the USA Copyrighted authorities for JESUS CHRIST. I believe it is a blessing legally written by hand. I am a witness to that. I put my finger on this book, a record kept by me not different persons. Believe it or not champion on the grounds who is LORD, our benefit, our Lord JESUS CHRIST no escaping that. *My destiny to inform. I am not a Democrat, with high ideals that would bring the Country down. I am an older individual tailored exactly with a conscious. I am a *political activist* maybe too involved the incident or not, no sliding. I can't let go. The real story here it is now I'm telling you it is benefiting, it is complete to others. I can't let go not running billboards Mt. Zion, definitely not Baptist, but the church of the living GOD, his name is JESUS CHRIST, Catholics. The saints in Nashville, please pray for me, cover me, the intended of this script, yes indeed! Oh LORD, I'm chained. Never forget in high places the champion to all mankind the rock to my people canonized to the young people, JESUS CHRIST. Say that again no hindrances, the champion to all, the rock to my people stayed canonized in Nashville, no matter what the situation we're destined. I've written a book this book and others for Him JESUS CHRIST. We're crazy about him. A wonderful counselor after the resurrection, a bright and morning star for a revolution that is what He has done for the kids. OH ELOHIM! GOD THE JUDGE IN THIS CITY JESUS CHRIST, HE IS THE GREATEST THING THAT HAS EVER HAPPENED TO THIS WORLD AND IN NASHVILLE, TENNESSEE AND ELSEWHERE A WONDERFUL COUNSELOR THE HUMAN MY REDEEMER JESUS CHRIST, FOR THE WHOLE EARTH. WE NEED MORE LIKE HIM. Spiritual attacks they will come, but he will never fail us hear that Latino's my own tribute? Mercy my GOD, save me from others as I write this book, this "*NEW ARTICLE.*" The LORD said unto me; you are alright by me. Don't get angry get up and read think about me, overlook the criticism they think they are right on their way to heaven. I view you a hundred times extra legally never skipped a beat. Woman finish the book, I AM your best friend. Think you for writing this book. It is this book behind you right now. It is significant you hear me. As you write this book you're not doomed by me, just set apart tell that to the President. Evil in Nashville, hear that Washington? Are you listening arm yourselves Baptist—of this generation, Pentecost a few. Are they listening authorities, the House of Representatives? Written by me a typical Southern African American preacher, the hunted this is true alone. May I repeat I'm not following a coattail like regular? You say, "Go to hell" your table. Now that you are at your table things are difficult, "*Get that Black woman out of here.*" Preachers they don't want you, you're behind your current allegations swing wide open. This execution VIP intended from the Kingdom. A new document and your righteousness displayed, we need help certainty. A miracle played technically the address Sister Barbara Payne. I feel something I can feel it right now. Read the *GOSPELS;* nothing is left on me. THE HOLY GHOST; Republicans, a change is coming your way be looking. I will topple them. See the proof.

ENDING

Thus saith the LORD; *REVELATION* 1:8 I am Alpha and Omega, (get the picture), the beginning and the ending, (of the time) saith the Lord which is, and which was, and which is to come, the ALMIGHTY. / CHRIST JESUS said; a miracle it takes a map holding courtesy. JESUS you are an architect the only one we need JESUS. Get the picture? I AM a custom builder. How am I? You nearly lost your mind my opinion, the devil he tackled you, worrying you all the time low temperature they are, worrying about them (the Jango) and your son Marco, and all of them Whites with fever. Don't worry about them and your baby child, they're not worth it believe me JESUS CHRIST, the Son of God you're the best to me. Typical your children they're not grounded no excuse for their behavior Pentecost. Know that GOD will look out for you.

*The Original Barbara Payne*

We understand a lot overwhelmed you a lot. Turn them off the racist's lobbyists. I know they hurt your feelings feeling racist's backlash anger, their like dinosaurs. Stay in your corner and be quiet; I will deal with them later those who committed racist's offense. Just keep working I'll be watching.

# ABOUT THE AUTHOR

*About the Author*

Ms. Barbara Payne is a member of the Apostolic Pentecostal denomination Church faith of the diocese in America. She stays true to the discourse her church teaches on matters concerning the adoption of the Apostles Doctrine. Definitely, she believes in that. Her belief in God Jesus Christ gave to her a writing breakthrough, an advantage from above for writing books people everywhere. Let me explain, the Lord came to visit her and waking up her mind writing fascinating stories this author. The stories she writes are not atheist in thought. He gave instructions to her to write books until this day on behalf of him. Her books are not pious in legalistic detection just a unique opportunity from God, making her a true success in life. Hallelujah! She works all alone. Her work it is a working deposit on her record up above in heaven, a now deposited. No job is ever too big for that.

## STUDY ACADEMIC CREDENTIAL

Ms. Barbara holds a Bachelor of Science Degree from Belmont University and she is very proud of that. She wants to earn a Master's degree.

## THE FORMATIVE YEARS

For Ms. Barbara's education in the formative years of her life individually educated at a primary school, in a pool with others in a three room classroom building in Ashland City, Tennessee. It was there where she was introduced to culture, and where she was introduced to the advantages of learning. The primary school was a social disadvantage one. Her concerns now are for the best education advantages afforded to African Americans and their children, and to all the children living in America. She ceases daily that moment every chance she gets.

## HELPING OTHERS HER ATTITUDE

Taking no advantage of other people it has been done too often. One of her main concerns in life is to lift everyone up, and showing no advantage; she taught that to her three children giving back to others. Help someone along the way. Giving back it is what matters in life, and giving back it is the antique of all values for you everywhere. Praise the Lord America! Help people out whenever you can—a true value in life on this life's journey.

www.ingramcontent.com/pod-product-compliance
Lightning Source LLC
Chambersburg PA
CBHW030335240426
43661CB00052B/1642